KLIMT

PHILIPPE THIÉBAUT

KLIMT
THE BIGGER PICTURE

PRESTEL
MUNICH · LONDON · NEW YORK

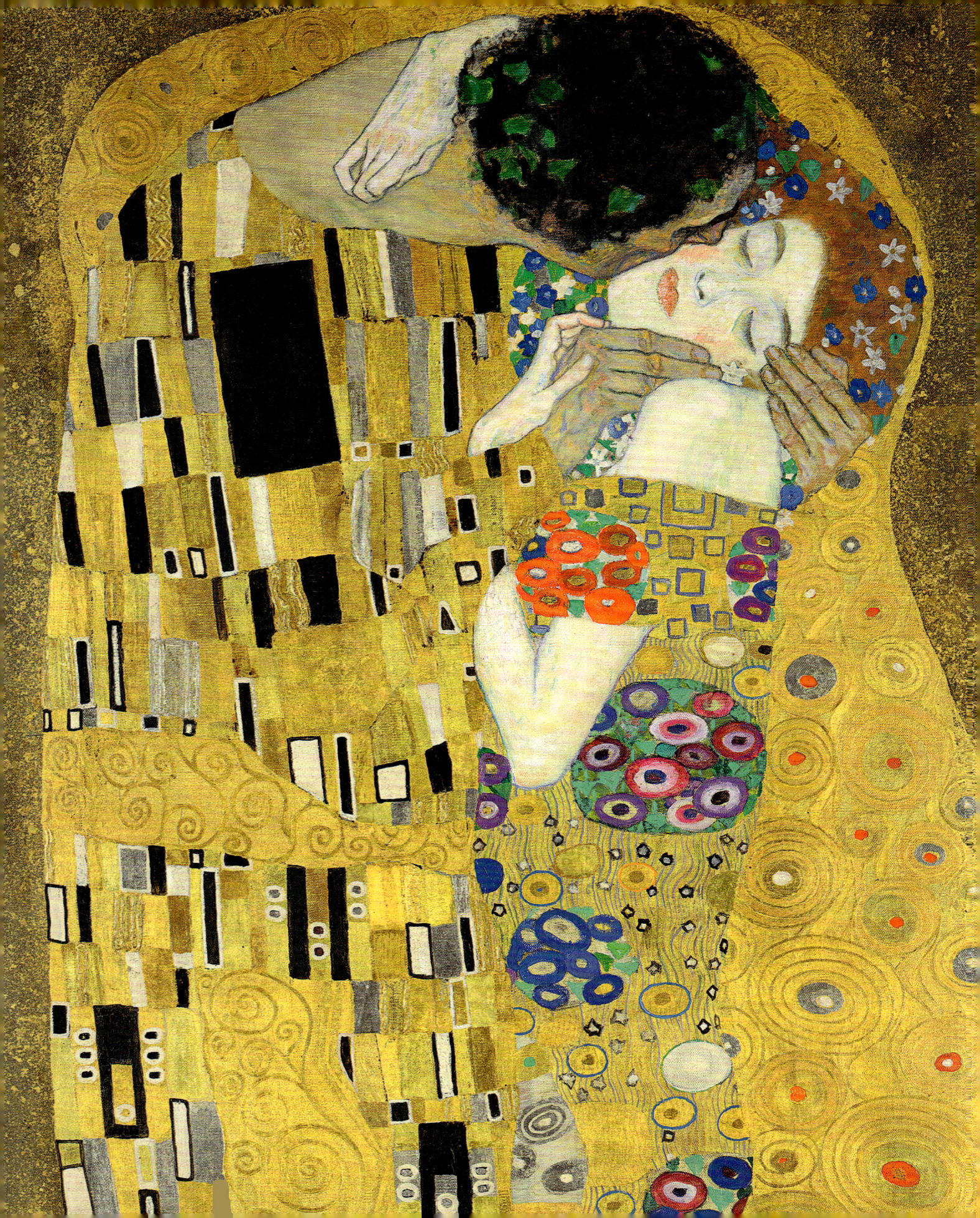

CONTENTS

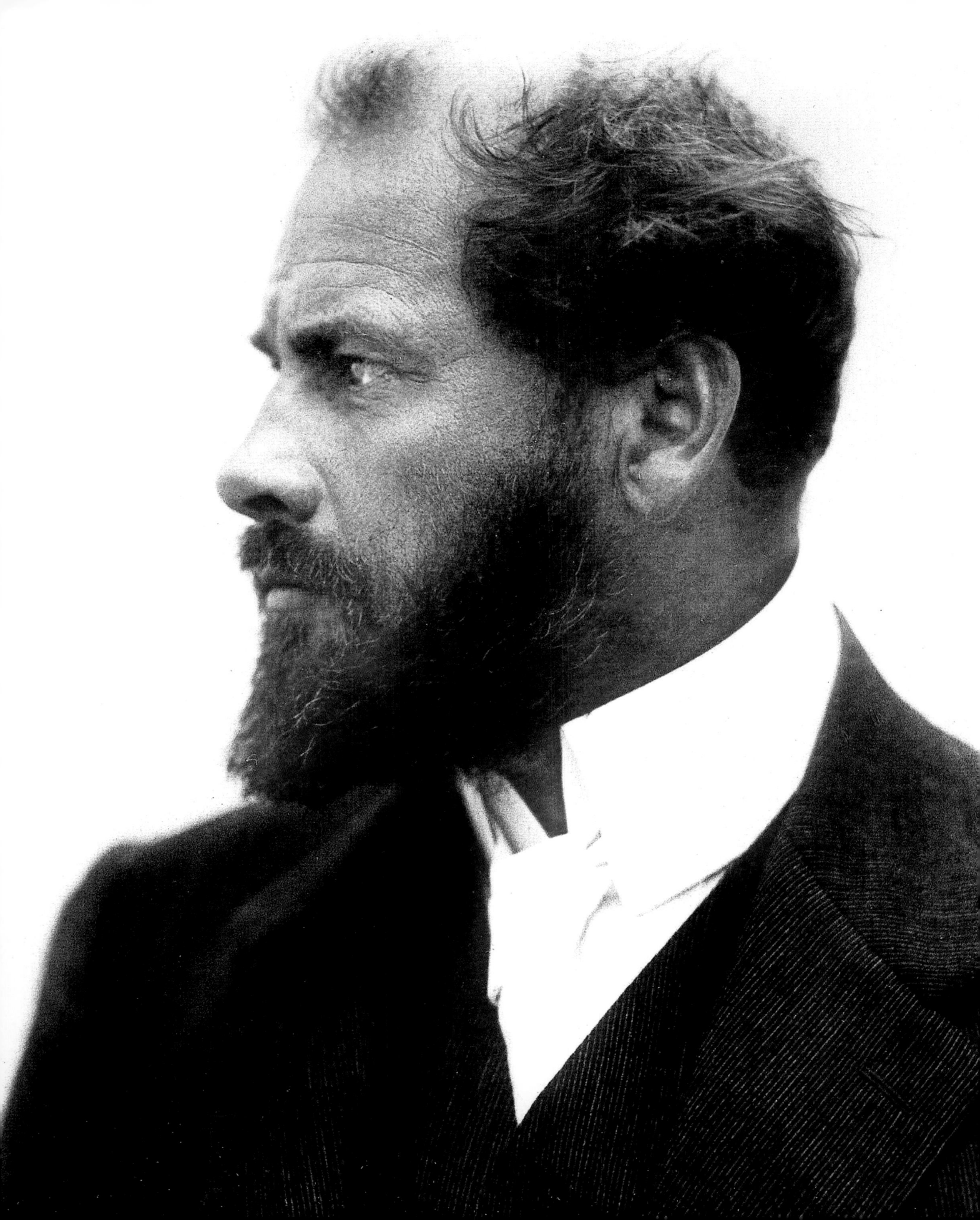

Introduction

At the turn of the twentieth century, a spirit of cultural renewal affecting every domain of life took hold of Vienna, turning the Austro-Hungarian Empire's capital into one of the prime hotbeds of a new style of art whose main objective was to create a living environment that met the needs and aspirations of "modern man".

Paradoxically, this extraordinary blossoming occurred at the same time as a crucial event in European political history of the second half of the nineteenth century: the disintegration of the Habsburg Empire during the reign of Franz Joseph, who had assumed the throne in 1848 after the abdication of his uncle Ferdinand I. In 1859, following the war for Italy waged against the empire by an alliance of France and the Kingdom of Sardinia, the Habsburgs lost Lombardy and Tuscany, along with Parma and Modena. In 1866, defeat at the Battle of Königgrätz ended the Austro-Prussian War, and the empire was forced to cede Venice and the rest of Venetia to the young Kingdom of Italy. Finally, France's defeat by Prussia in 1871 marked the beginning of German unification and the supremacy of Berlin in the German-speaking countries.

The misfortune did not spare the imperial family. On 19 June 1867, Franz Joseph's younger brother, who had been crowned Emperor Maximilian I of Mexico in 1864, was shot by republicans. In 1889, Crown Prince Rudolf committed suicide at the age of thirty at his hunting lodge in Mayerling after killing his mistress, Marie Vetsera. On 10 September 1898, Empress Elisabeth, of fragile mental health and exhausted by her dietary regimens and the never-ending travels that she undertook in a quest to remedy her depression, was killed in Geneva by an Italian anarchist. Finally, on 28 June 1914, Archduke Franz Ferdinand, the emperor's nephew and heir to the throne, was also assassinated, in Sarajevo, along with his wife. This tragic event led Austria-Hungary to declare war on the kingdom of Serbia; as is

Portrait of Gustav Klimt,
c. 1905, photograph (detail)

well known, the conflict was not contained to the Balkans, but led to the formation of alliances and ultimately to the First World War.

Despite all the blows struck against his empire, Franz Joseph managed to encourage the fulfilment of his capital's economic, artistic and cultural potential. Inspired by the urbanism of Georges-Eugène Haussmann, the official opening of the Ringstrasse, on 1 May 1865, was the first bold move in this campaign. Opulent residential buildings, tree-lined sidewalks, promenades for pedestrians and riders, new public buildings along the route of the old city walls: all of these created a convivial location prized by the upper bourgeoisie. Around the time of the Ring's development, Gustav Klimt quickly found himself involved in the creation of the very finest architectural decoration as part of the urbanization project, particularly because his studies had prepared him well to take on a project of this kind.

Born in 1862 in Baumgarten, a village in the suburbs of Vienna, Gustav Klimt was the second son in a family of four girls and three boys. His father was a chiseller and engraver who worked with precious metals; his son Georg (1867–1931) followed in his footsteps. Gustav enrolled in the School of Arts and Crafts (now the University of Applied Arts). The school was founded in 1868 and relocated in 1877 to the Stubenring, near the Museum of Art and Industry (now the Museum of Applied Arts). The museum, which was modelled after the South Kensington Museum (now Victoria and Albert Museum) in London, was founded in 1864. The School of Arts and Crafts consisted of four departments: architecture, sculpture, figurative painting and decorative painting, each including appropriate draughtsmanship training. In accordance with the vision of the school's director, Rudolf Eitelberger, the institution aimed to break down barriers between the "major" and "minor" arts, that is, between the fine and decorative arts. This institution is where Gustav – and his younger brother Ernst (1864–1892), who matriculated one year later – received sound training in decorative painting, which would quickly earn them renown once they completed their studies.

In 1883, the brothers opened a collective studio that they called the Künstler-Compagnie, or Artists Company, in the sixth district of Vienna with classmate Franz Matsch (1861–1942). The same year, they received a major commission to decorate the ceilings and curtain of the theatre in Reichenberg (now Liberec, Czech Republic) that had been built by two Viennese architects, Ferdinand Fellner (1847–1916) and Hermann Helmer (1849–1919). The following year, in 1884, the trio was once again hired by the Fellner-Helmer agency, which was constructing a theatre in Fiume (now Rikeka, Croatia). The collaboration of the two teams continued in 1885 and 1886 with the theatre in Karlsbad (now Karlovy Vary, Czech Republic), with the Künstler-Compagnie once again responsible for the ceilings and stage curtain.

This was followed by the first major Viennese commission: on 20 October 1886, the imperial council of architecture hired the Klimt brothers and Franz Matsch to paint the ceilings of the two grand staircases in the new Burgtheater, built on the Ring by the architect Karl von Hasenauer (1833–1894) according to plans developed in collaboration with Gottfried Semper (1803–1879), one of the pre-eminent

German architectural theoreticians of the time. In *The World of Yesterday: Memoirs of a European,* published in German in 1942 and in English in 1943, Stefan Zweig, recalling the city where he grew up, stressed the Burgtheater's crucial role in Viennese culture: "The first glance of the average Viennese into his morning paper was not at the events in parliament, or world affairs, but at the repertoire of the theatre, which assumed so important a role in public life as hardly was possible in any other city. For the Imperial theatre, the Burgtheater, was for the Viennese and for the Austrian more than a stage upon which actors enacted parts; it was the microcosm that mirrored the macrocosm, the brightly coloured reflection in which the city saw itself".

The Historical Museum of the City of Vienna also asked the Künstler-Compagnie to immortalize the interior spaces of the old Burgtheater, built on the Michaelerplatz in the eighteenth century and partially renovated in the mid-nineteenth century, before the building's demolition. Some years later, in 1890, the gouache that Gustav Klimt painted for this commission won him the Emperor's Prize, in the amount of four hundred gold ducats. Two years previously, Franz Joseph had awarded him the Gold Cross for Artistic Merit for his work decorating the new Burgtheater. Considering that Hasenauer, an architect whom the emperor regarded very highly, had called on the talent of the three young men in 1884 to decorate the Hermesvilla, built for Empress Elisabeth on a former hunting ground east of Vienna, Gustav Klimt was clearly poised to establish himself as a major figure in Viennese architectural decoration. The ensuing decade would confirm his status.

In 1890, the Künstler-Compagnie was commissioned to work on one of the largest construction projects on the Ringstrasse, which had broken ground twenty years before: the celebrated Kunsthistorisches Museum, or Museum of Art History. As at the Burgtheater, Klimt was charged with decorating the ceiling of a grand staircase. He created eight spandrels and five intercolumnar pictures there. The building was inaugurated on 17 October 1891.

Following the death of Ernst Klimt from pericarditis, the Künstler-Compagnie was dissolved the following year. This did not keep Gustav Klimt and Matsch from pursuing a career in officialdom, however. In 1894, the board of the University of Vienna entrusted them with decorating the Great Hall of a new building, designed by Heinrich von Ferstel (1828–1883). Klimt's task was to paint the allegories of *Philosophy, Medicine* and *Jurisprudence,* as well as the ten spandrel panels on the theme of these allegories. Matsch was assigned the allegories of *Theology* and the *Victory of Light over Darkness.*

Success was not in the cards this time. Klimt opted to distance himself from the flamboyant, theatrical spirit of the Ringstrasse, manifested by the illusionist allegories of Hans Makart (1840–1884). Although his respect for allegory remained undiminished, he nevertheless departed from traditional iconography, which he judged insufficient for visualizing subjects relating to the human condition – precisely the subjects of the university's commission. The project ended in disaster. A first scandal erupted in March 1900 with the presentation of *Philosophy*. Eighty-seven professors signed a petition against the picture because of its despairing iconography. Protests grew in 1901 and 1903, when *Medicine* and then *Jurisprudence* were unveiled. In response to the incomprehension and hostility that his work provoked, Klimt wrote a letter in April 1905 to the Ministry of Culture and Education in which he withdrew the commission and announced that he would return his thirty-thousand-crown advance – made possible by the support of a patron, who lent him the money. The academics' rejection of his allegories was due to the pictures' implacable pessimism, which threw into doubt the notion of progress and the redeeming character of the sciences taught at the university. The conquests of science and reason, the victory of medicine over illness and the establishment of equality and justice were challenged by the representation of humanity as fragile and suffering, trapped in a system that ineluctably led to death. Symbolizing humanity's distress and precarity, these nude, ravaged and falling bodies not only went against the spirit of the commission; it amounted to a frontal attack on it. Even more powerfully, Klimt's three allegories presented a coherence for which justification could be found in the philosophy of Arthur Schopenhauer, who considered the human condition inevitably unhappy and whose writings exerted a profound influence on the cultural and artistic life of the era. Although it is difficult to make definitive pronouncements about Klimt's philosophical knowledge, his friendships with eminent men of letters – including leaders of the Jung-Wien (Young Vienna) movement such as Hermann Bahr (1863–1934) and Peter Altenberg (1859–1919) – suggest that Klimt was close to the literary milieu.

Even as he was working on the allegories commissioned by the university, which he thought of as evidence of his art's philosophical ambitions, Klimt attacked the conservatism of Viennese institutions and came to lead a group of young artists who protested the policies of the Künstlerhaus, or Artists' House, which he had joined in 1891. Built in 1864 on a parcel between the Ringstrasse and Karlsplatz, the Künstlerhaus was home to the annual exhibitions of the Cooperative Society of Viennese Painters, Sculptors and Architects. Wishing to increase public awareness of new works, Klimt and his artist friends criticized the Künstlerhaus for its partiality to works upholding tradition as well as its disorderly exhibition of the works it chose. On 25 May 1897, just two months after the opening of the twenty-fifth exhibition, they left the Künstlerhaus and founded the movement known as the Vienna Secession, whose full name is the Austrian Association of Visual Artists Vienna Secession. Just a year after its founding, it had its own building, built by one of its members, the architect Joseph Maria Olbrich (1867–1908), providing impressive proof of the separatist group's vitality. There, the Secessionists worked towards the objective stated in the motto engraved in golden letters on the lintel above the entryway: "Der Zeit ihre Kunst / Der Kunst ihre Freiheit" (To every age its art, to every art its freedom).

In contrast to the grand display of the Künstlerhaus, the Secession opted for smaller exhibitions, consisting of works that were meticulously selected and hung according to collective deliberation. Member artists were to show their most recent works, all the while fulfilling another self-appointed mission: opening their exhibition hall's doors to foreign artists also in search of novelty. Each of the twenty-three exhibitions organized by the group was a unique production, in terms of both the works selected and the arrangement of the space. The peak of this policy was doubtlessly the 1902 exhibition titled *Beethoven,* directed by the architect Josef Hoffmann (1870–1956), a friend of Klimt's. The event gave Klimt the space to display his decorative talent on a frieze that unfolded on three walls of a room allocated solely to him. The following year, in November 1903, a monographic exhibition paid homage to him as the leader of the Secession. This time, the designer was Koloman Moser (1868–1918), the movement's most multidisciplinary artist. As with all the Secession exhibitions, the contrast to the Künstlerhaus's decorative overload was chasmic. The single decorative element was the grey-painted moulding that bordered each display wall, which were white. The lighting fixtures and the white-lacquered furnishings were also designed by Moser.

In these exhibitions, the architectural setting, designed to be harmonious with the works on display, contributed in large part to the successful joining of "major" and "minor" arts, giving heft to the designer-architects' work. This intended role for the decorative arts in the new "modern" style was concretized in 1903, with the creation of a cooperative dedicated to the artistic production of everyday items: the Wiener Werkstätte, the workshop of the Secession. But discord in the Secession was not far behind, forcing the Wiener Werkstätte to present their first exhibition not in the group's exhibition hall but in Galerie Miethke, a private gallery. Klimt's close identification with the designer-architects and artisans had led to the formation within the Secession of a sort of clique, called the "stylists". Before long, they were in conflict with the "naturalists", led by the painter Josef Engelhart (1864–1941), who advocated a more traditional approach to painting and argued for exhibitions dedicated solely to easel painting.

In 1905, the break was complete: Klimt and fifteen other artists left the Secession. Now without an exhibition space, they were offered a property on which Hoffmann built an ensemble of temporary exhibition spaces, which were named the Kunstschau, or Art Show. The first event took place in the spring of 1908, and even as it gave consideration to the widest range of fields of artistic creation, it accorded the lion's share to Klimt and the Wiener Werkstätte. A second event took place the following year, and it was here that the young Egon Schiele (1890–1918) had his first chance to show a comprehensive overview of his work. But the Kunstschau soon halted its activity to make way for the Concert Hall, built by the duo of Fellner and Helmer from 1911 to 1913.

After the passionate dispute over the paintings meant for the university, Klimt would never again accept a public commission. However, to meet his needs, he could count on a solid network of patrons from Viennese high society; meanwhile, in complete support of his work, prominent figures in art criticism including the writer Hermann Bahr and the Hungary-born journalist Ludwig Hevesi (1843–1910) delivered analyses of his paintings that are among the most refined ever written.

Klimt's admirers – many of whom were Jewish – belonged to the industrial *grande bourgeoisie* and sat on the boards of the empire's largest corporations. These were true art lovers with great artistic culture. Moreover, their wives, often aesthetes in their own right, played a major role in the artists' social circle. It was hardly unheard of for the wives to occasionally pose for the maestro. Two people who clearly demonstrate Klimt's links with his patrons are August Lederer (1857–1936) and Otto Primavesi (1868–1926).

Lederer was indisputably the foremost collector of Klimt's works. A great industrialist, he held stakes in distilleries in Vienna, Galicia and Hungary. He was the one who bought *Philosophy* and *Jurisprudence* and entrusted their display in his Bartensteinstrasse home to Josef Hoffmann. He also owned the *Beethoven Frieze,* and he asked Klimt to paint his wife, Serena; his mother-in-law, Charlotte Pulitzer; and his daughter, Elisabeth, who became the Baroness Bachofen von Echt.

Klimt made the acquaintance of Primavesi in 1905. A banker from Olmütz in northern Moravia (now Olomouc, Czech Republic), he owned major shares in the Moravian association of sugar manufacturers and in several jute-spinning facilities, and was also a shareholder in the Wiener Werkstätte. He commissioned Hoffmann to build him a villa at Winkelsdorf, the site of flamboyant costume parties in which Klimt participated. Primavesi commissioned Klimt to paint a portrait of his wife, Eugenia, a Viennese actress nicknamed Mäda; and one of their daughter Mäda Gertrude. These are two of the most accomplished works of Klimt's late career.

Alongside his work as a portraitist, Klimt dedicated more and more time to landscape painting. This genre represents forty percent of his total work. These landscapes were mainly done during the summers he spent on the banks of the Attersee, a lake near Salzburg, Upper Austria, with his in-laws, the Flöges.

In 1891, Gustav's younger brother Ernst Klimt had married Helene Flöge (1871–1936), the daughter of a manufacturer of meerschaum pipes. Following the deaths of Ernst and his father, Klimt not only had to provide for his mother and an unmarried sister; he also assumed the role of tutor for his niece Helene. This led to a relationship with Emilie Flöge (1874–1952), Helene's sister and "the love of Klimt's life", according to a statement by the son of August and Serena Lederer.

This relationship has always been the subject of a question that is difficult to answer: was it sexual, or did it remain platonic? According to some of Klimt's biographers, he suffered from a masculine disorder that Sigmund Freud called "psychical impotence" in "the behaviour of love", consisting of the inability to commit to one woman and a preference for random encounters. Klimt forthrightly evoked his sexual appetites in a small 1915 self-portrait in which he is reduced to his genitals, confirming the writer Arthur Schnitzler's observation in 1912 that the painter resembled a vigorous faun. In 1993, the Austrian art historian and gallerist Christian Nebehay claimed that Klimt was the father of at least fourteen children.

Whatever the true nature of their certainly unconventional relationship, it was Emilie that Klimt called to his bedside as he was about to die, on 6 February 1918, of a lung infection, which he had contracted at the hospital; he had been admitted to treat a thrombosis that left his right side paralyzed. "I believe that I will never recover from Klimt's death", said Hoffmann, with whom he had shared the Secession's greatest moments of glory. "I must recognize that I am no longer myself."

Klimt's painted oeuvre, consisting of about 230 works, may seem modest. But aside from the fact that Klimt worked very slowly, the cultural agenda of the Anschluss – the annexation of Austria by Nazi Germany in 1938 – and the destruction wrought during the Second World War have deprived us of one of the most decisive milestones of Klimt's career, the *Faculty Paintings,* which, along with other works, belonged to August Lederer. Confiscated in 1938 by the Nazis, the Lederer collection was stored at Schloss Immendorf, a castle in Lower Austria that the German forces burnt when faced with the advance of the Red Army. After the war, many battles were waged by the descendants of the families pillaged by the Nazis, to recover works by Klimt that had belonged to their parents. The most famous is the case of Maria Altmann, niece of Adele Bloch-Bauer, who in 2006 regained possession of her aunt's portrait, an absolute icon of Klimt's oeuvre.

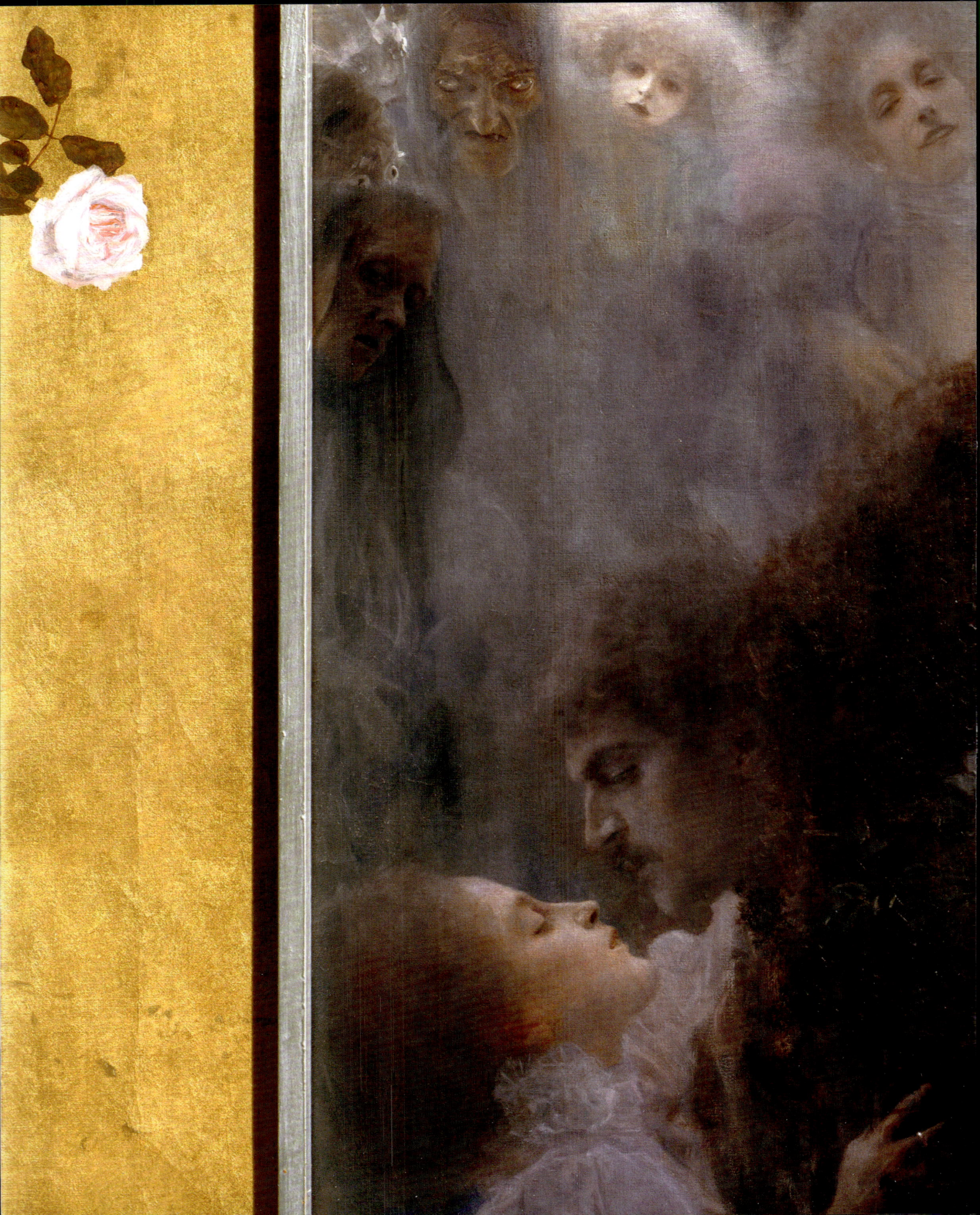

Klimt and the Ringstrasse

Renaissance Revival was the dominant style when Gustav Klimt was training at the School of Arts and Crafts in Vienna, where the grandiose façades of government buildings and upper-bourgeois residences rose along the Ringstrasse. Typified by the work and flamboyant personality of the painter Hans Makart, it was so prevalent that the critic Ludwig Hevesi thought it was on its way to becoming a national style. Today, the art of Makart – based on allegory, illusionism and formal profusion – is considered a prime example of historicism. It should be noted that Hevesi, who actively championed the Vienna Secession, saw in the work of Makart and his studio the development of a "modern" aesthetic and a decorative style that he deemed "psychological".

With the support of his professor, the painter and engraver Ferdinand Julius Laufberger (1829–1881), the young Klimt joined the team of Makart assistants responsible for executing the master's studies for Vienna's historical pageant, which commemorated the silver anniversary of Emperor Franz Joseph I and Empress Elisabeth.

Shortly before Makart's death, in 1884, the Klimt brothers – this time, on the recommendation of Julius Victor Berger (1850–1902), Laufberger's successor – were asked to decorate the empress's apartments in the Hermesvilla. Several years later, between 1897 and 1899, the banker and industrialist Nikolaus Dumba (1830–1900), whose home office at Parkring 4 was considered exemplary of the Neo-Renaissance style – commissioned Gustav Klimt to decorate the music salon and Franz Matsch the dining room. Sadly, Klimt's works *Music* and *Schubert at the Piano*, which had been added to the Lederer collection after Dumba's death, were destroyed in the Schloss Immendorf fire of 1945.

Klimt bears the closest resemblance to Makart in his paintings intended for a series of engravings titled *Allegories and Emblems,* a commission for the Vienna publishing house Gerlach & Schenk. With a sensuality evoking Makart's female figures, *Allegory of Fable* (pp. 20–21), painted in 1883, stands out against a fanciful forest landscape, surrounded by animals featured in Aesop's famous fables: on one side, the lion and the mice, and on the other, the fox and the swan. In *Allegory of Idyll* (pp. 18–19), the subject – a young woman showing a bird's nest to two children – is inscribed in a tondo supported by two young male nudes whose pose and musculature certainly owe a great deal to Michelangelo, and also to the English painter Edward Burne-Jones, Klimt's Pre-Raphaelite contemporary. *Allegory of Idyll* reflects Klimt's talent for integrating a subject within an ornamental structure, an aptitude that would fully blossom in the ceiling decorations of the Burgtheater's grand staircase, a commission that was awarded to the Künstler-Compagnie.

Established by the theatre's director, Adolf von Wilbrandt (1837–1911), the program was different from previous theatrical productions by the Künstler-Compagnie, which were essentially based on allegories featuring assorted characters in period costumes and musical genres. This time, the objective was to evoke the history of theatre across the centuries. Three works dedicated to antiquity fell to Gustav. He was to depict *The Altar of Dionysus* (pp. 24–25), *The Cart of Thespis* and *The Theatre at Taormina* (p. 23). To render the classical character of such subjects, the painter turned his back on Makart and looked to the Neoclassicism of David and Ingres, as well as to historical Realism; he took care to maintain verisimilitude using precise details from archaeological excavations and studies. In this, Klimt's compositions show clear affinities with works by his British contemporary Lawrence Alma-Tadema and the French artist Jean-Léon Gérôme. Sharing an impeccable technique, these works engage in meticulous and colourful historical recreation, with depictions of nudes that are simultaneously cold and sensual. Shakespeare's theatre, also painted by Klimt, is illustrated with a scene from *Romeo and Juliet* in a performance at the Globe Theatre in London. It is noteworthy that no matter what era he was depicting, Klimt always created a connection between the stage event and the audience to emphasize that theater was part of society. Nor did he shy away from representing himself at the Globe, in gentleman's garb, alongside his brother Ernst and Matsch (pp. 26–27).

The same year, in 1890, Klimt was summoned to the construction site at the grand staircase of the Kunsthistorisches Museum (Museum of Art History), on which Makart had worked. Klimt was appointed to execute the paintings for eight spandrels and three intercolumniations (pp. 28–29). The commission was to represent different eras of art in an allegorical form; Klimt was to depict ancient Egypt, classical antiquity and the Italian Renaissance. As at the Burgtheater, draughtsmanship had precedence over colour, and the figures emanate a feeling of cold precision.

In the early 1890s, Klimt's easel painting most clearly reflected the distance he had put between his work and that of Makart. Two paintings are particularly revelatory of the unmistakable divergence of the two artists. First, the portrait of Josef Pembaur (1848–1923; p. 30), an eminent figure in the contemporary musical world, in which the figure of Apollo, a universal symbol of art's struggle in the quest for modernity, announced an iconographic program that would be important to the Secession. The other, *Allegory of Love* (p. 31), painted in 1895 as part of a second series of allegories ordered by the publishing house Gerlach, shows a contemporary couple about to kiss. Above them, faces – some ominous – emerge from a crepuscular fog, symbolizing the ages of woman: from the sunny little girl to the radiant young woman to the dishevelled crone, presaging a pessimism that Klimt would develop in his future allegories.

Allegory of Love,
1895, oil on canvas, 60 × 44 cm, Wien Museum, Vienna (p. 14, detail; see p. 31)

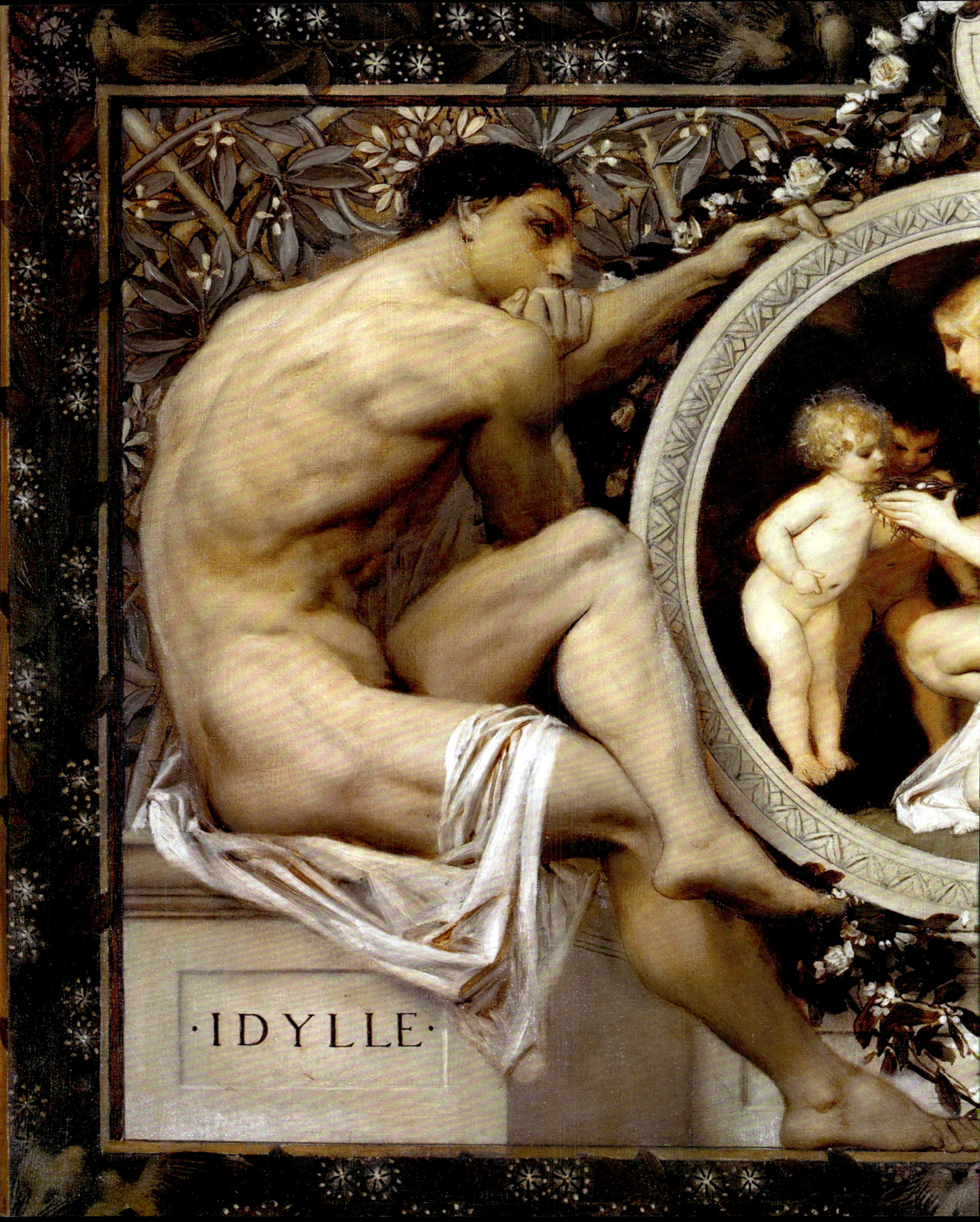

·IDYLLE·

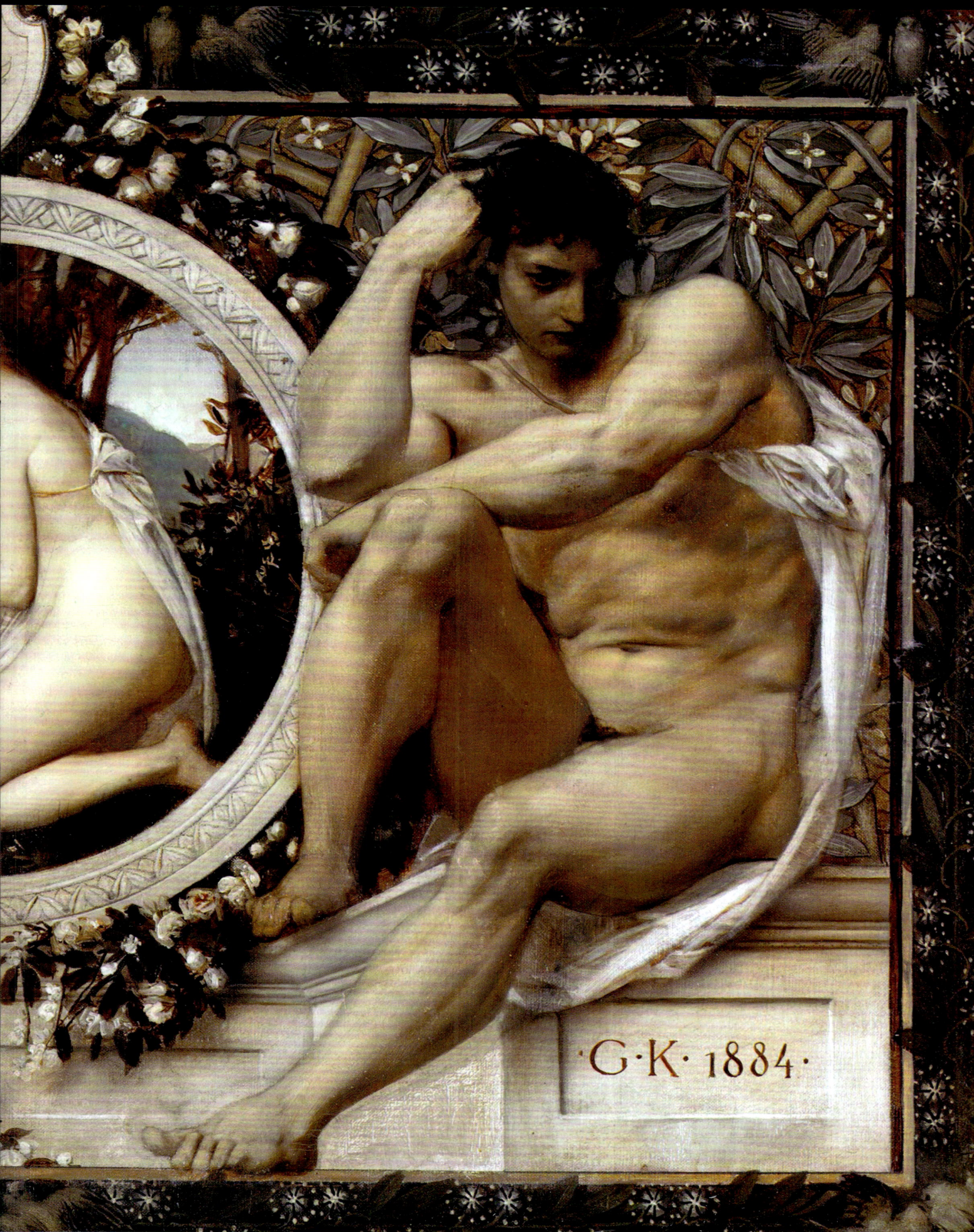

·G·K·1884·

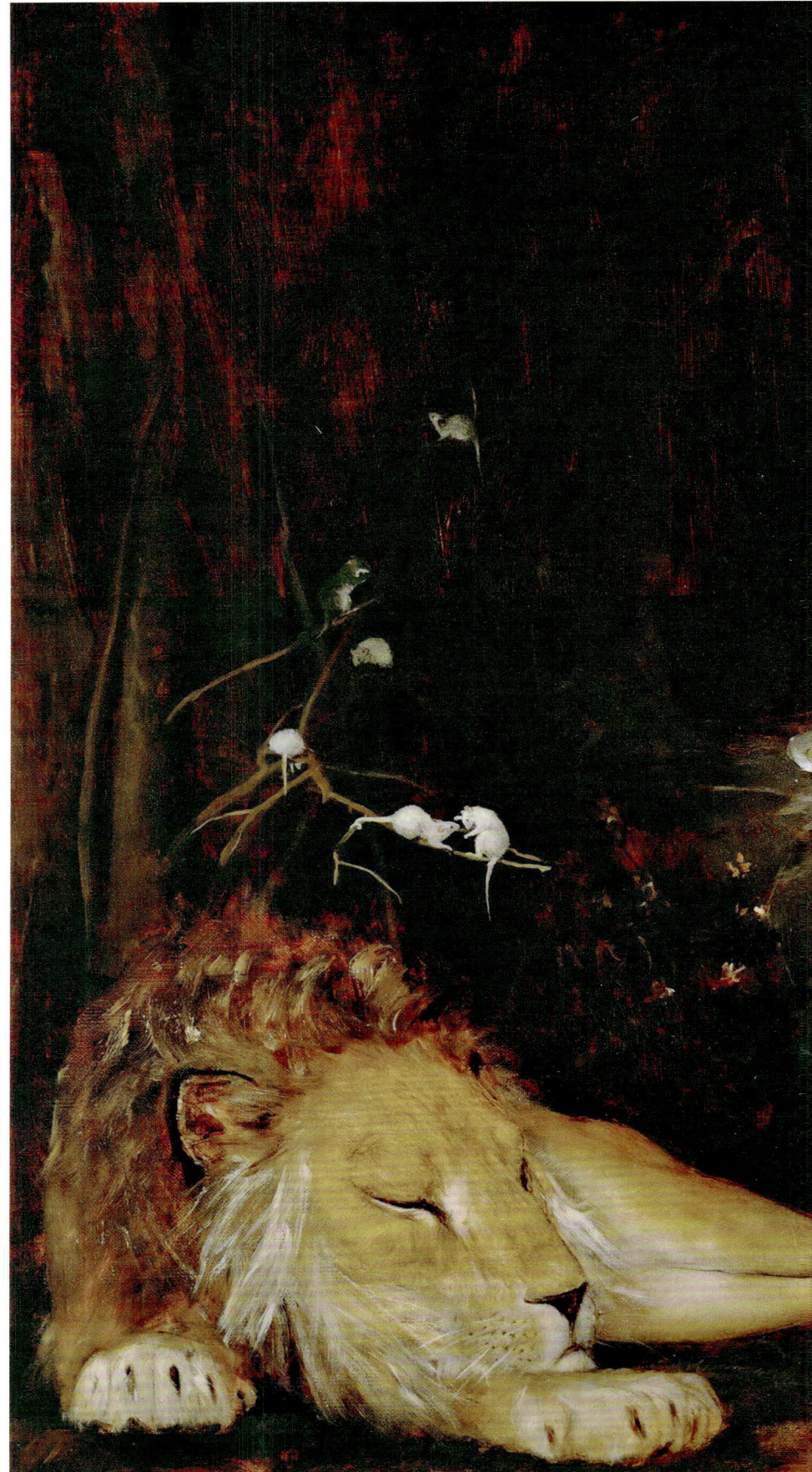

Allegory of Idyll,
1884, oil on canvas,
49.5 × 73.5 cm,
Wien Museum, Vienna
(preceding spread)

Allegory of Fable,
1883, oil on canvas,
84.5 × 117 cm,
Wien Museum, Vienna

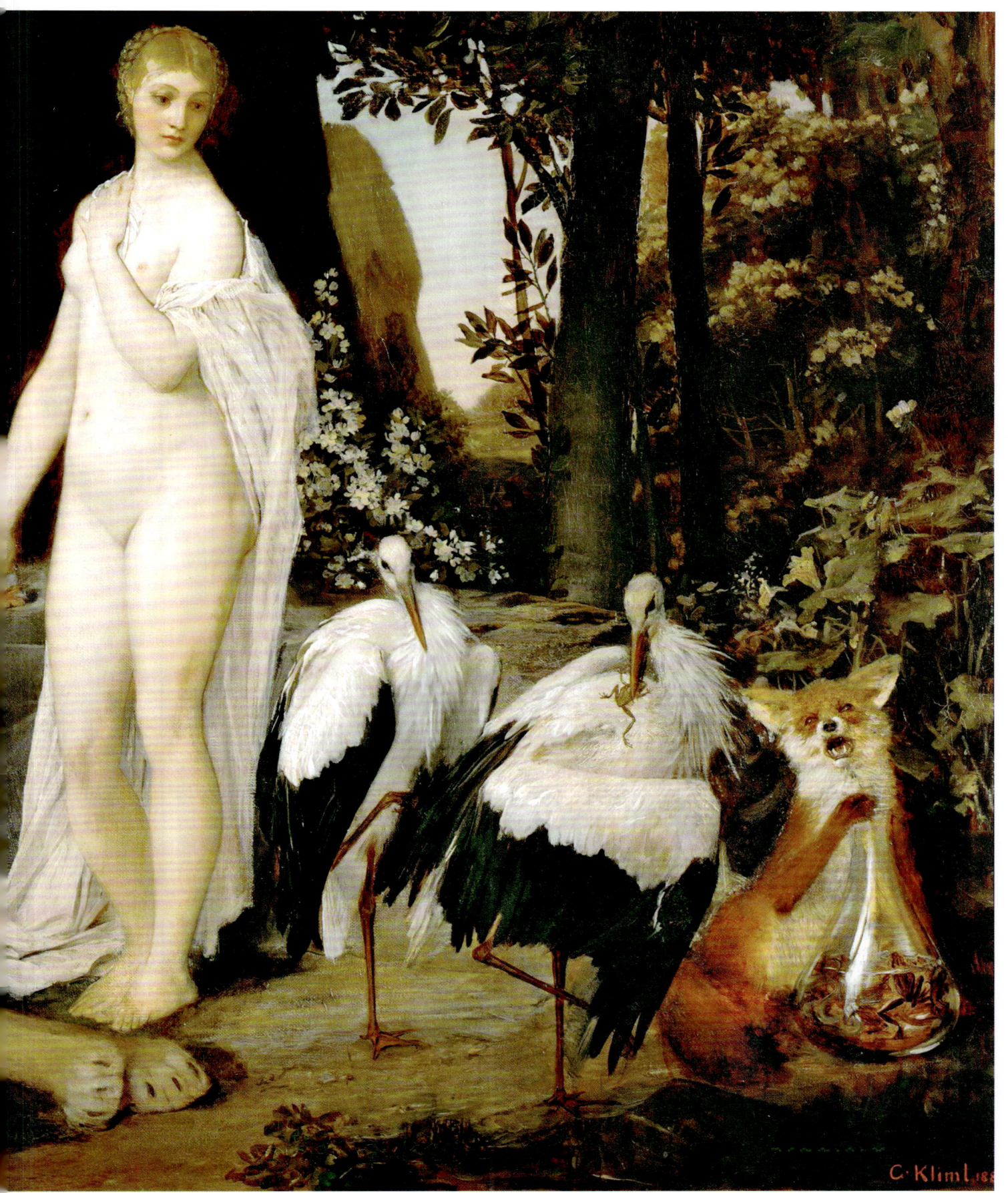

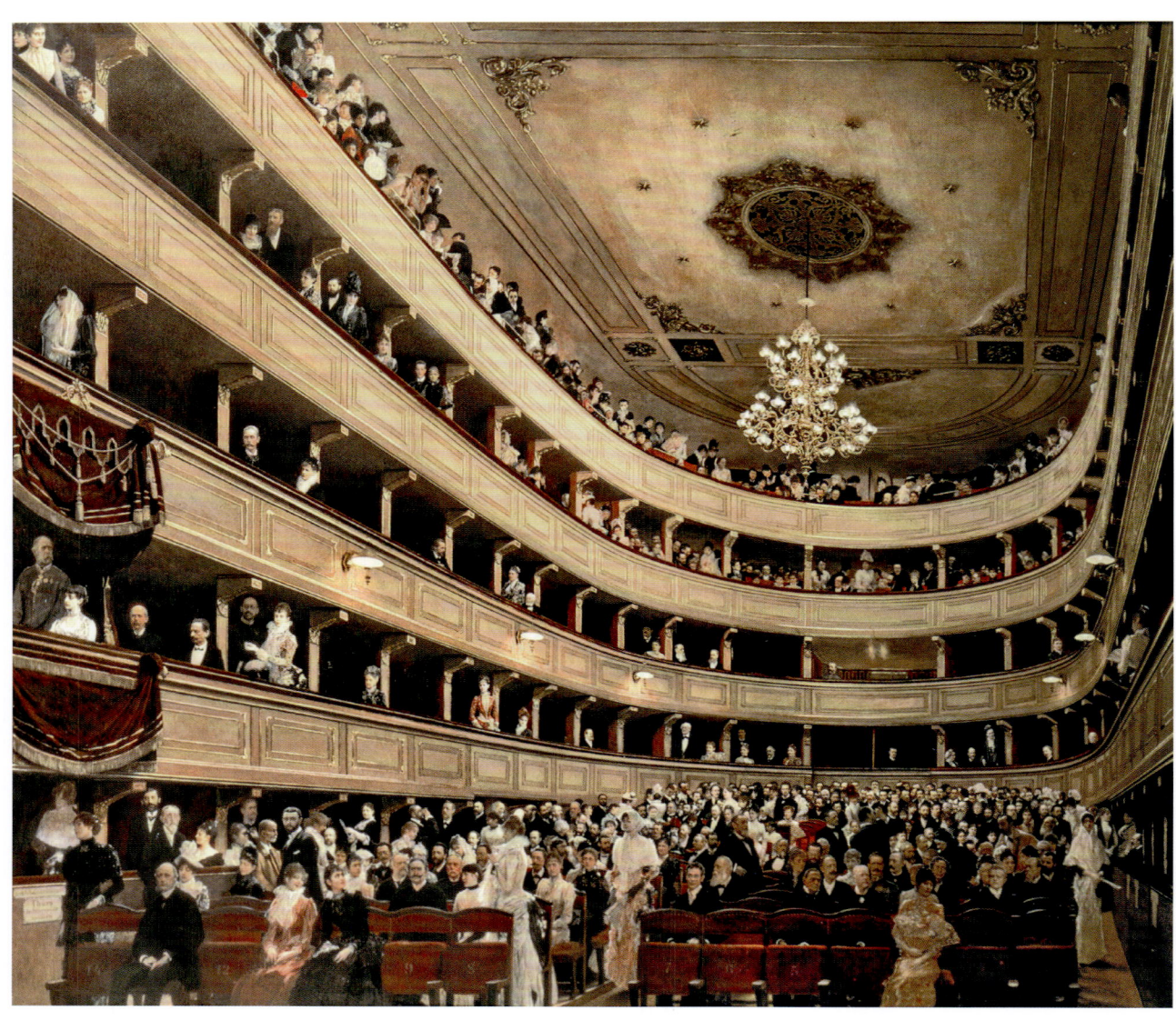

Interior View of the Old Burgtheater, 1888/1889, gouache on paper, 91.2 × 103 cm, Wien Museum, Vienna (above)

The Theatre in Taormina, 1886–1888, oil on marble plaster, *c.* 750 × 600 cm, Burgtheater, Vienna (opposite, detail)

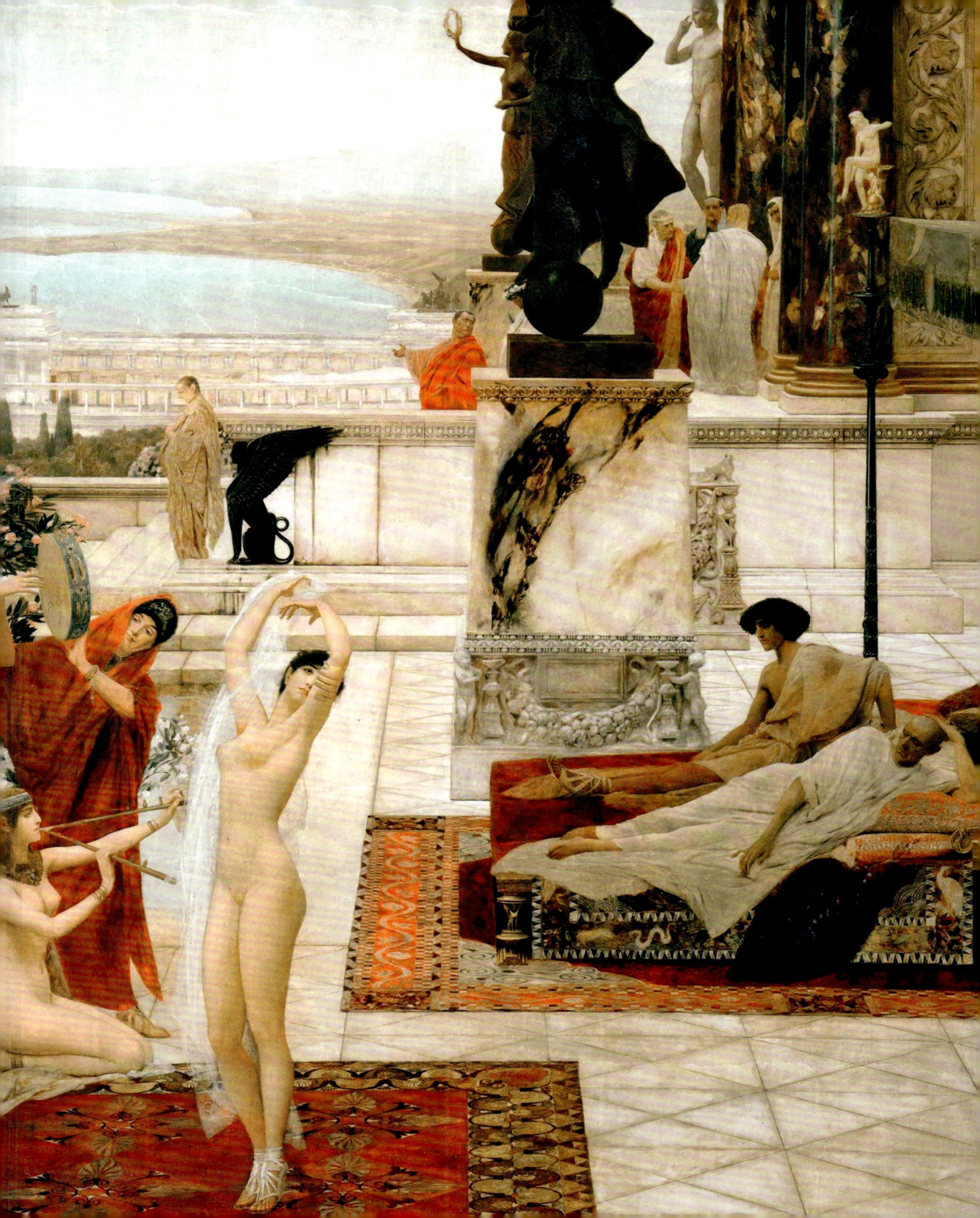

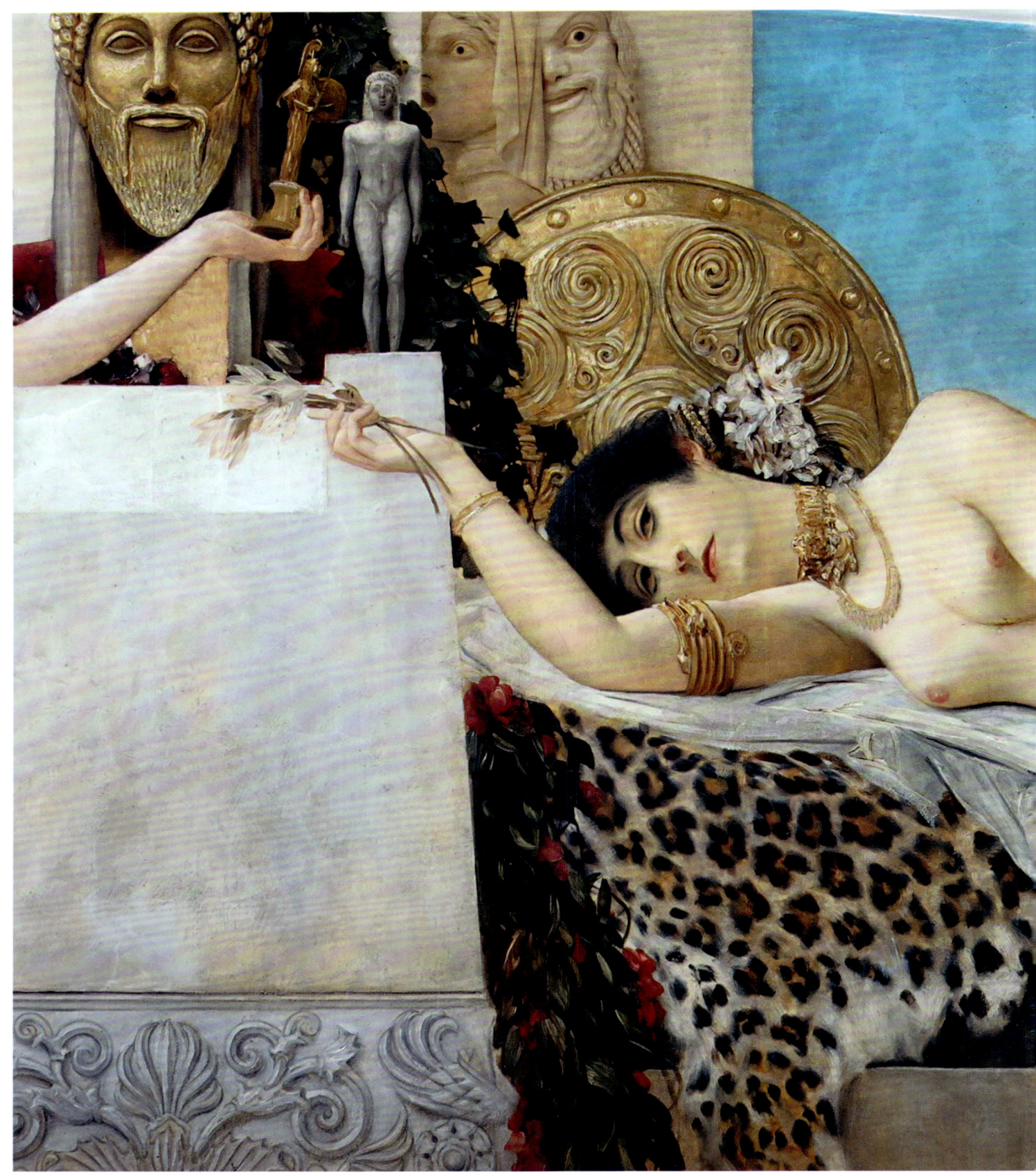

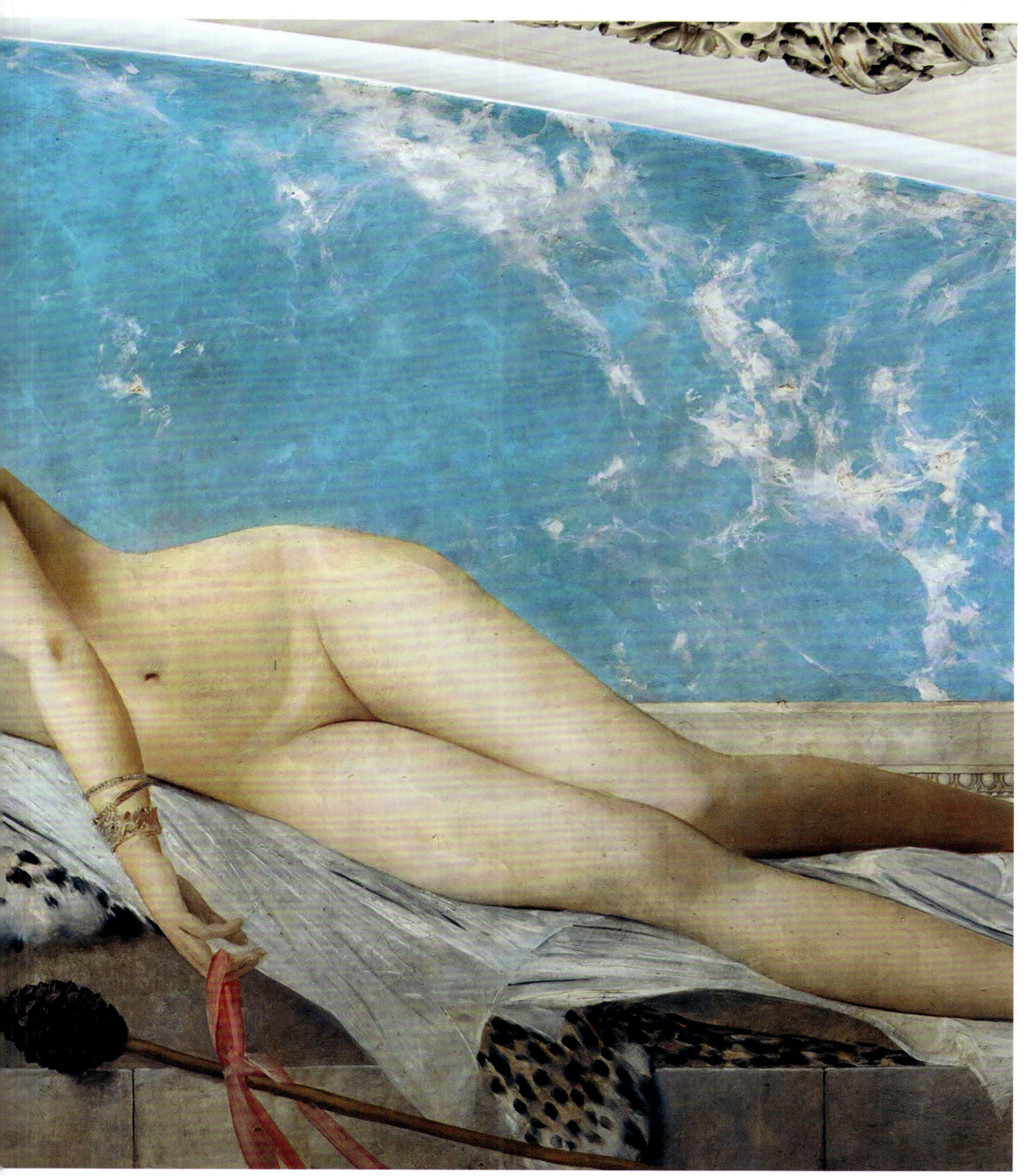

The Altar of Dionysus, 1886–1888, oil on marble plaster, *c.* 160 × 1200 cm, Burgtheater, Vienna (detail)

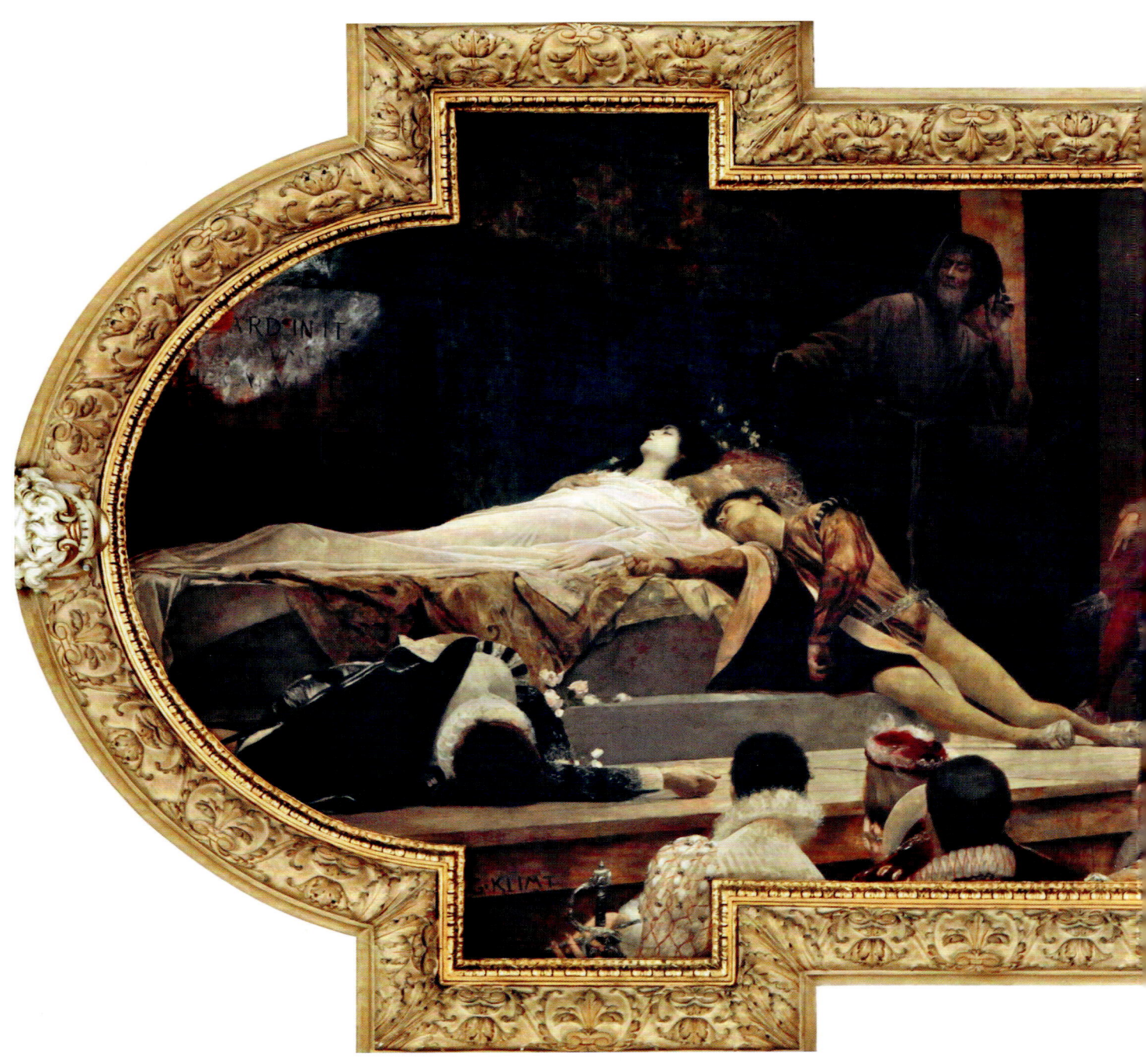

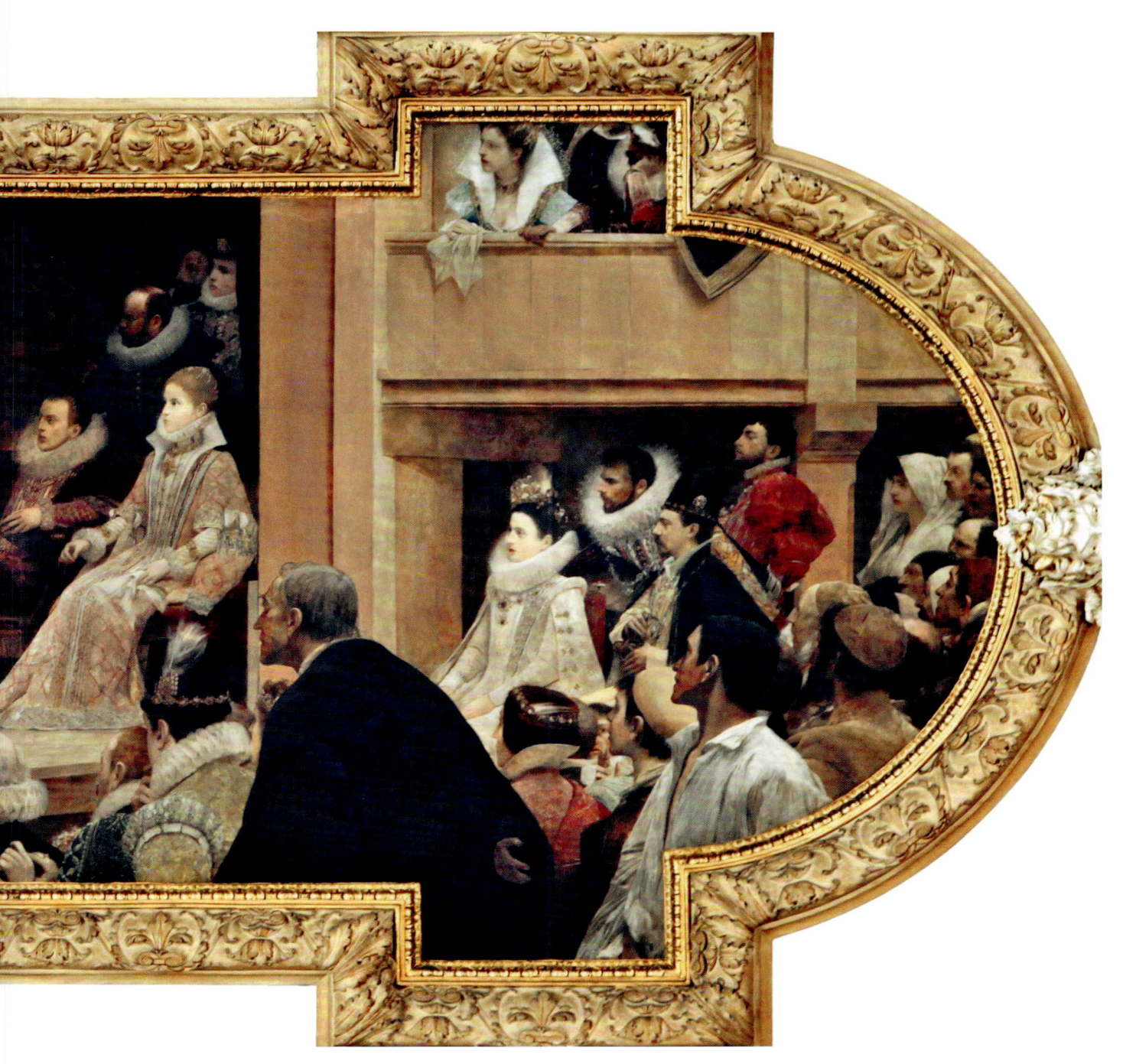

Shakespeare's Globe Theatre, 1886–1888,
oil on marble plaster, *c.* 280 × 600 cm, Burgtheater, Vienna

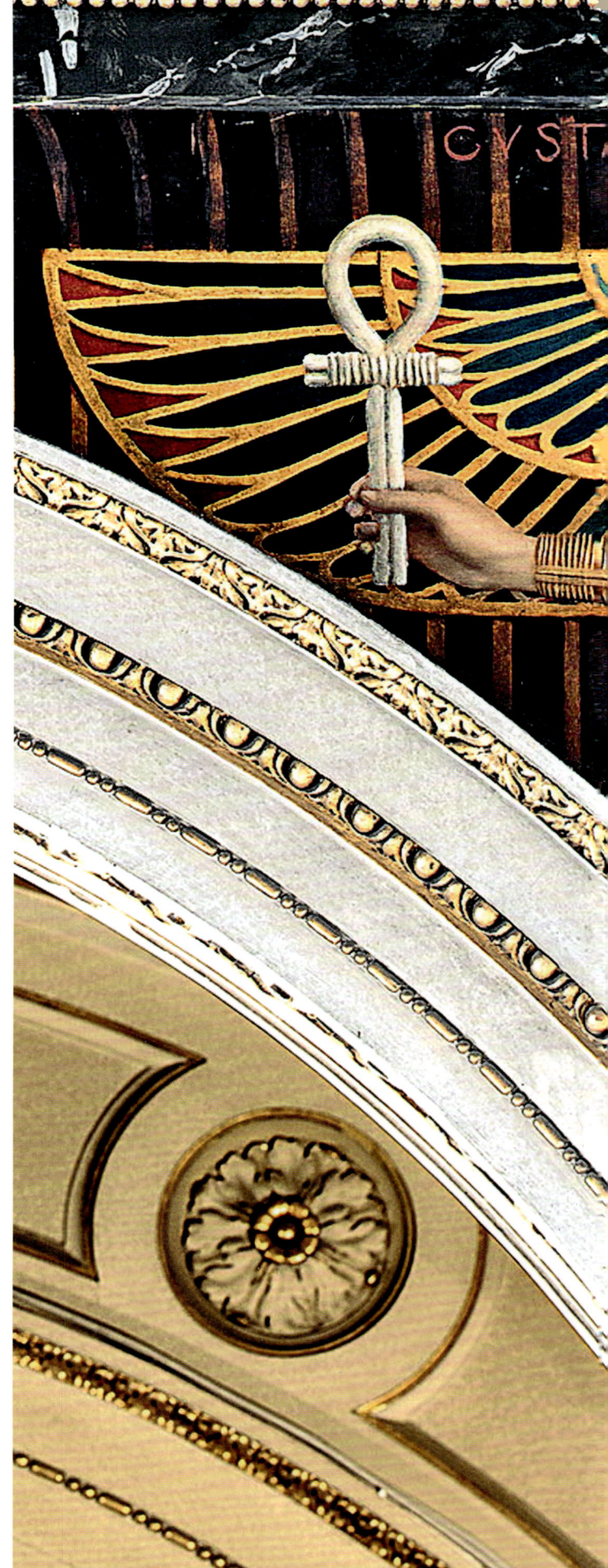

**Egyptian Art (Nekhbet and
Sarcophogus with Isis Statuette),**
1890/1891, oil on canvas,
230 × 230 cm,
Kunsthistorisches Museum, Vienna

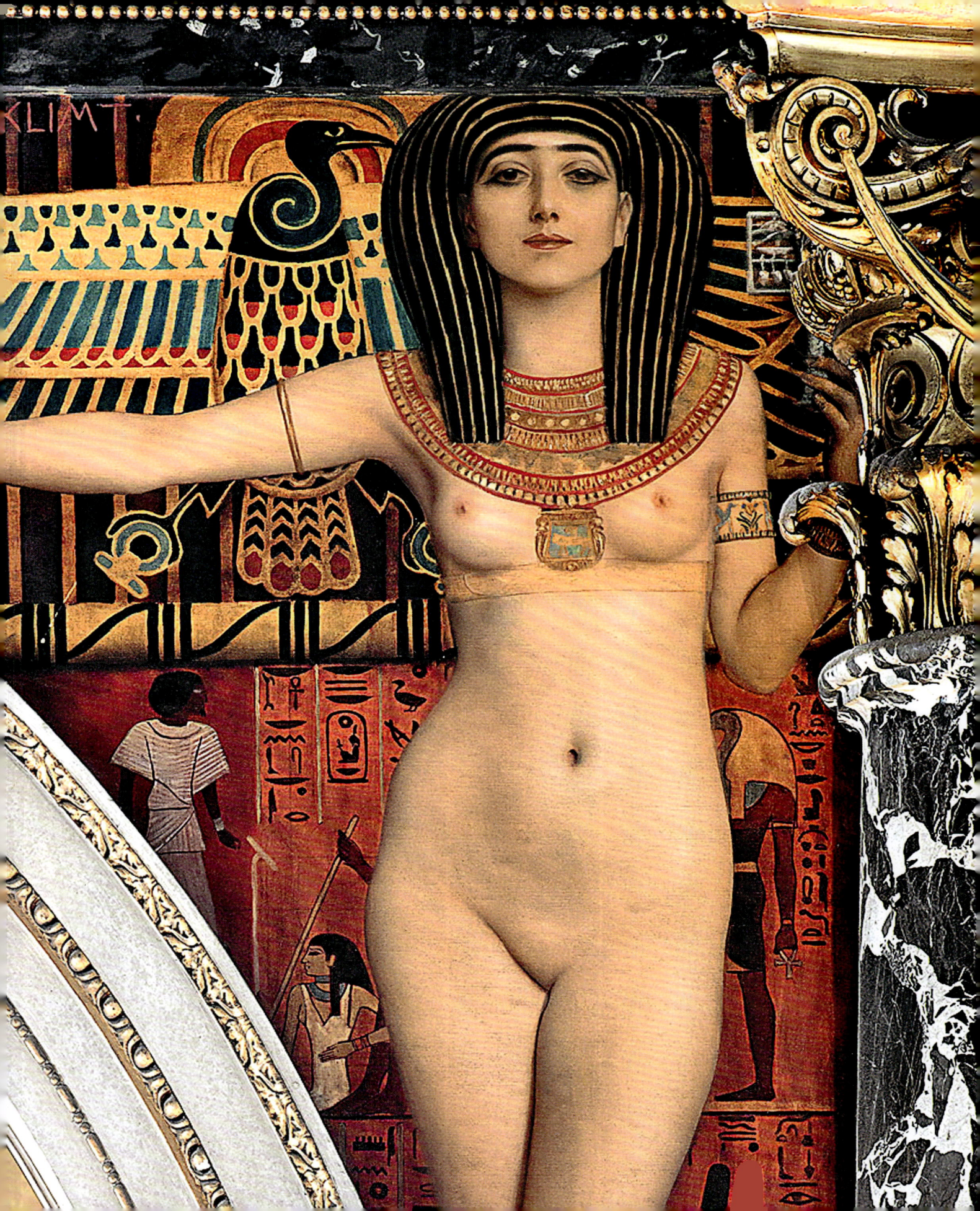

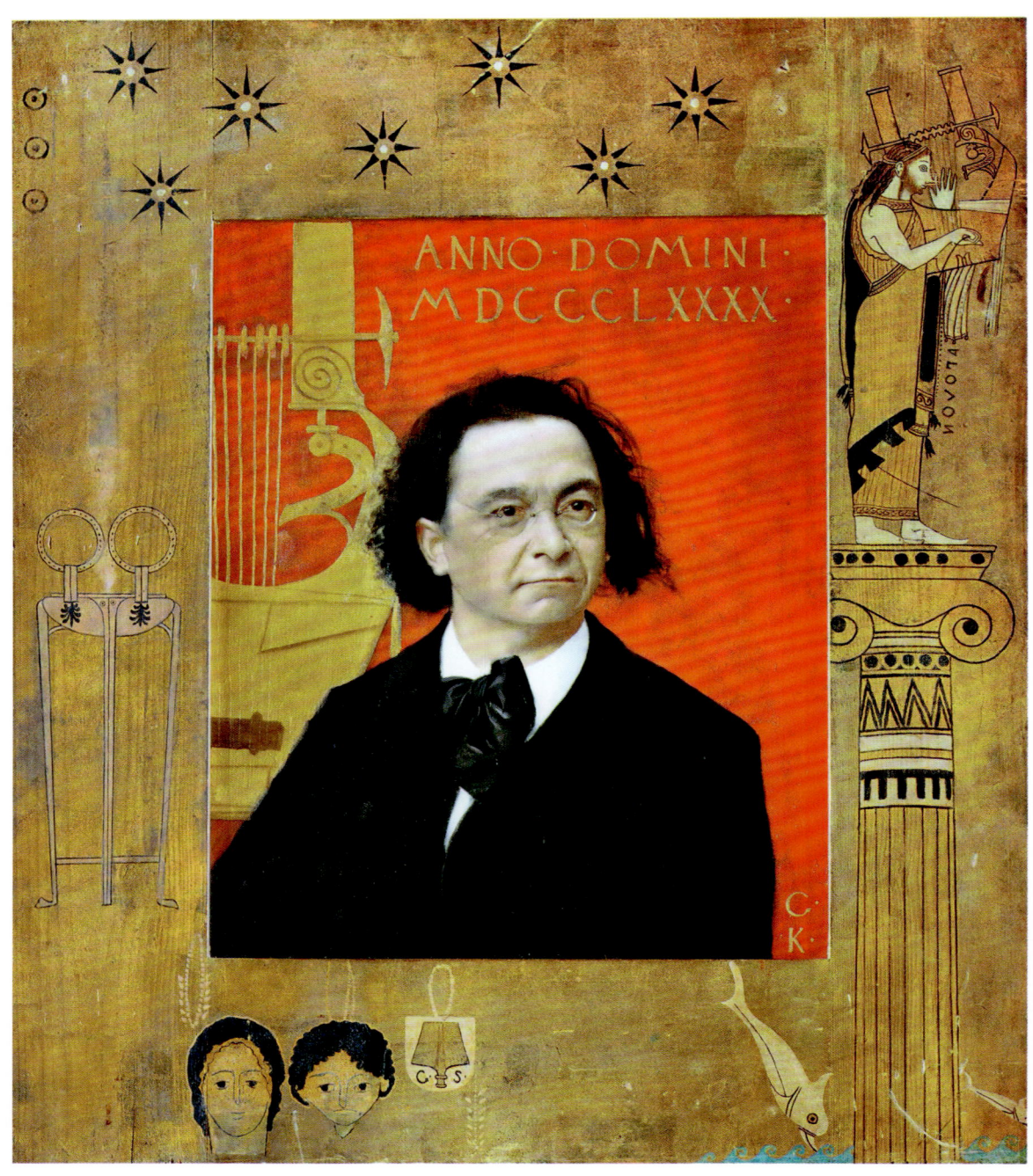

Portrait of the Pianist Josef Pembaur, 1890, oil on canvas, 69 × 55 cm,
Tiroler Landesmuseum – Ferdinandeum, Innsbruck (above)

Allegory of Love, 1895, oil on canvas, 60 × 44 cm, Wien Museum, Vienna (opposite)

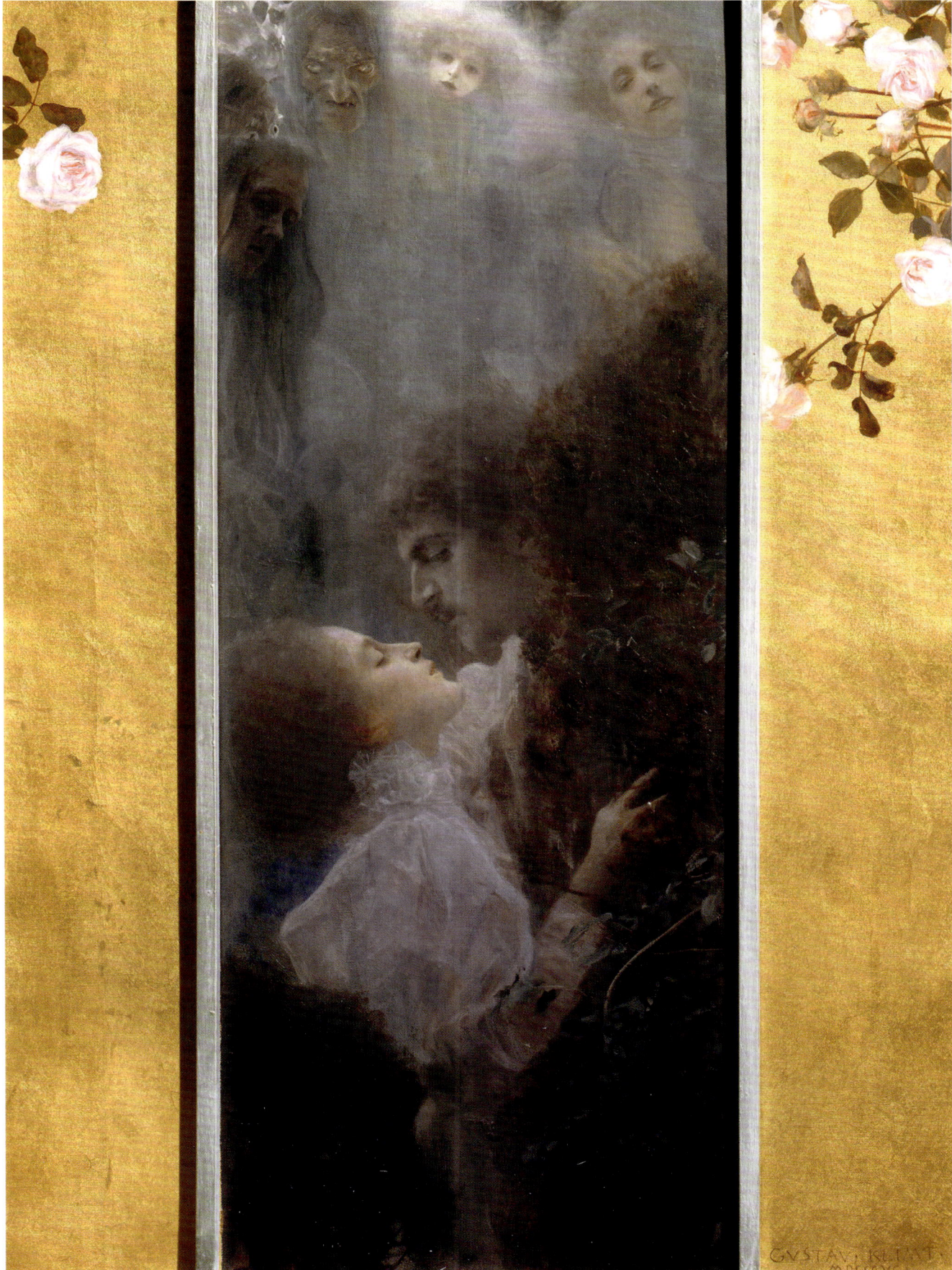

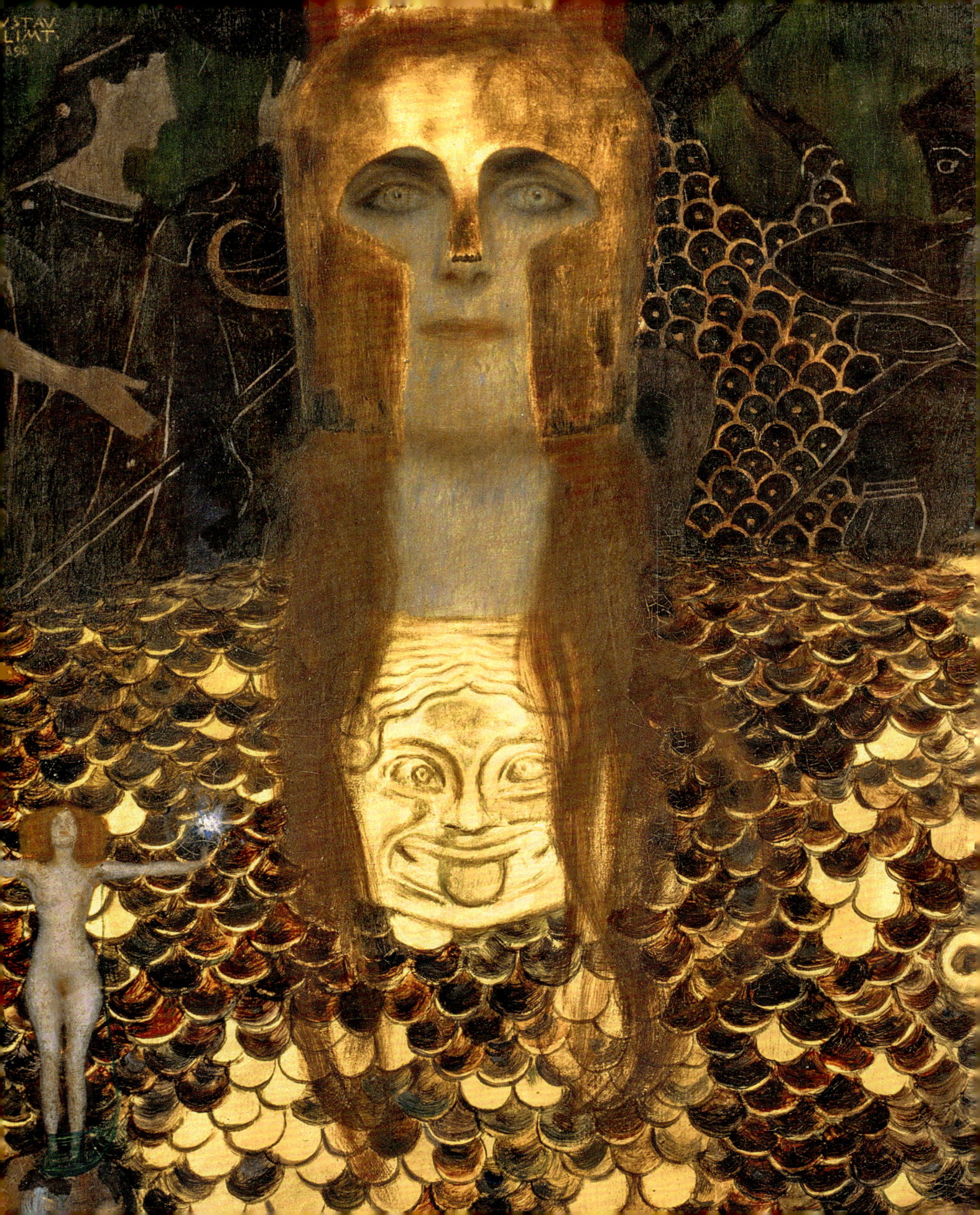

The Vienna Secession

Klimt adamantly expressed his creative energy in the poster that he designed in April 1898 for the Secession group's first exhibition (p. 39). Theseus fighting the Minotaur under the protection of Athena was emblematic for a generation of artists in revolt against a cultural milieu that they considered outdated. Since January, these artists had had a first-rate medium at their disposal: the journal *Ver Sacrum* (Sacred Spring), whose fiery temper was summarized in a statement attributed to the writer Hermann Bahr: "We wish to declare war on sterile routine, on rigid Byzantinism, on all forms of poor taste. … We must have the strength to destroy and radically tidy up." Klimt's visual message was even more effective because his composition lacked depth and accorded plentiful space to emptiness, two characteristics resulting from his familiarity with Japanese prints.

In the first version of the poster, the Greek hero's genitals were visible. Censors, however, required Klimt to hide the scandalous organs, and in the final version, he concealed them behind a tree trunk.

The goddess of justice reappeared as the protector of the Secession's activities in *Pallas Athene* (p. 32), which debuted in 1898 at the group's second exhibition. This utterly fearsome protector, with her unyielding face, strong jawline and glacial gaze, resembles the works of the Belgian Symbolist painter Fernand Khnopff. A battle in the background evokes, like that of Theseus, the Secessionists' work as well: the struggle of Heracles and Triton, transcribed from a piece of Athenian pottery from the sixth century BCE.

In *Pallas Athene*, Klimt substituted a small, red-headed female nude holding a mirror for the traditional Nike. In March 1899, she would reappear, life-sized, with the title *Nuda Veritas* (p. 38), bearing a motto in black letters on a gold background that was borrowed from the poet Friedrich Schiller: "If your deeds and your art cannot please everyone, please a few. To please many is terrible." There is nothing academic about this work's nudity. On the contrary, with her abundant red hair strewn with daisies, her slightly insolent gaze, her slender body and her flamboyant pubic hair, the subject was provocatively modern despite the rigidity of her pose, which incited Hevesi, the fine critic, to see in her a "Secessionist Isis". The serpent at her feet, which appears to have pulled down the transparent blue veil that had concealed her nudity, may symbolize temptation and vice. Could this be Eve? In search of a new visual language, Klimt clearly explored the mysterious perspectives that the Symbolists held dear. The same can be said for *Music I* (pp. 36–37), created in 1895, a modern, delicate figure silhouetted against a starry night sky, absorbed in the music of a voluminous antique zither. How could one possibly not think of Friedrich Nietzsche – whose seminal work *The Birth of Tragedy* was published in 1872 and reissued in 1886 – for whom music connected humankind with the cosmos and revealed the most deeply buried feelings of the spirit?

Like the Symbolist painters, Klimt also created more alarming images of femininity by returning, for example, to the biblical figures Judith and Salome (pp. 40–41). In these works, both heads – that of Holofernes and that of John the Baptist – are not merely brandished but are reduced to decorative accessories, making the women into contemporary femmes fatales, wearing "dresses of the modern day, made up in fabrics that are more or less in fashion", as Hevesi noted.

The Secession gave Klimt a magnificent opportunity to put his decorative painting talents to good use. The Vienna group inarguably achieved its objective to turn its exhibition hall into a temple of art with its fourteenth exhibition, which opened on 15 April 1902. Designed entirely by Josef Hoffmann, it was dedicated to the display of *Beethoven,* which the German sculptor Max Klinger (1857–1920) had just completed after six years of work. For the occasion, Klimt's frieze of the same name (pp. 44–50; fold-out p. 50), measuring thirty-four metres in length, was installed on the upper part of three walls in the left-side room. The first wall depicts humanity's longing for happiness as it supplicates a knight resplendent in golden armour. On the back wall, hostile forces rage around the giant Typhon, a monstrous winged ape with a serpent's tail that Zeus confronted twice; to his left are the Gorgons, above whom hover Sickness, Madness and Death, while to his right are shown Lust, Immodesty and Intemperance. After overcoming these obstacles, the longing for happiness, under the guidance of Music and Poetry, resumes its path on the right-hand wall, finding fulfillment in the form of an intertwined nude couple. With its undeniably erotic character, this embrace hardly corresponds with the fraternal and universal embrace celebrated in the *Ode to Joy* at the end of Ludwig van Beethoven's Ninth Symphony. Another interpretation was proposed in the 1970s, in which the armoured hero's virility is annihilated following the journey past the hostile forces and the final embrace symbolizes the triumph of the woman, who lives in harmony with the flow of the cosmos. In light of this Freudian approach, the *Beethoven Frieze* is as much an homage to Beethoven's genius as it is an example of the omnipresence of the duality of Eros and Thanatos in Klimt's work.

Pallas Athene,
1898, oil on canvas, 75 × 75 cm, Wien Museum, Vienna (p. 32, detail)

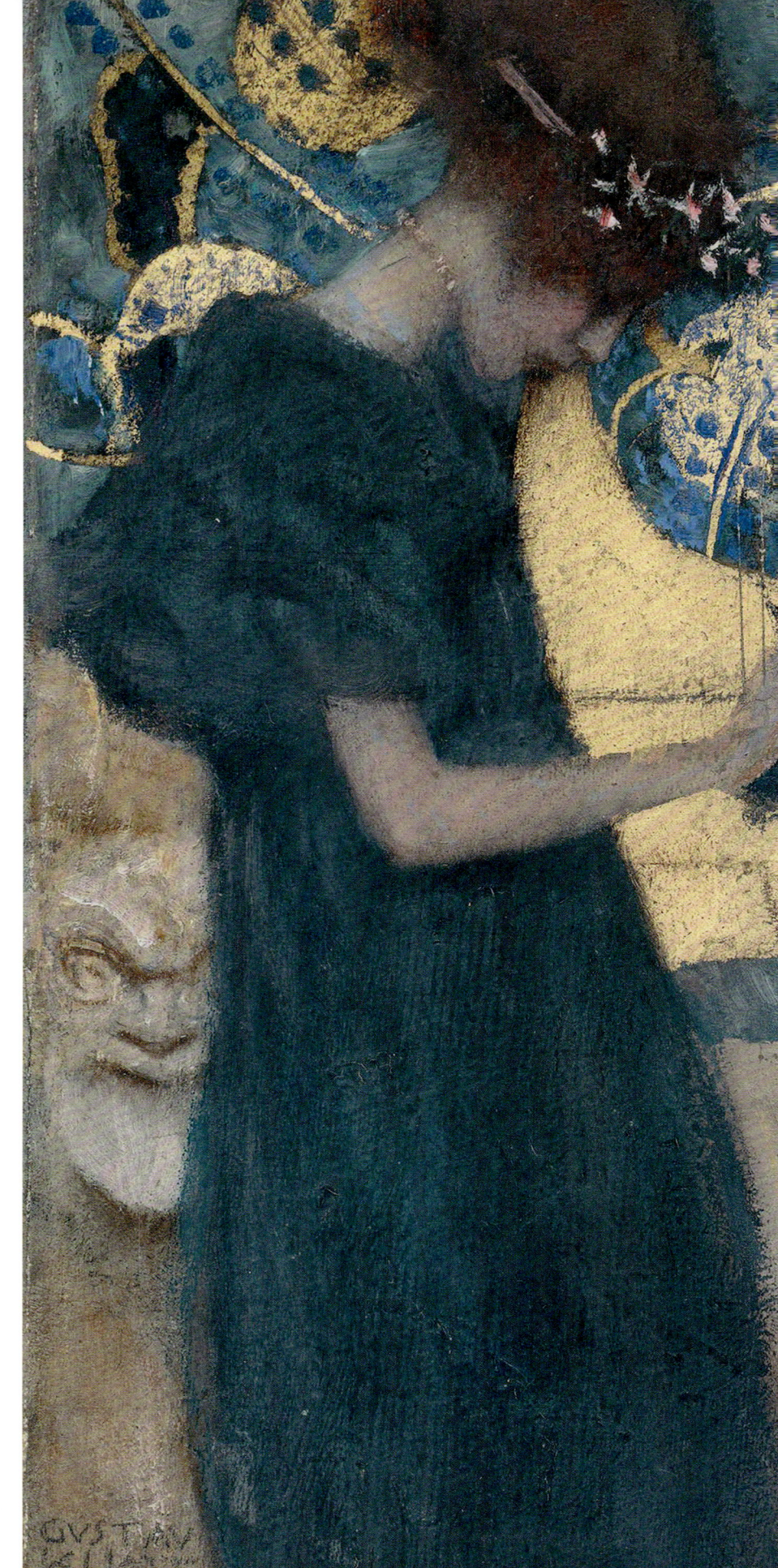

Music,
1895, oil and gold on canvas,
27.5 × 35.5 cm,
Bayerische Staatsgemäldesammlungen –
Neue Pinakothek, Munich (detail)

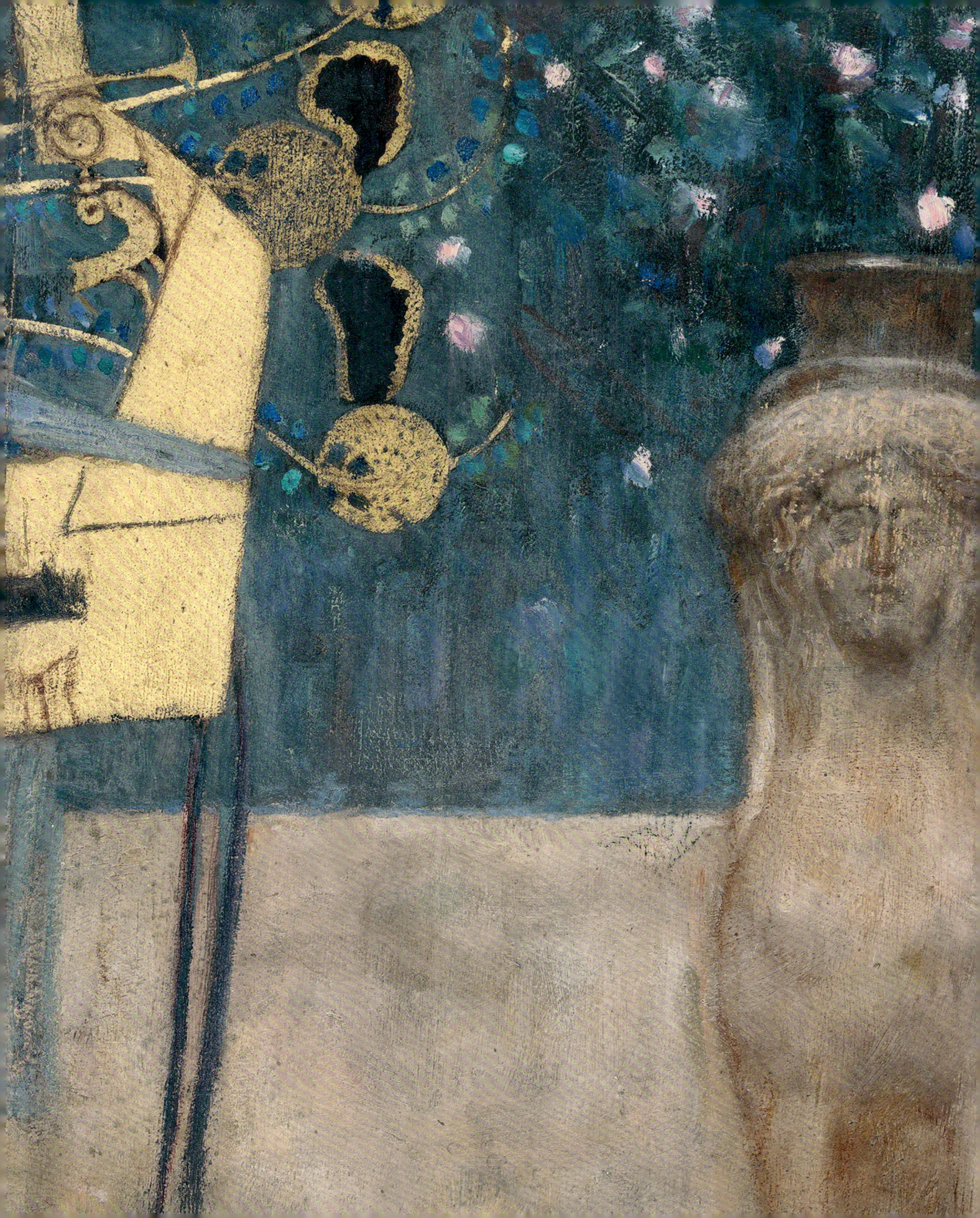

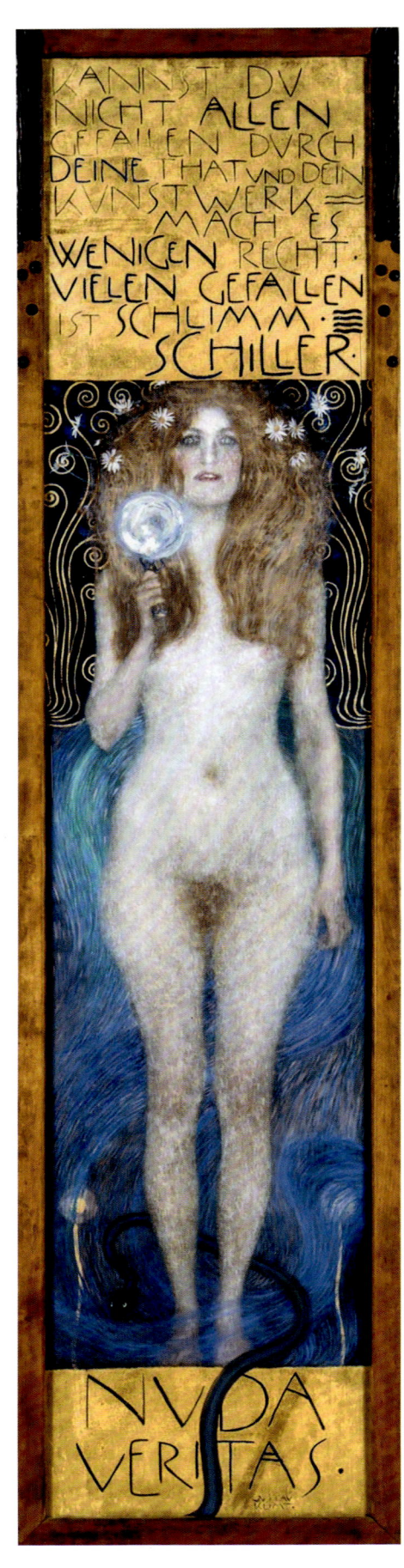

Nuda Veritas,
1899, oil on canvas,
252 × 56.2 cm,
Österreichisches
Theatermuseum, Vienna
(left)

**Poster for the first exhibition
of the Vienna Secession,**
1898, colour lithograph,
64 × 47 cm,
private collection
(opposite)

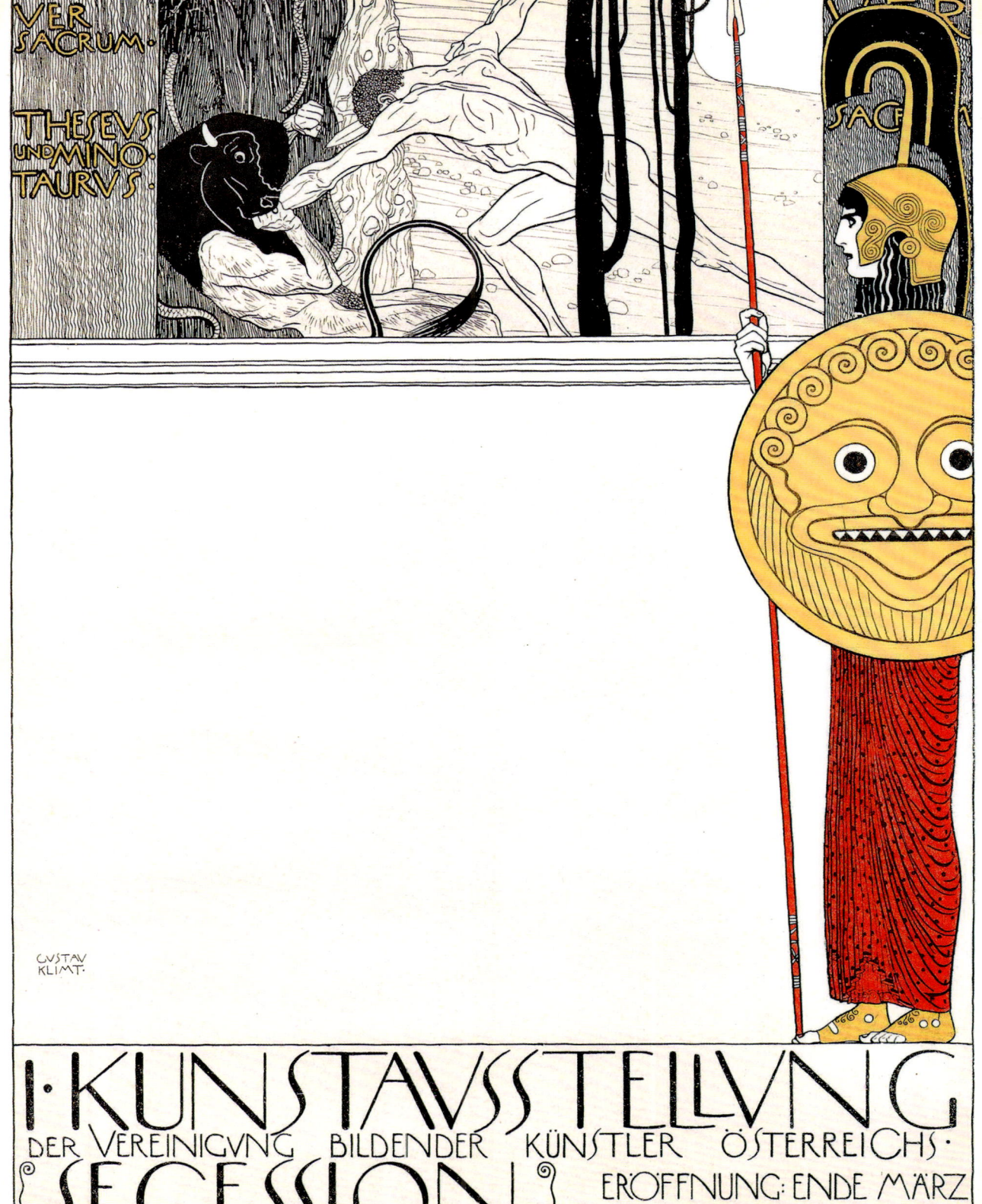

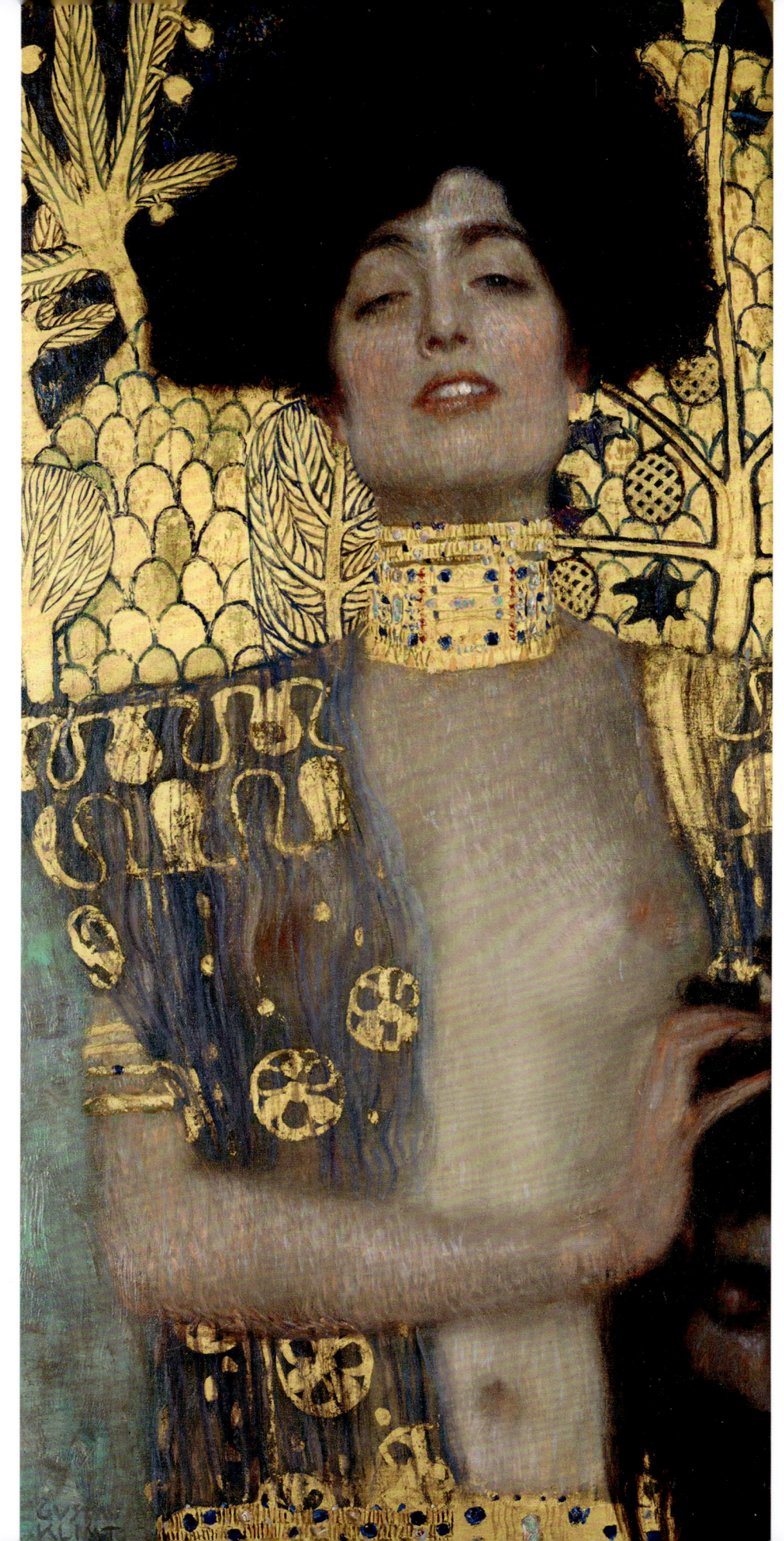

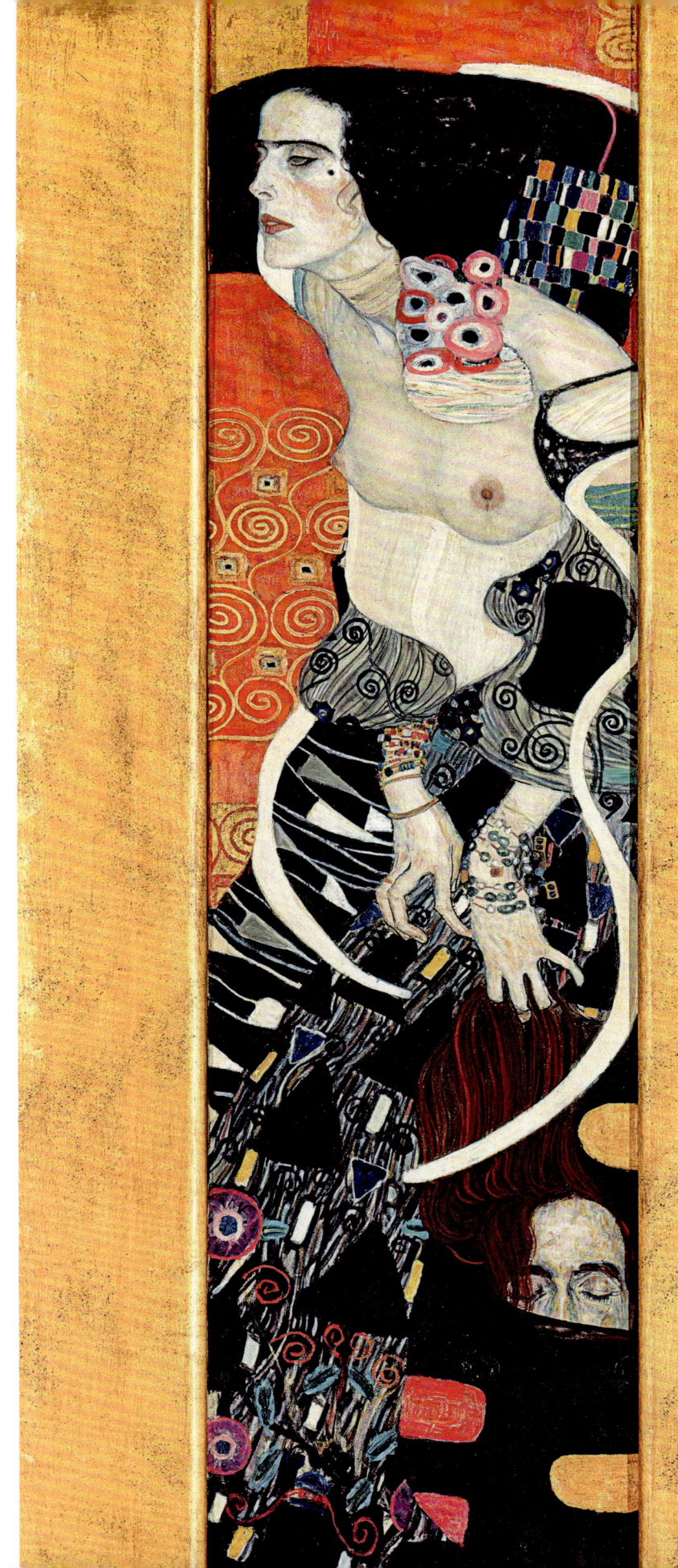

Judith I,
1901, oil and gold on canvas,
84 × 42 cm,
Österreichische Galerie Belvedere, Vienna
(opposite, detail)

Judith II (Salome),
1909, oil on canvas,
178 × 46 cm,
Fondazione Musei Civici di Venezia, Venice
(right, detail)

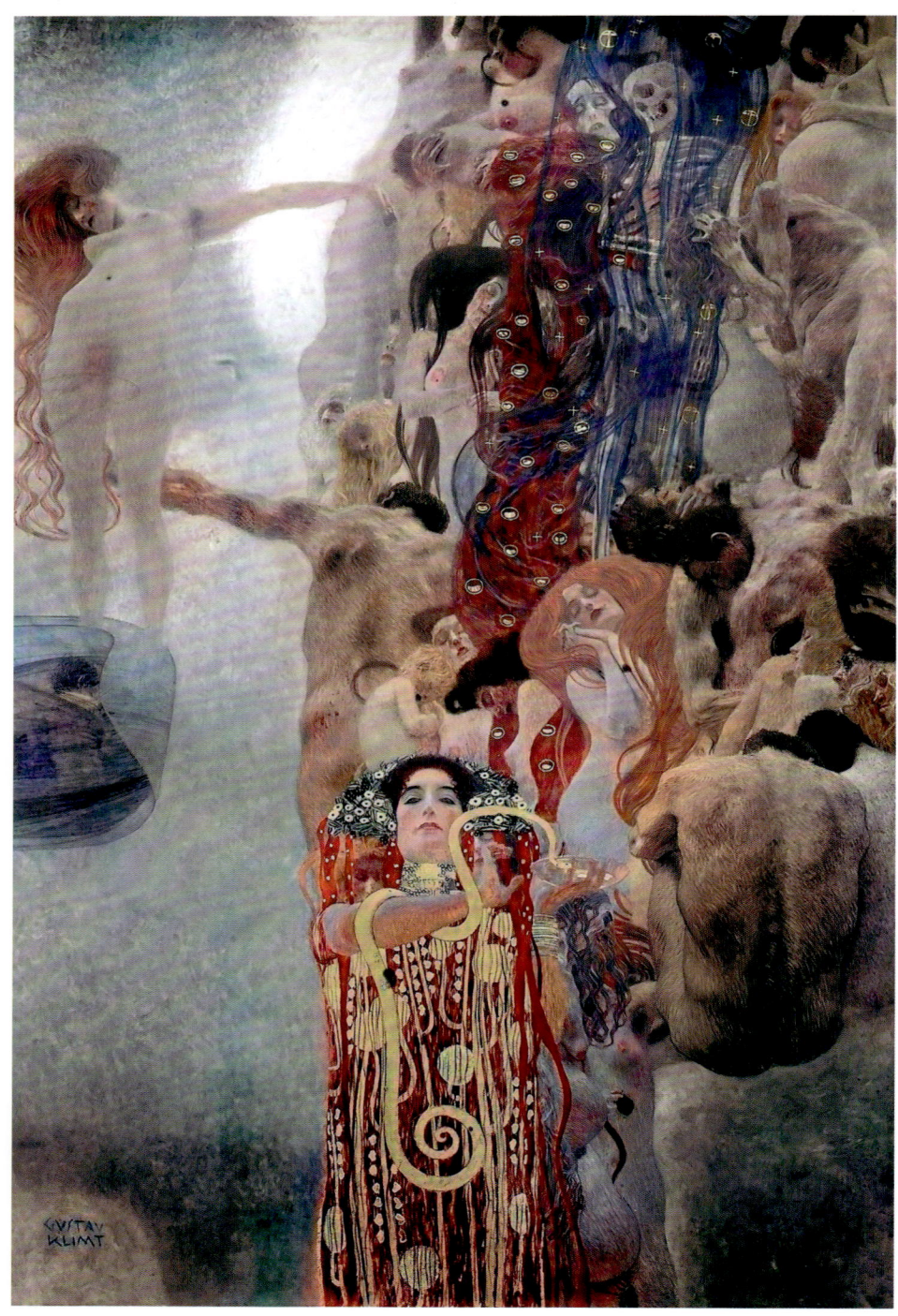

Medicine, destroyed in the 1945 fire at Schloss Immendorf and
colour scheme reconstructed with artificial intelligence, 430 × 300 cm,
Österreichische Galerie Belvedere, Vienna, in partnership with Google (above)

Hygieia (detail from *Medicine,* opposite)

The Beethoven Frieze, The Gorgons (pp. 44–45, detail of central wall),
Poetry and **Longing for Happiness** (pp. 46–49, details of right-hand wall)
1901/1902, charcoal, graphite, black and coloured chalk, red chalk,
pastels, casein paint, gold, silver, gilt stucco, applications,
215 × 3,414 cm, Secession Building, Vienna

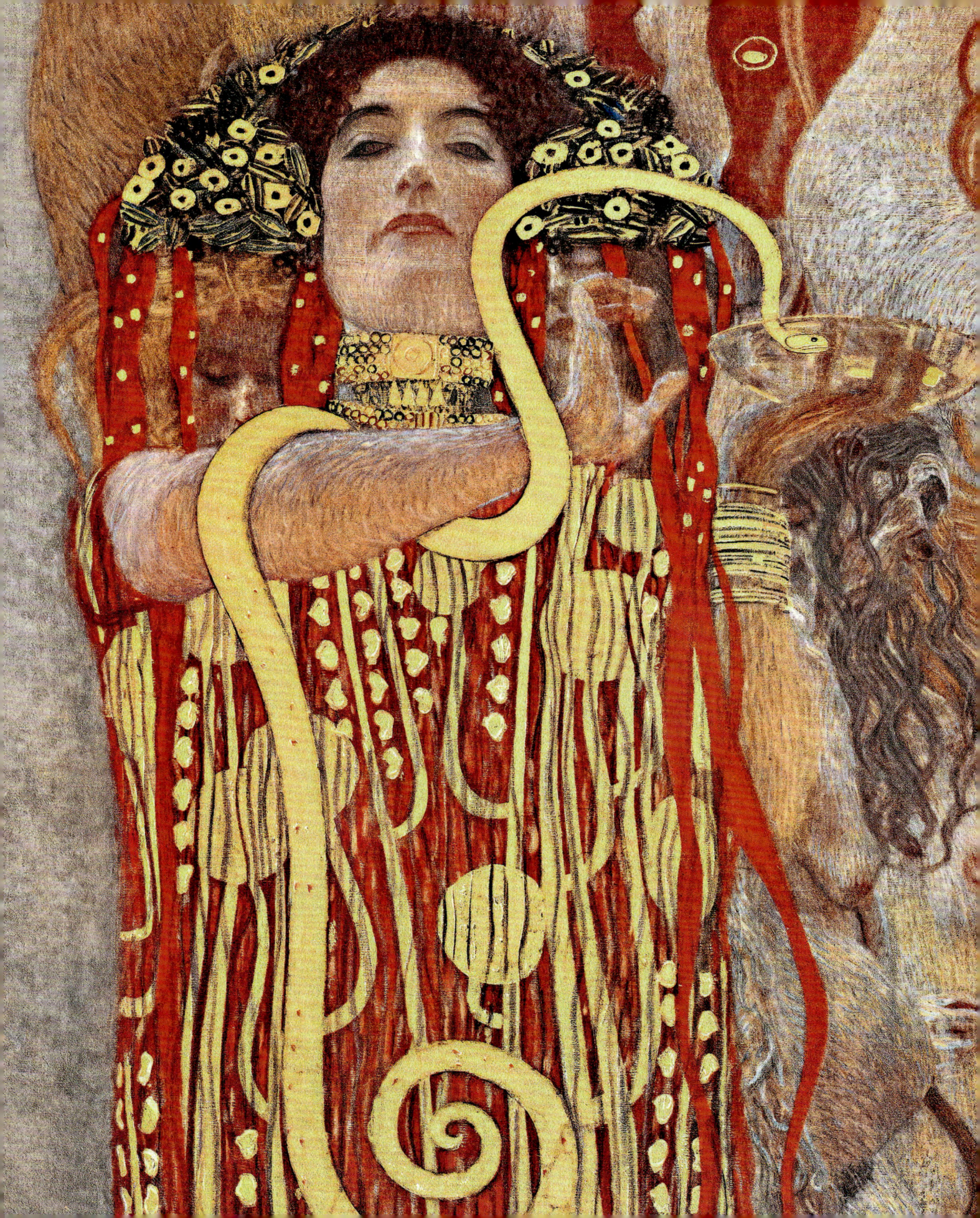

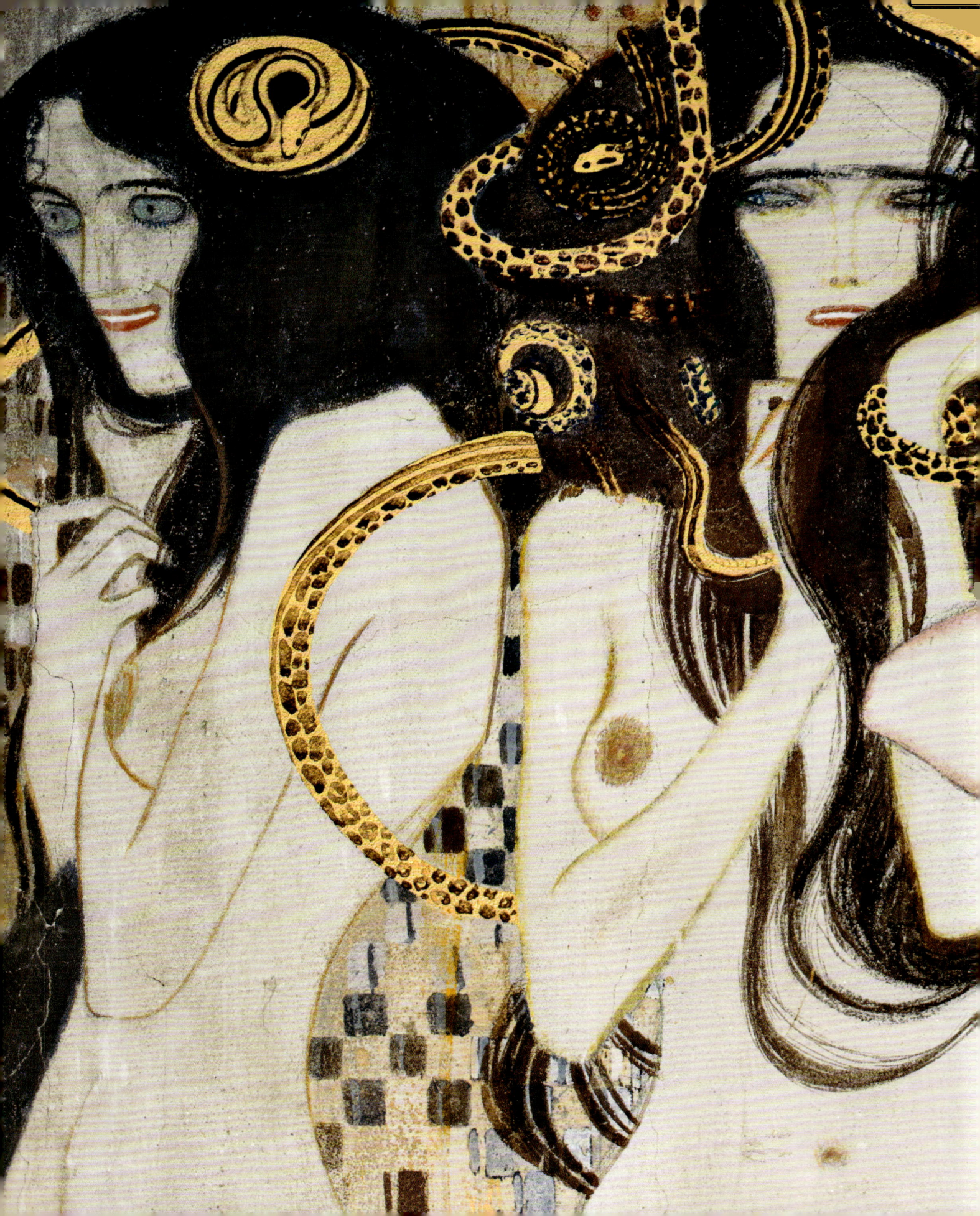

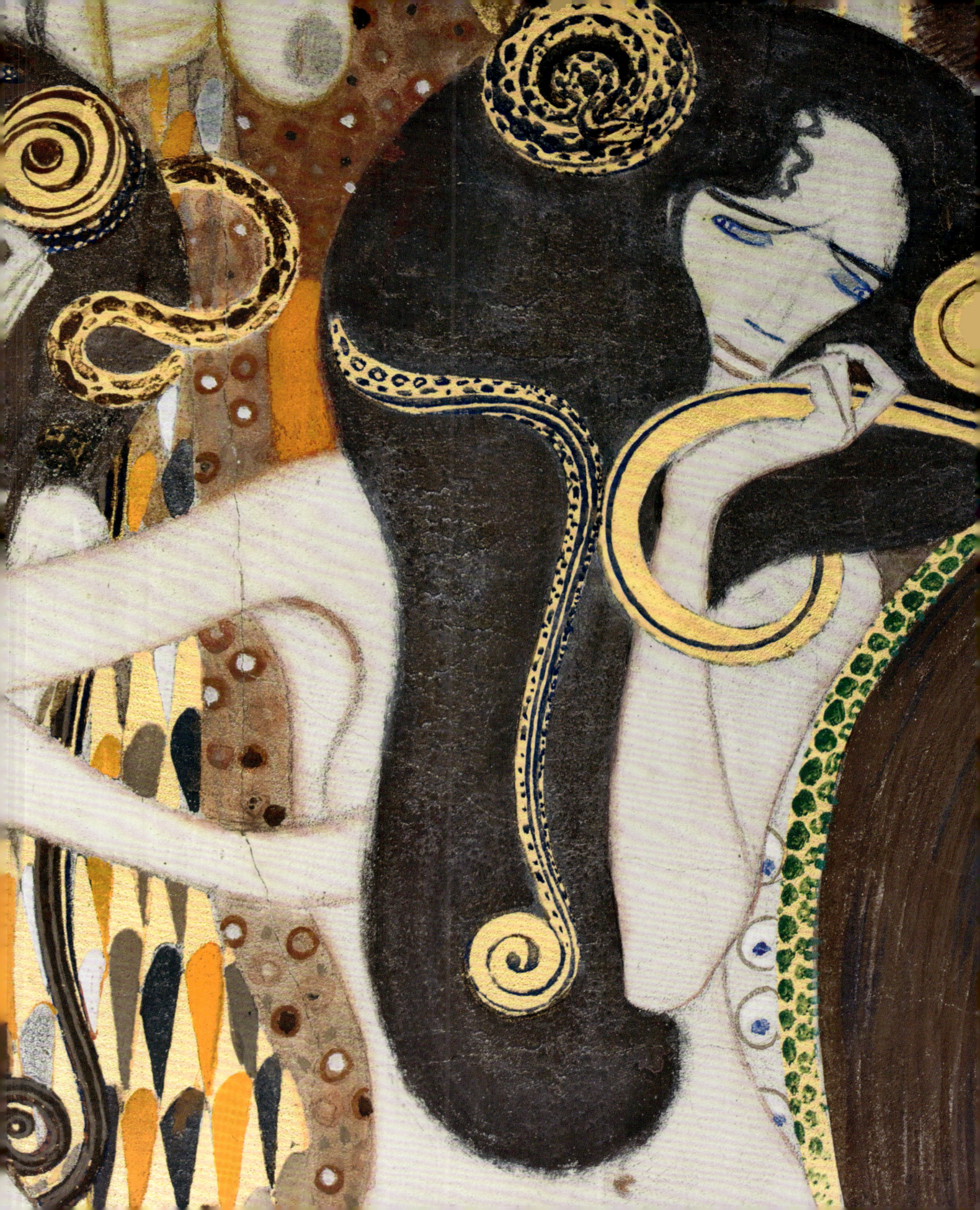

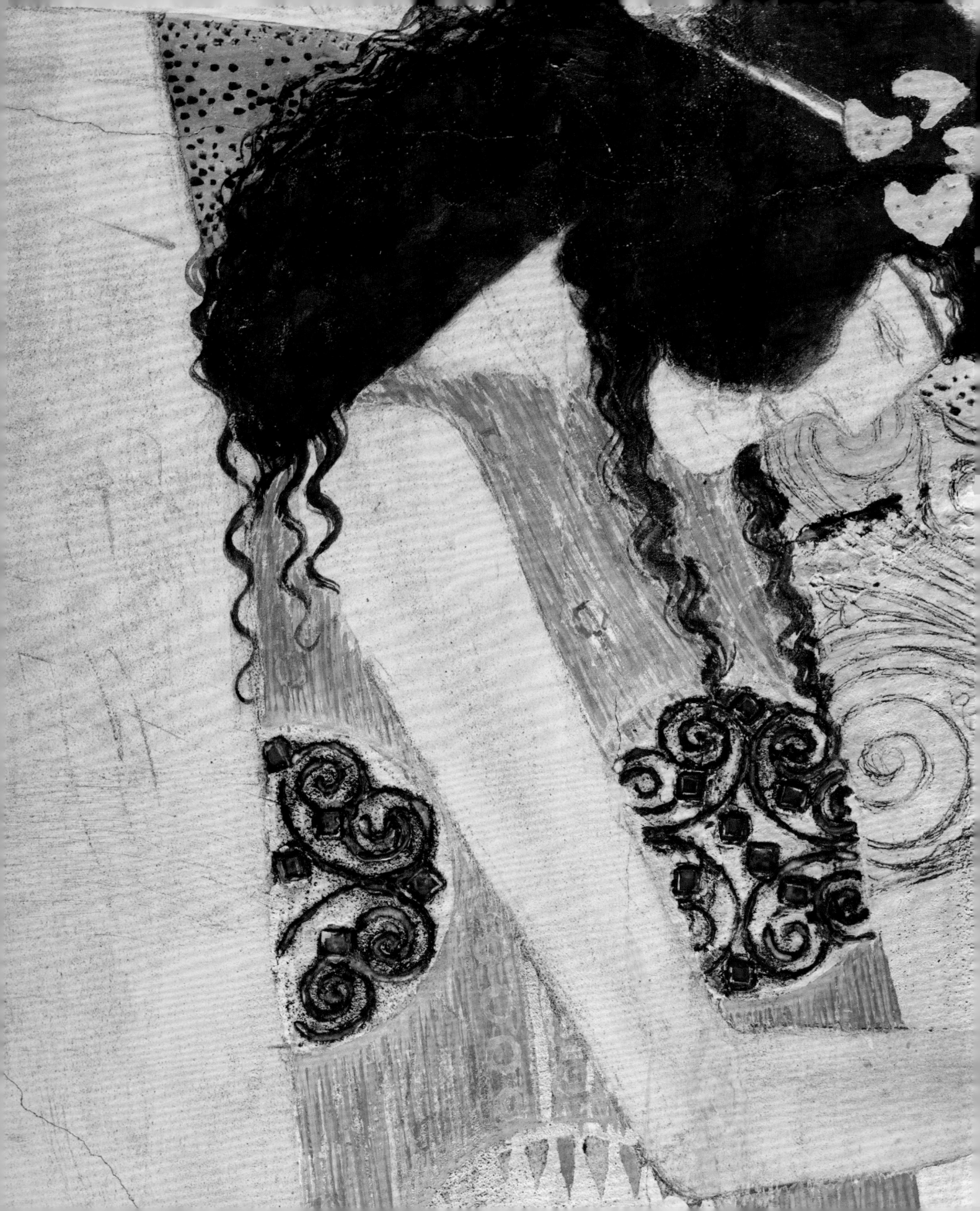

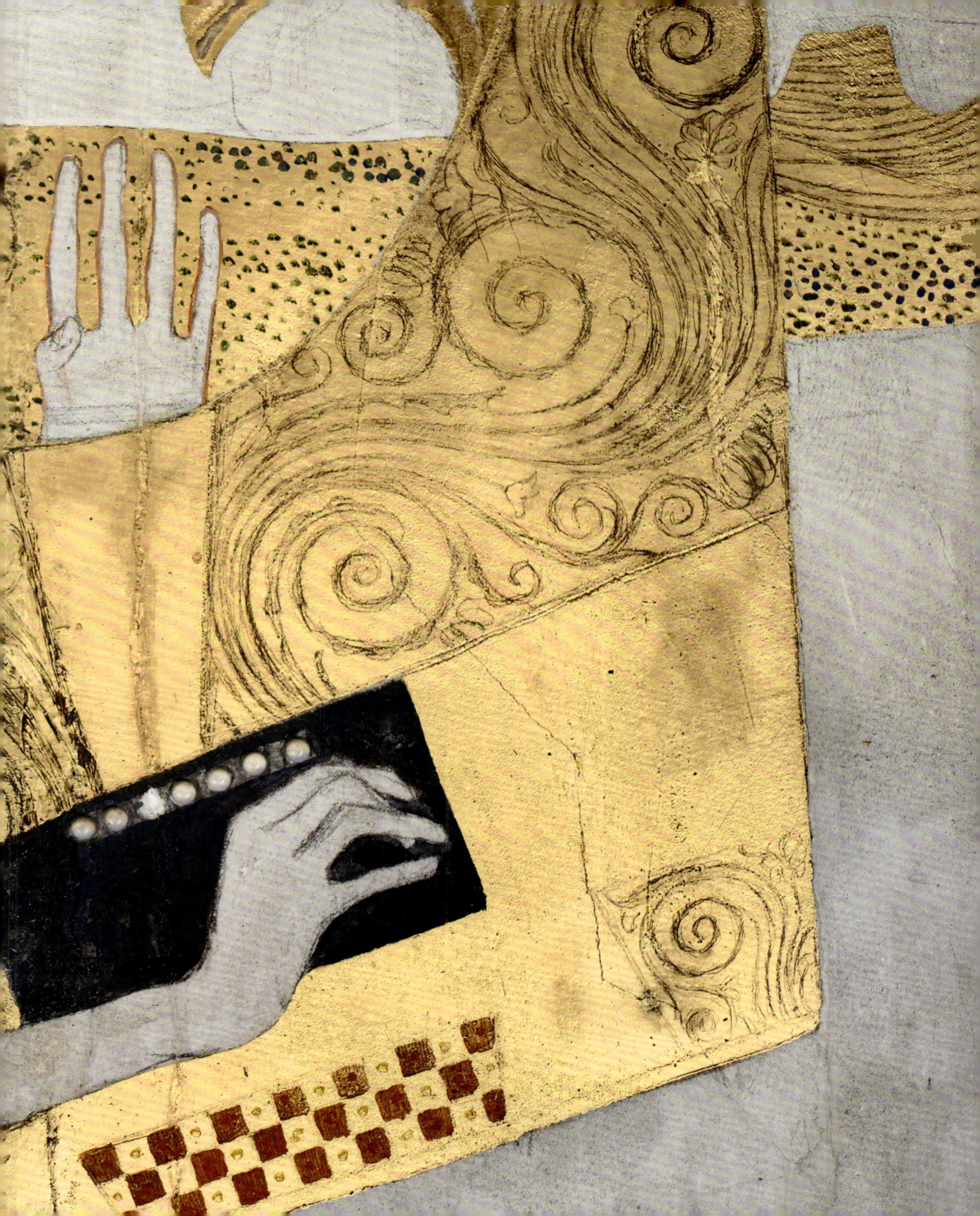

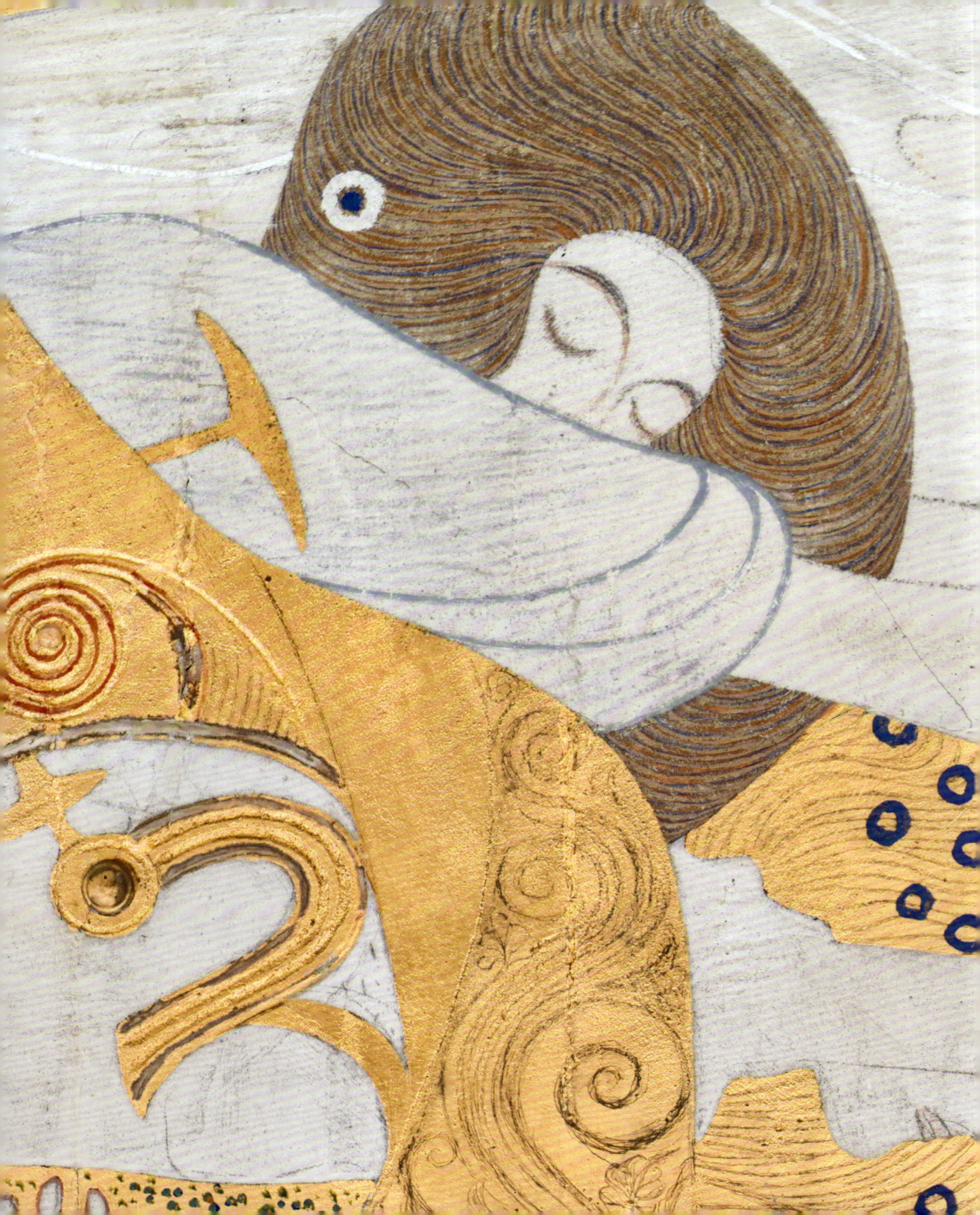

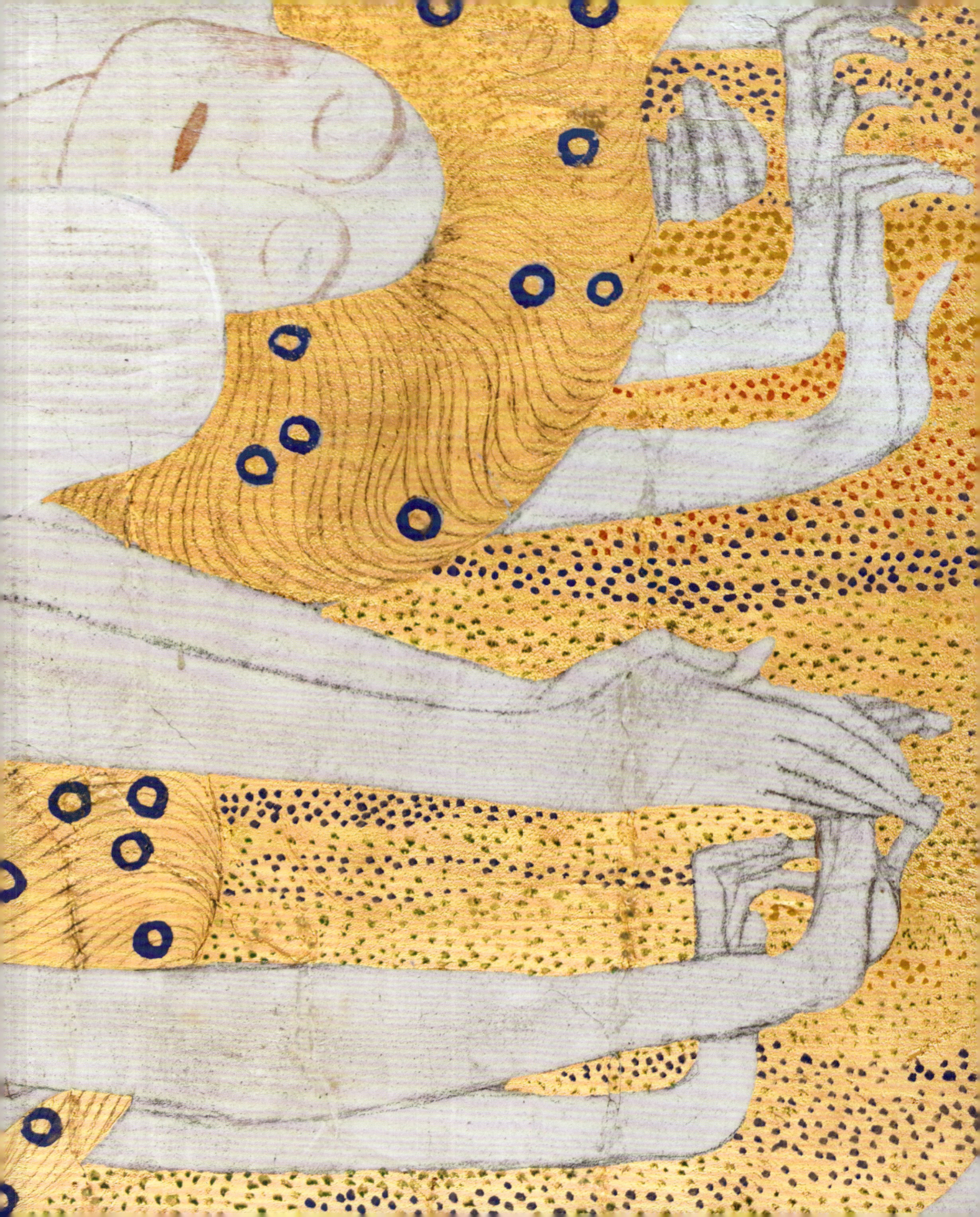

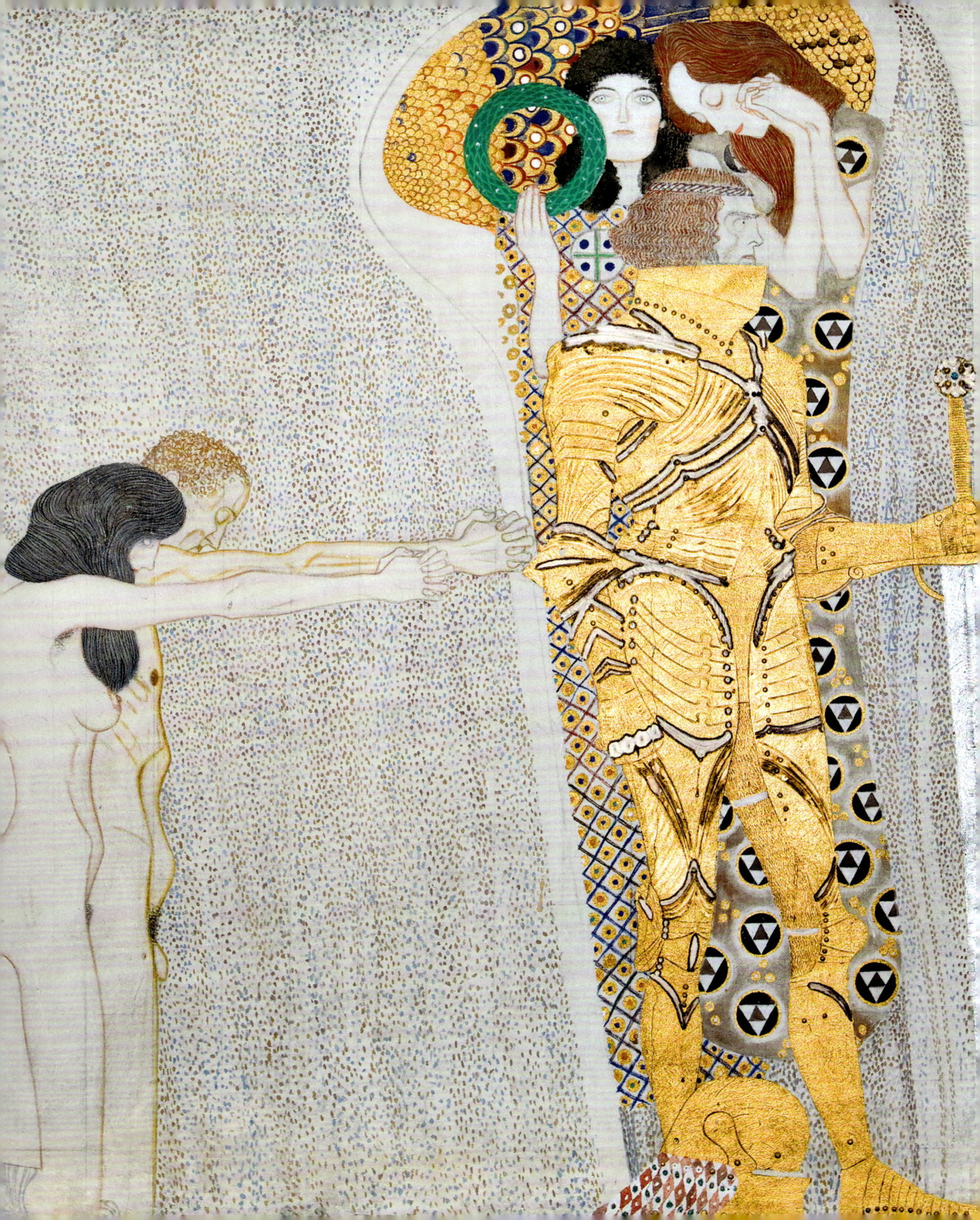

The Beethoven Frieze

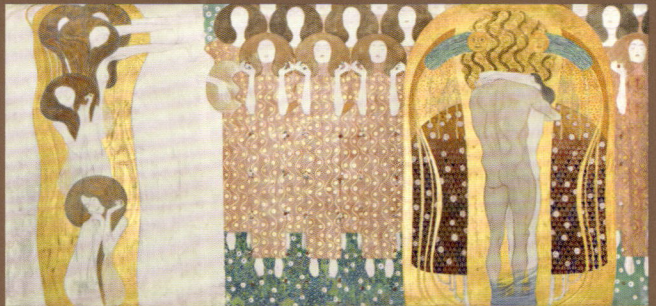

In 1902, the *Beethoven Frieze* formed the starting point in a presentation designed by Josef Hoffmann that culminated with Max Klinger's *Beethoven* sculpture at the centre of the Secession Building. Following the temporary display, the frieze remained *in situ* through the Klimt retrospective in November 1903. When this exhibition closed its doors, the industrialist Carl Reininghaus acquired the frieze and then sold it to August Lederer in 1915. Due to persecution under the Nazis, his wife, Serena, and son, Erich, were forced to give up their collection before fleeing Austria. After the war, Lederer sought restitution for his stolen paintings. The court decided in his favour and issued an order prohibiting the export of the frieze. In 1973, following long negotiations, the Austrian state acquired the work for fifteen million schillings and proceeded to restore it. Since 1985, it has been on display in the lower level of the Secession Building, in a space that is identical in size to the 1902 installation.

Beethoven Frieze, 1901/1902, casein paint and charcoal on lime plaster, gold leaf, semi-precious stones and mother-of-pearl, 215 × 3,414 cm, Secession Building, Vienna

Beethoven Frieze (detail of central wall), 1901/1902, *Ode to Joy* (open fold-out)

Beethoven Frieze (detail of left wall), 1901/1902, *Well-Armed Strong One* (left page)

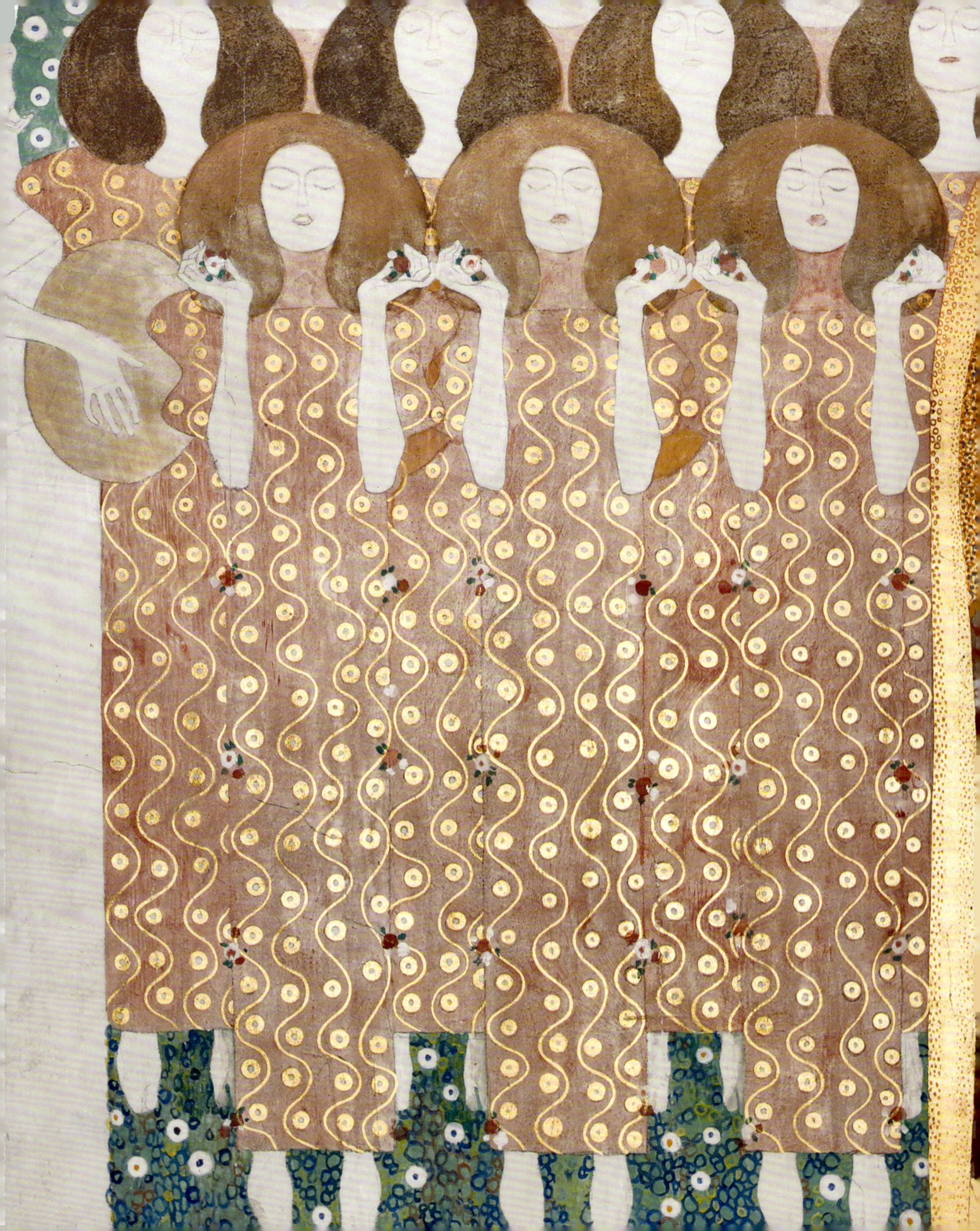

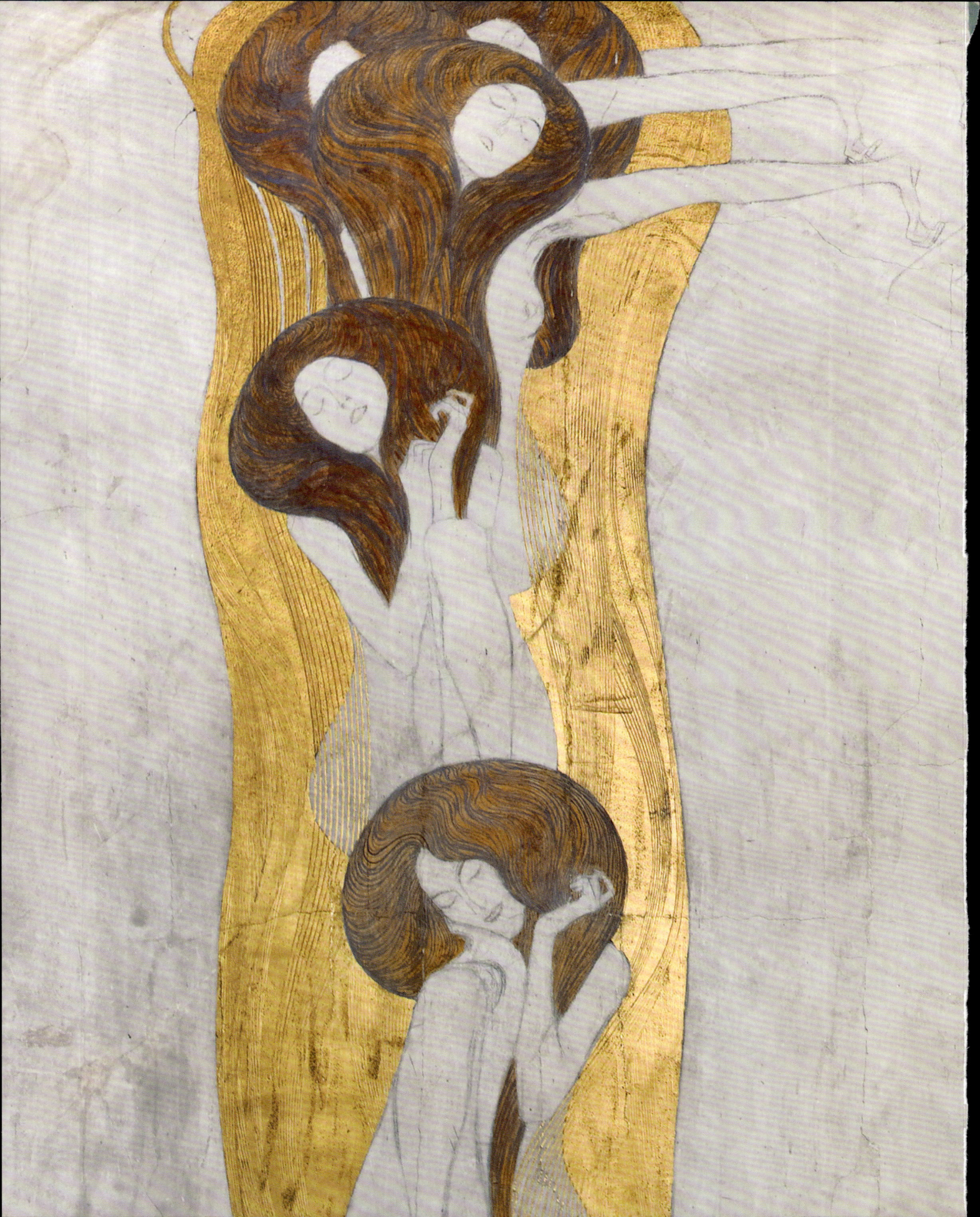

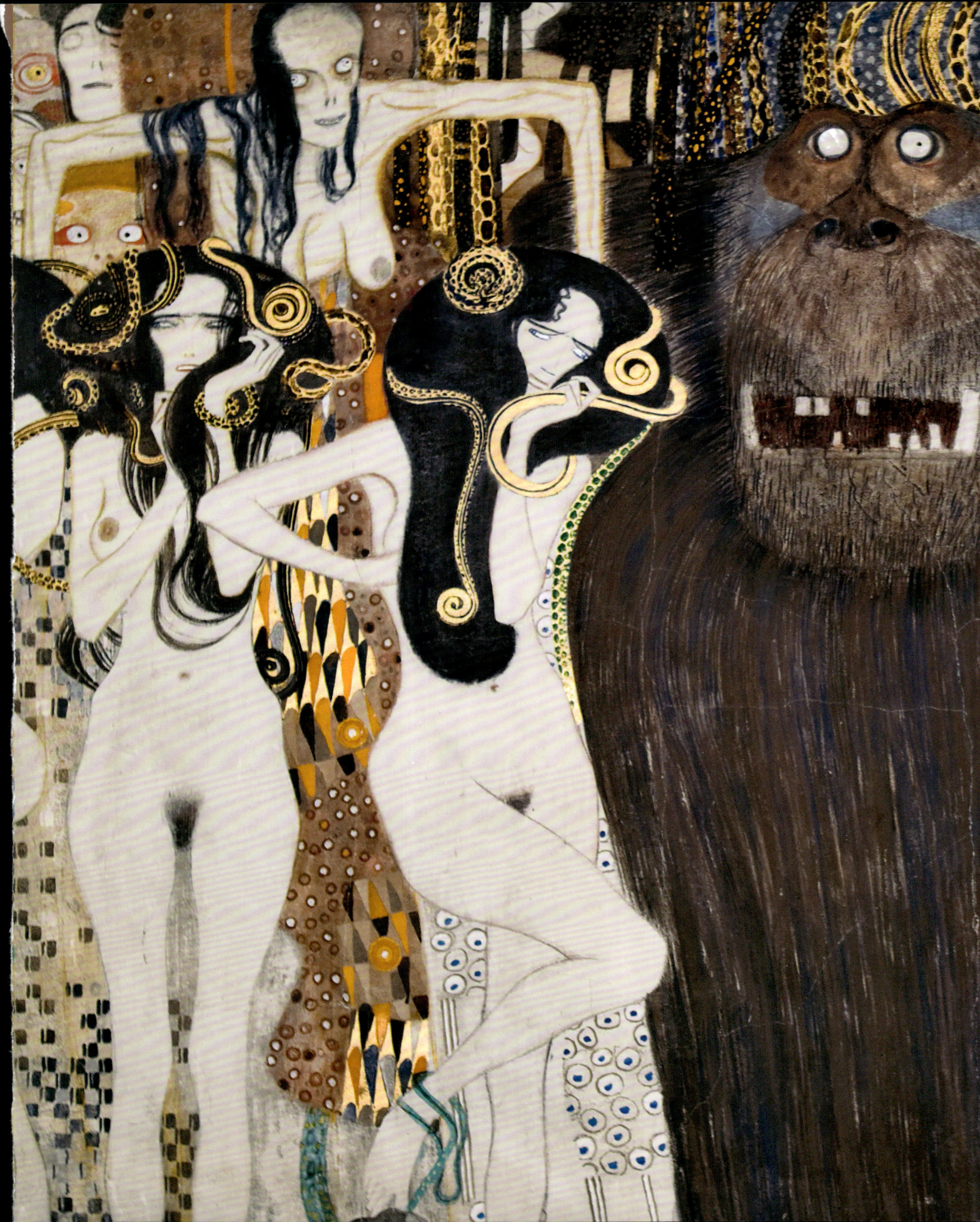

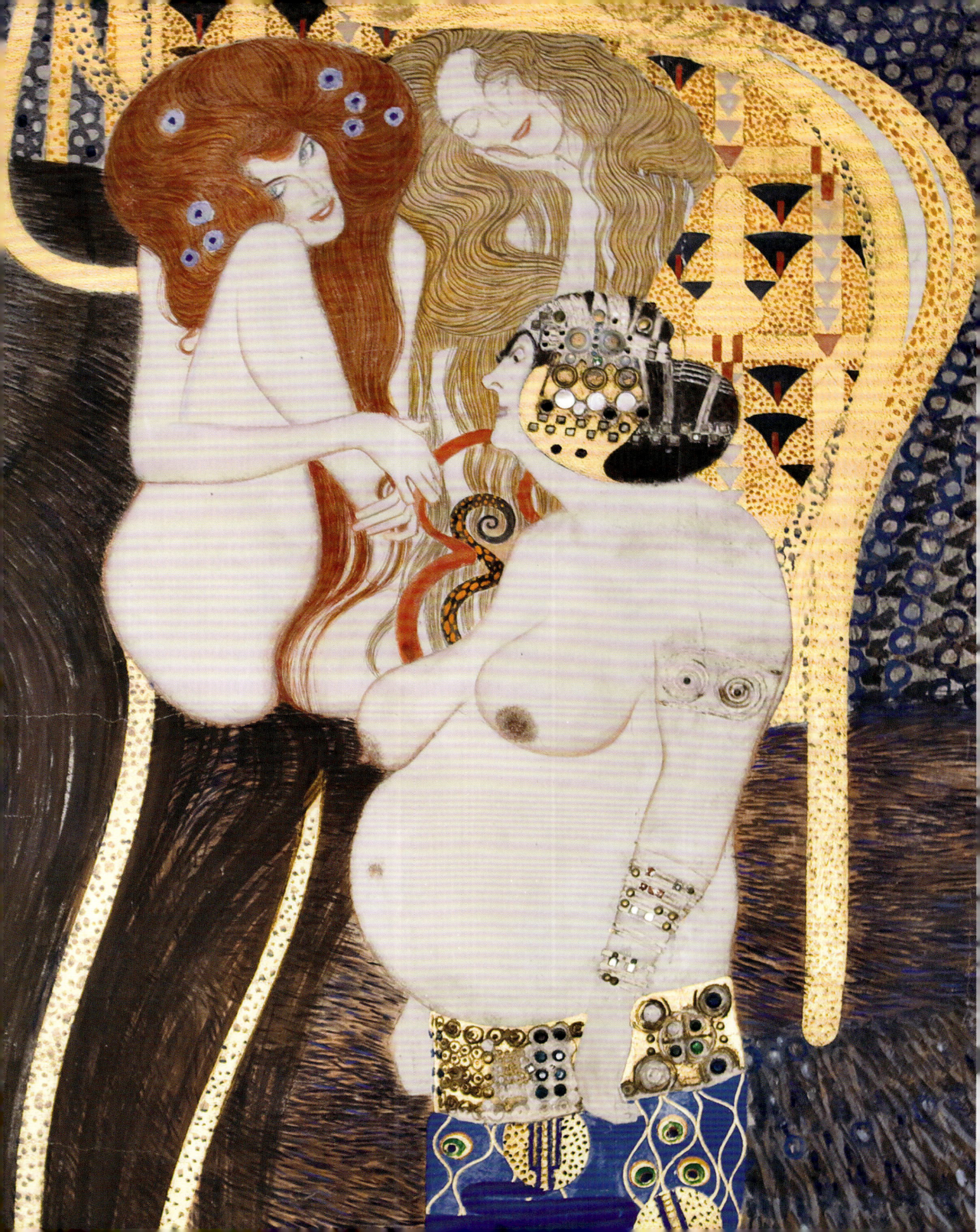

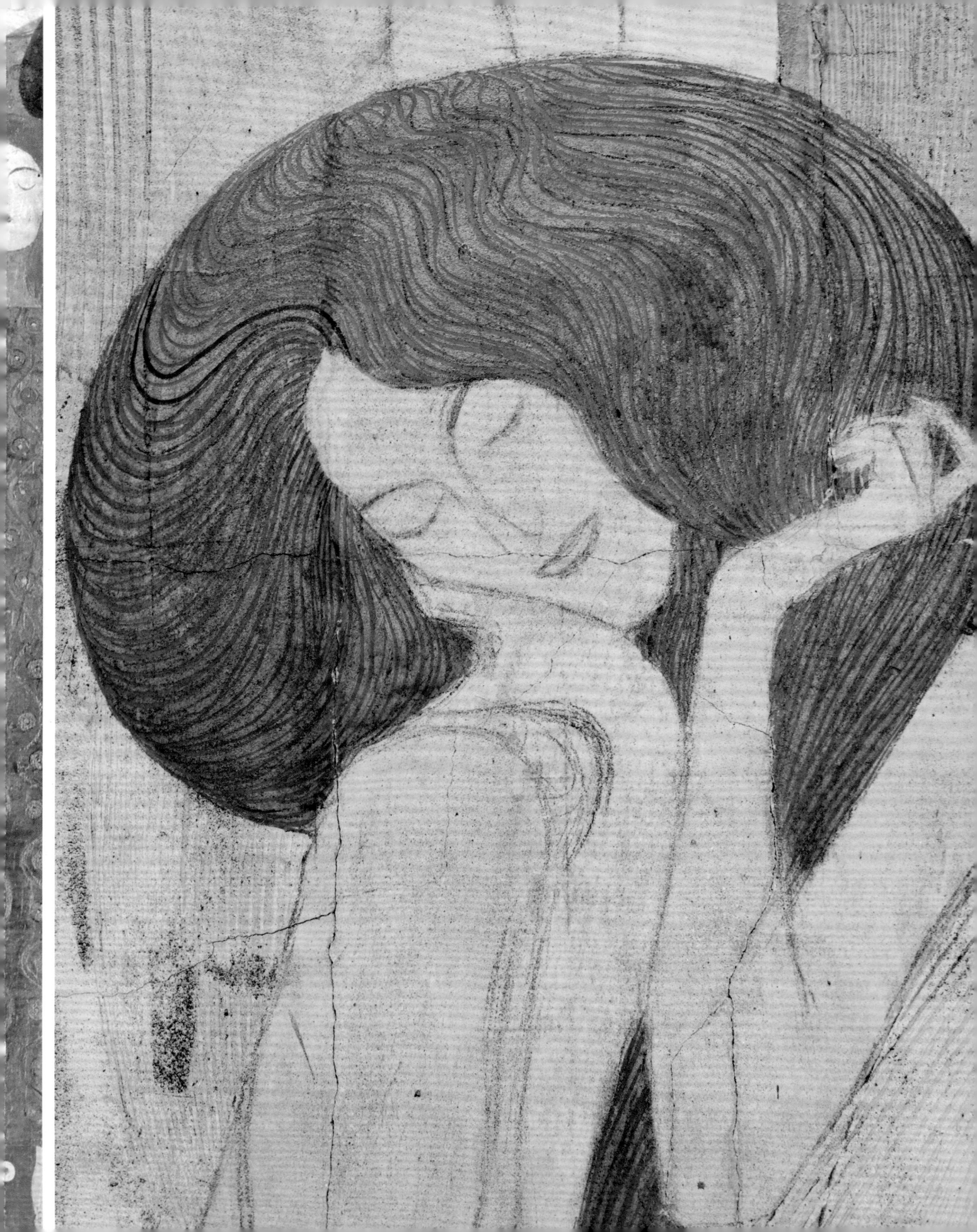

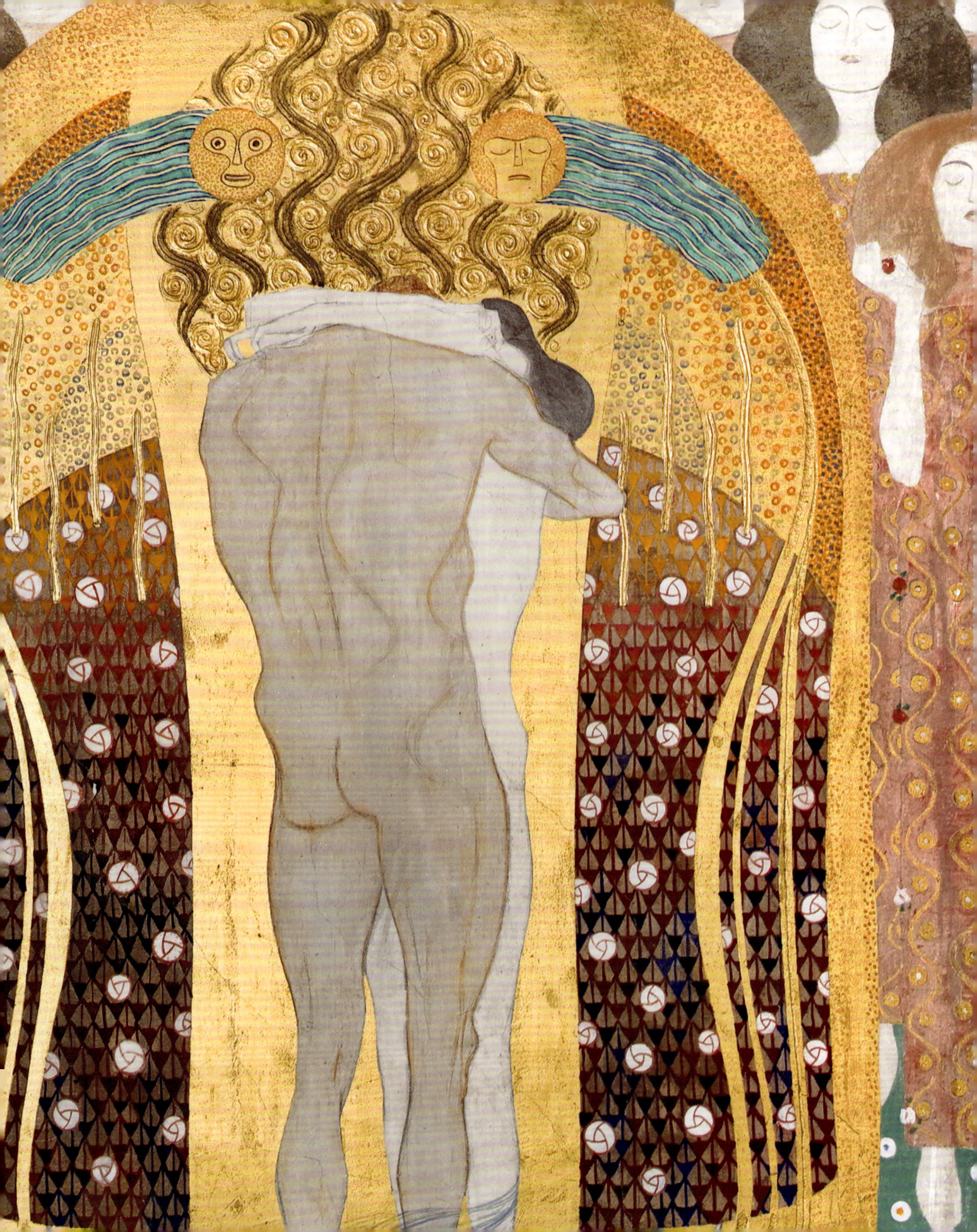

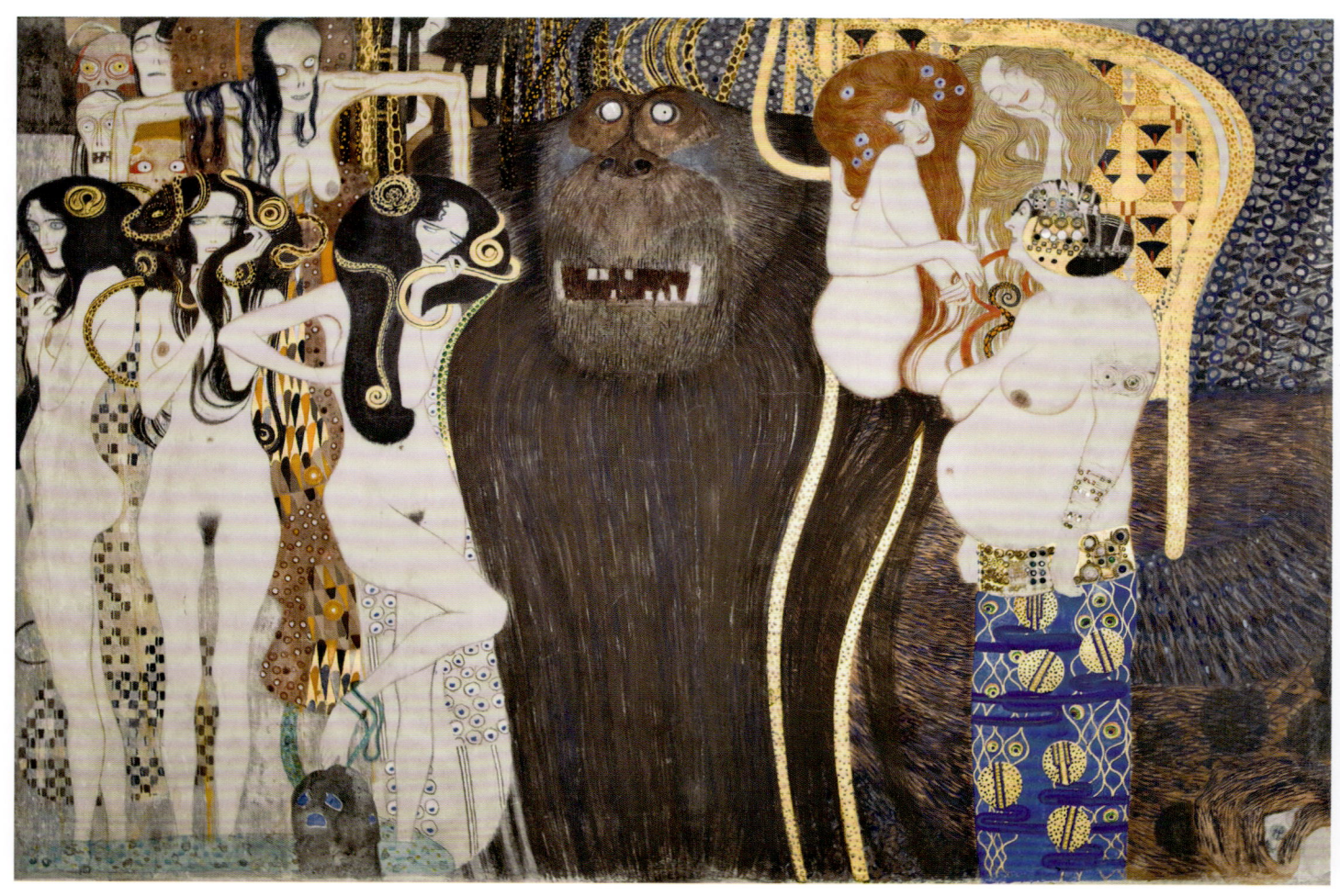

The Hostile Forces and The Gorgons (detail of central wall), 1901/1902, casein paint and charcoal on lime plaster, gold leaf, semi-precious stones and mother-of-pearl, 215 × 314 cm, Secession Building, Vienna (above, detail)

Gnawing Sorrow (detail of central wall), 1901/1902, 215 × 315.5 cm, Secession Building, Vienna (right page)

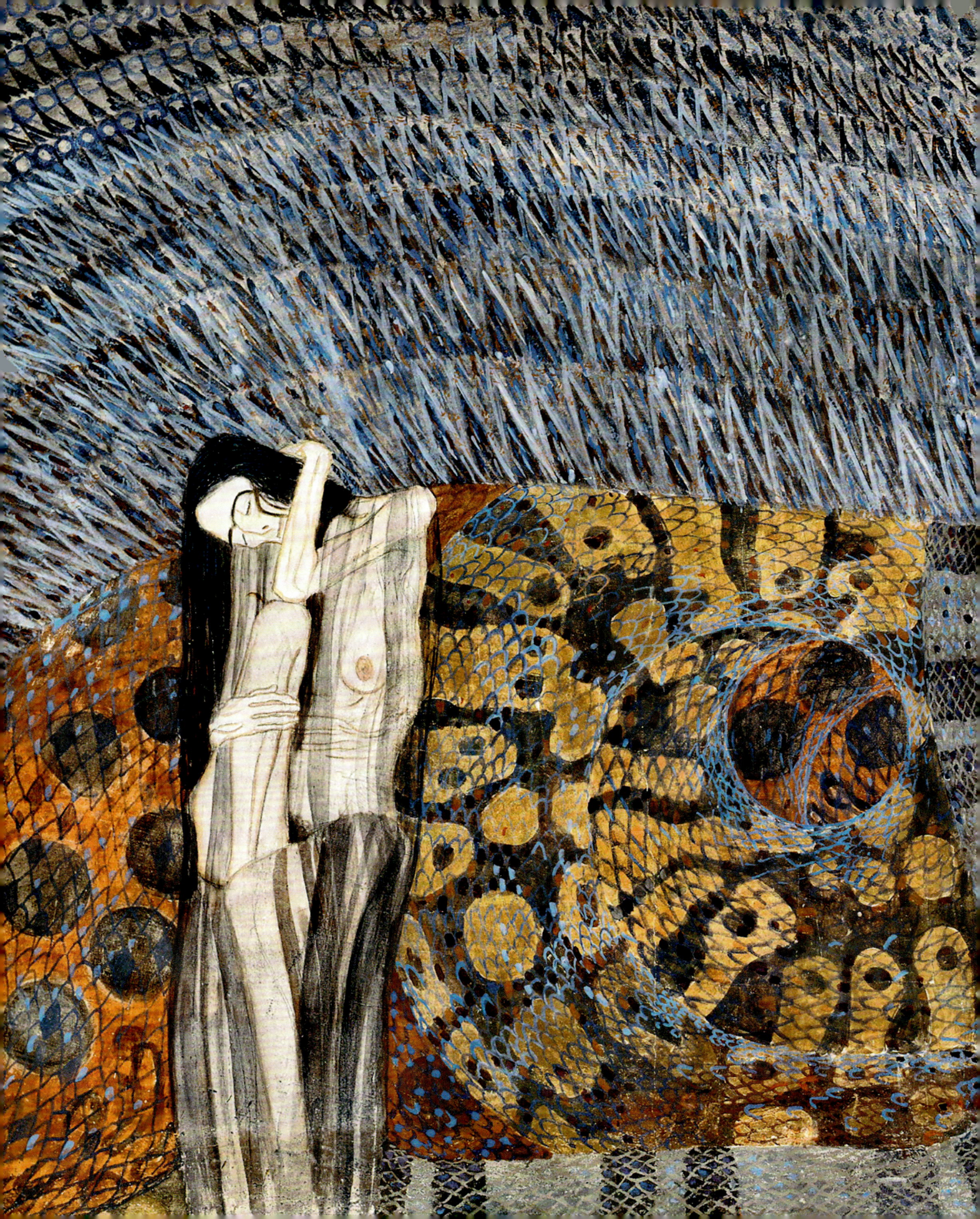

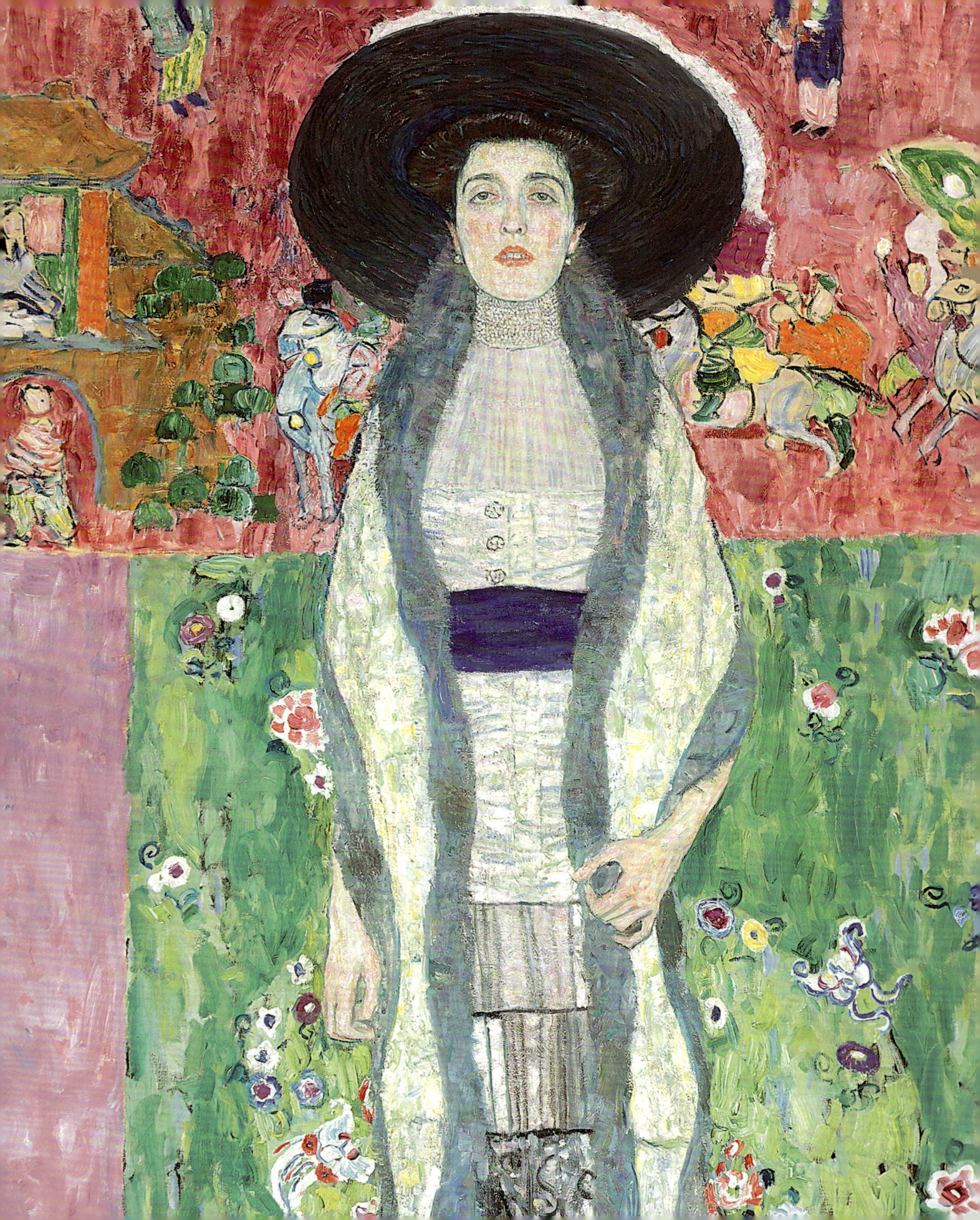

Portraits of Women

The unshakeable support of Vienna's industrial and financial high society gave Gustav Klimt freedom to apply his expertise in the area of female portraiture. Ludwig Hevesi, writing in 1903, saw this as the beginning of a new era. This stunning gallery of personalities presents an unusual image of the elegance and refinement of the upper middle class at the turn of the twentieth century.

Sonja Knips (1873–1959; p. 57), the daughter of a major general of the Austro-Hungarian Empire and the wife of a steel magnate, is the subject of the first of these portraits. It was shown in November 1898 at the second Secession Exhibition. Enveloped in a silky dress, light in both colour and weight, her body appears to lack all depth, as the artist's attention is concentrated on the attractive, even-featured face that casts upon the world a tranquil, perhaps detached gaze. In her right hand, the model holds a morocco-bound booklet, given to her by Klimt, containing the various sketches made in preparation for the portrait.

The treatment of Sonja Krips's dress, and of those of Marie Henneberg (1851–1931; p. 58) – the wife of the famous art photographer Hugo Henneberg – and Hermine Gallia (1870–1936; p. 56) – the wife of the commercial director of the Auer gas lamp manufacturer – evoke the famous palette of whites developed by James McNeill Whistler in the 1860s. In the meantime, in contrast to Whistler, Klimt quickly abandoned neutral backgrounds and came closer to the technique of Fernand Khnopff, whose full-length portraits of women clothed in white are set against two-dimensional, carefully structured backgrounds. This is particularly the case in the portrait of Margaret Stonborough-Wittgenstein (1882–1958; p. 62), the daughter of the industrialist Karl Wittgenstein and elder sister of the philosopher Ludwig Wittgenstein and the pianist

Paul Wittgenstein. This portrait was commissioned by the model's father in 1905, the year of her wedding to the New York businessman Jerome Stonborough. Enveloped in yet another light-coloured, vaporous dress, the young woman's figure is somewhat eclipsed by the background wall, designed as a splendid decorative arrangement of great sophistication.

Klimt further developed this notion in his portrait of Fritza Riedler (1860–1927; p. 63), the wife of a Viennese imperial adviser and professor at the Technical University of Munich. The image, dated 1906, is stripped of all depth. The model is shown seated in a chair apparently produced by the Wiener Werkstätte. A small semi-circular stained-glass window forms a halo around her face, as if it were part of her hairstyle, not unlike the arrangements of hair of the Spanish children painted by Diego Velázquez. The dominance of the decorations on the model is heightened by the gold and silver leaf arranged behind her face. This is the beginning of Klimt's so-called Golden Period, which is already evident in the 1890 portrait of Josef Pembaur (p. 30) and *Pallas Athene* of 1898 (p. 32), and which reached its pinnacle with the portrait of Adele Bloch-Bauer in 1907 (fold-out p. 72).

This trend, fittingly called Byzantine, reflects the strong impression that mosaics in the Basilica of San Vitale in Ravenna made on Klimt in December 1903. It would give way in the early 1910s to less-overwhelming backgrounds, inspired largely by Japanese prints, which, incidentally, Klimt collected. Henceforth, a panoply of Far Eastern birds, animals and figures would be deployed behind the model, in the style of wallpaper or drapery. This East Asian style would enchant Adele Bloch-Bauer, who commissioned a second portrait in 1912. Elisabeth Bachofen von Echt (1867–1943; p. 69), the daughter of August Lederer, clothed in a floral-patterned coat, seems to force a path through a crowd of Asian figures; similarly, Friederike Maria Beer (1891–1980; p. 68), whose enthusiasm for the clothing styles launched by the Wiener Werkstätte was unconditional, melts into a melee of Asian warriors. On the other hand, the intense yellow field that serves as a background in the portrait of Eugenia Primavesi (1874–1963; p. 72), who was also a customer in the Wiener Werkstätte fashion boutiques, can be explained by the fact that the painting is unfinished: exasperated by Klimt's slowness, the client took it away in a gesture of impatience.

Klimt's interest in contemporary fashion may have been piqued by his relationship with Emilie Flöge. We know that in the summer of 1904, the young woman opened a fashion boutique with her sisters, and the Wiener Werkstätte was contracted to do the interior furnishings. Meanwhile, in Klimt's sumptuous 1902 portrait of Flöge (pp. 59–61), the reality of contemporary style is almost erased. The face is reproduced with infinite delicacy; the slender figure is entirely concealed under a dress. Certainly, although its cut may evoke the so-called reform movement, which took hold of women's fashion at the very start of the twentieth century, its pattern is completely fanciful. The serpentine blue lines that descend the length of the body, accompanied by various partly gilded patterns, literally transform the underlying feminine anatomy into pure ornamentation. On the other hand, from 1907 to 1909, Klimt painted a small number of busts of women whose clothing is undeniably contemporary, without conforming to the modernity of the Wiener Werkstätte. The abundance of red hair, the thin, red lips and the half-closed eyes, exalted by hats and boas, certainly stem from the then-current idea of the femme fatale.

Portrait of Adele Bloch-Bauer II,
1912, oil on canvas, 190 × 120 cm, private collection (p. 52, detail; see p. 66)

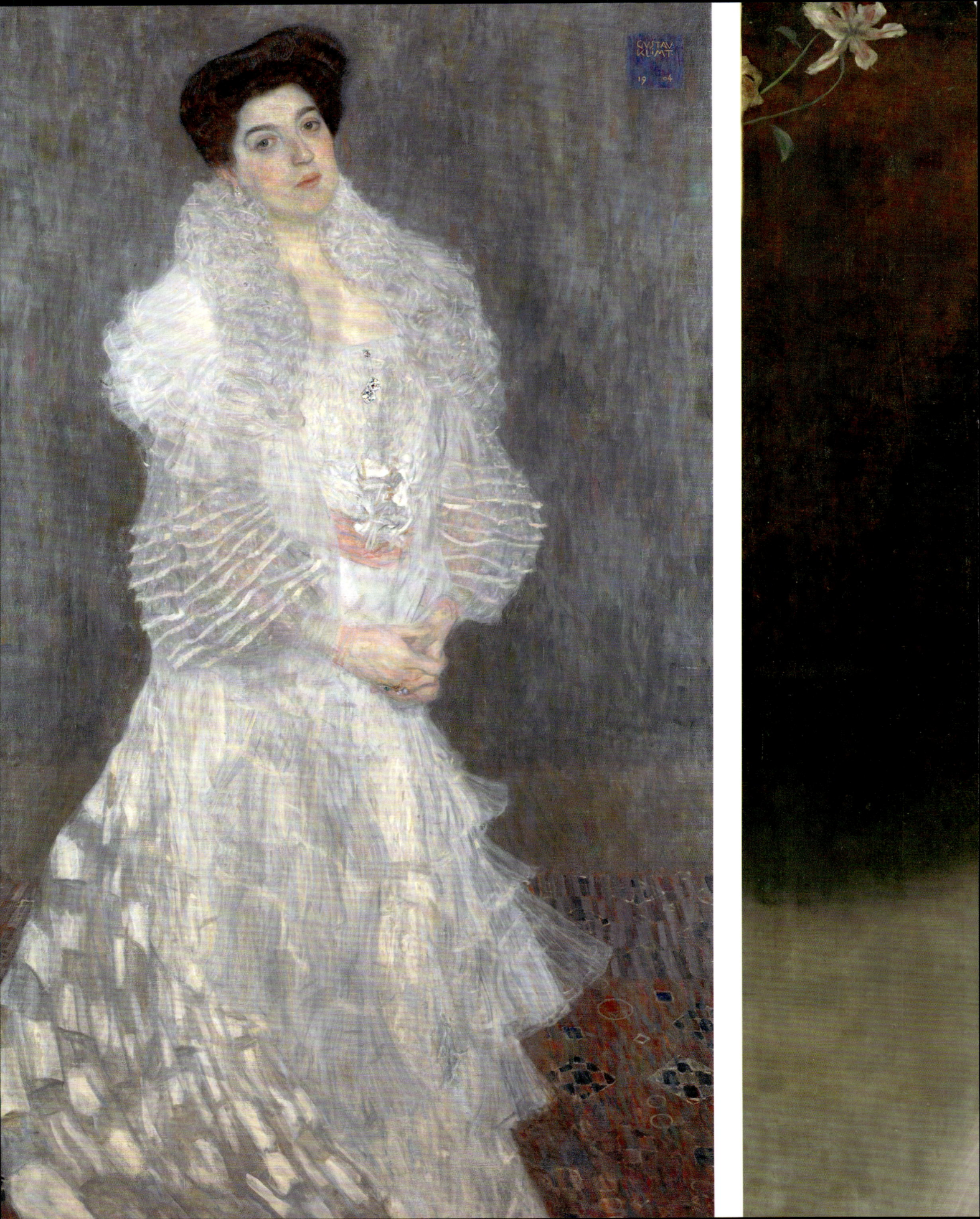

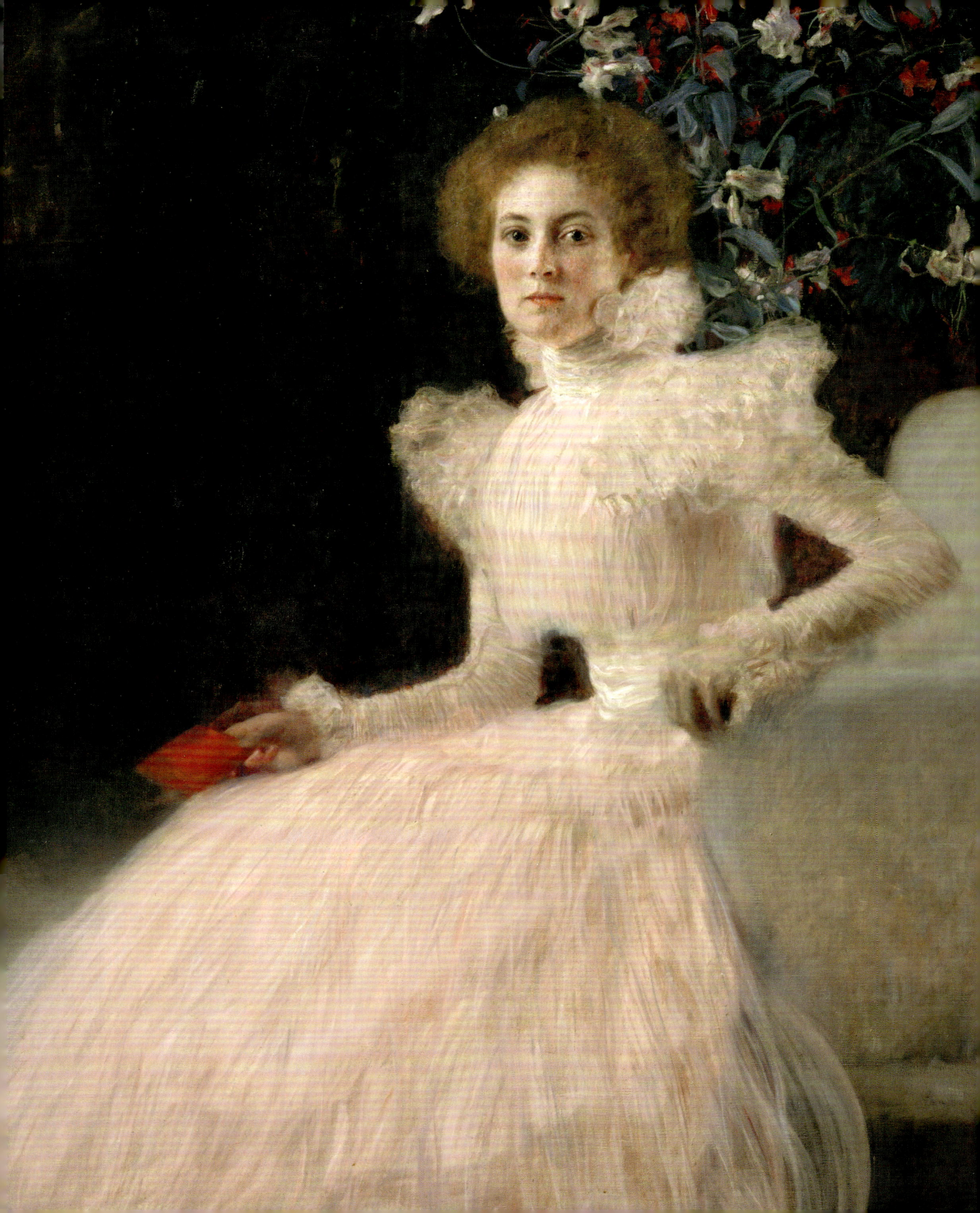

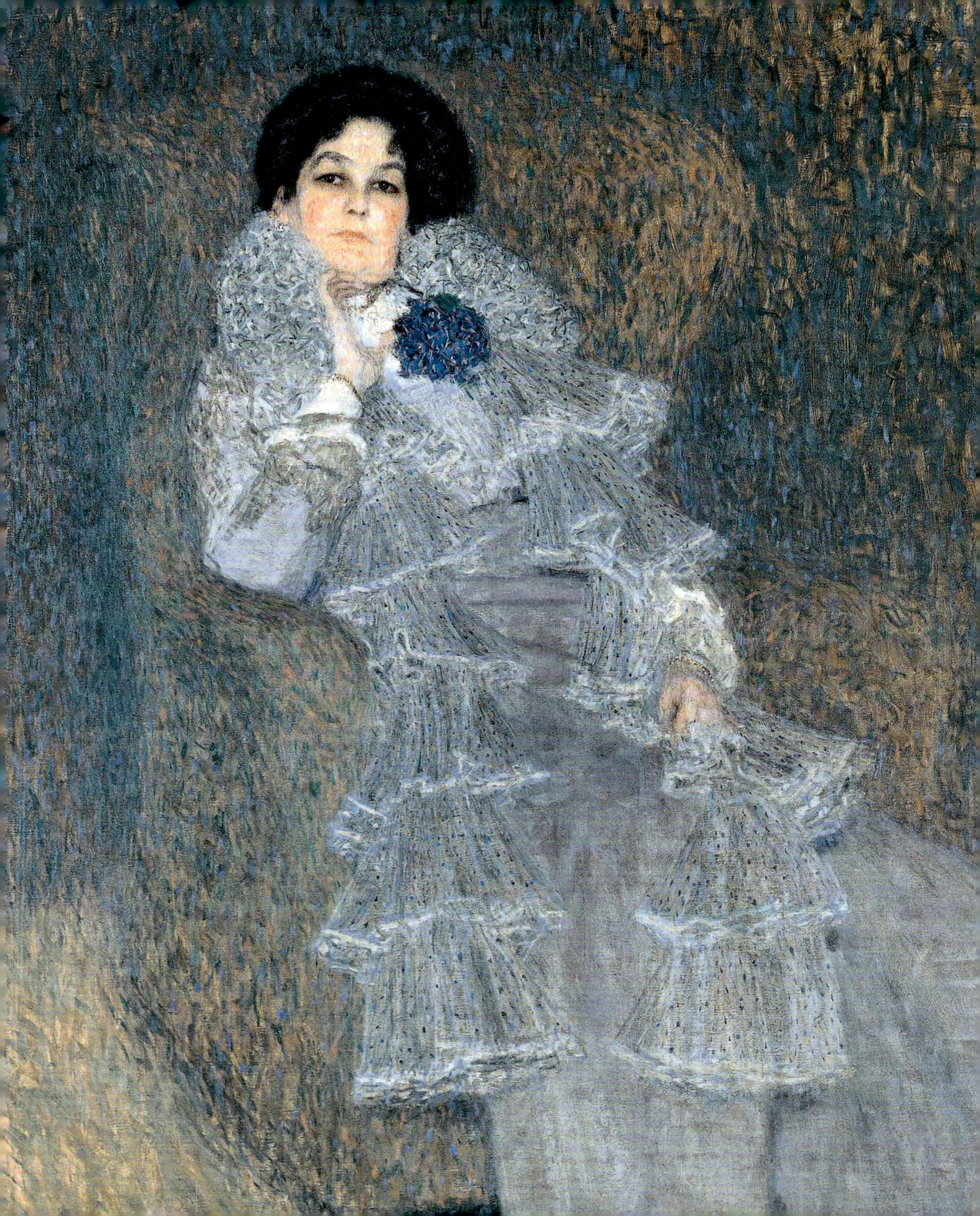

Portrait of Hermine Gallia,
1904, oil on canvas,
170.5 × 96.5 cm,
National Gallery, London
(preceding spread on left, detail)

Portrait of Sonja Knips,
1898, oil on canvas,
145 × 146 cm,
Österreichische Galerie
Belvedere, Vienna
(preceding spread on right, detail)

Portrait of Marie Henneberg,
1901/1902, oil on canvas,
140 × 140 cm,
Kunstmuseum Moritzburg
Halle (Saale)
(left, detail)

Portrait of Emilie Flöge,
1902/1903, oil and gold leaf
on canvas,
181 × 84 cm,
Wien Museum, Vienna
(right; following spread, detail)

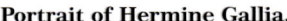

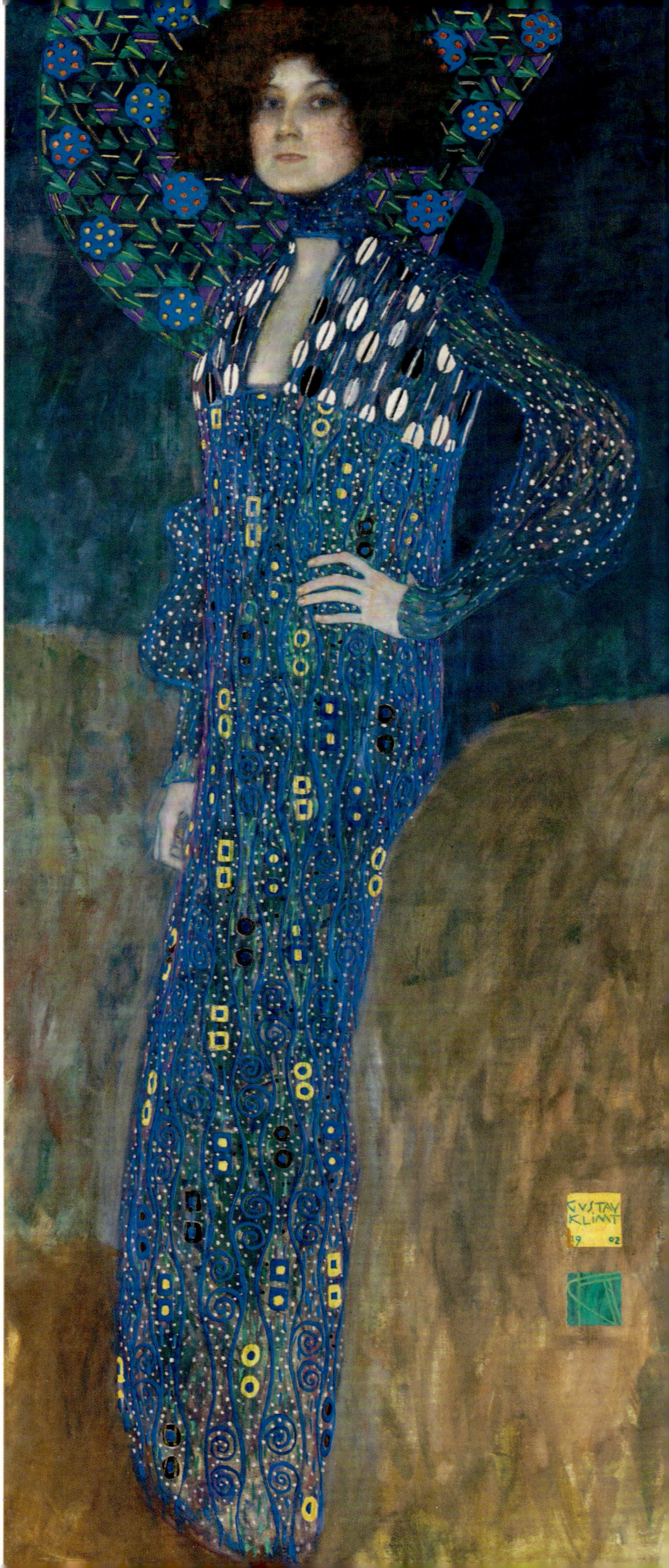

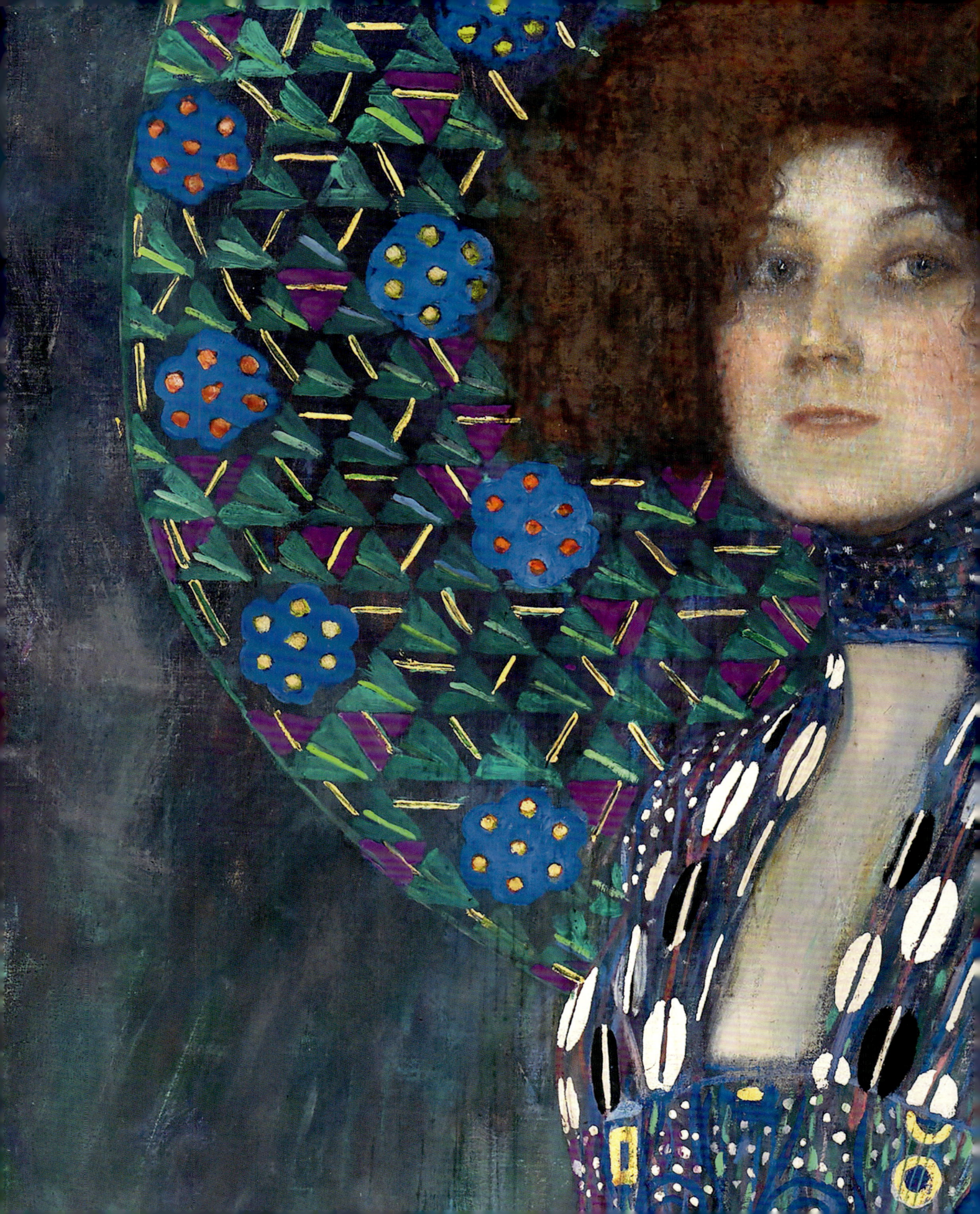

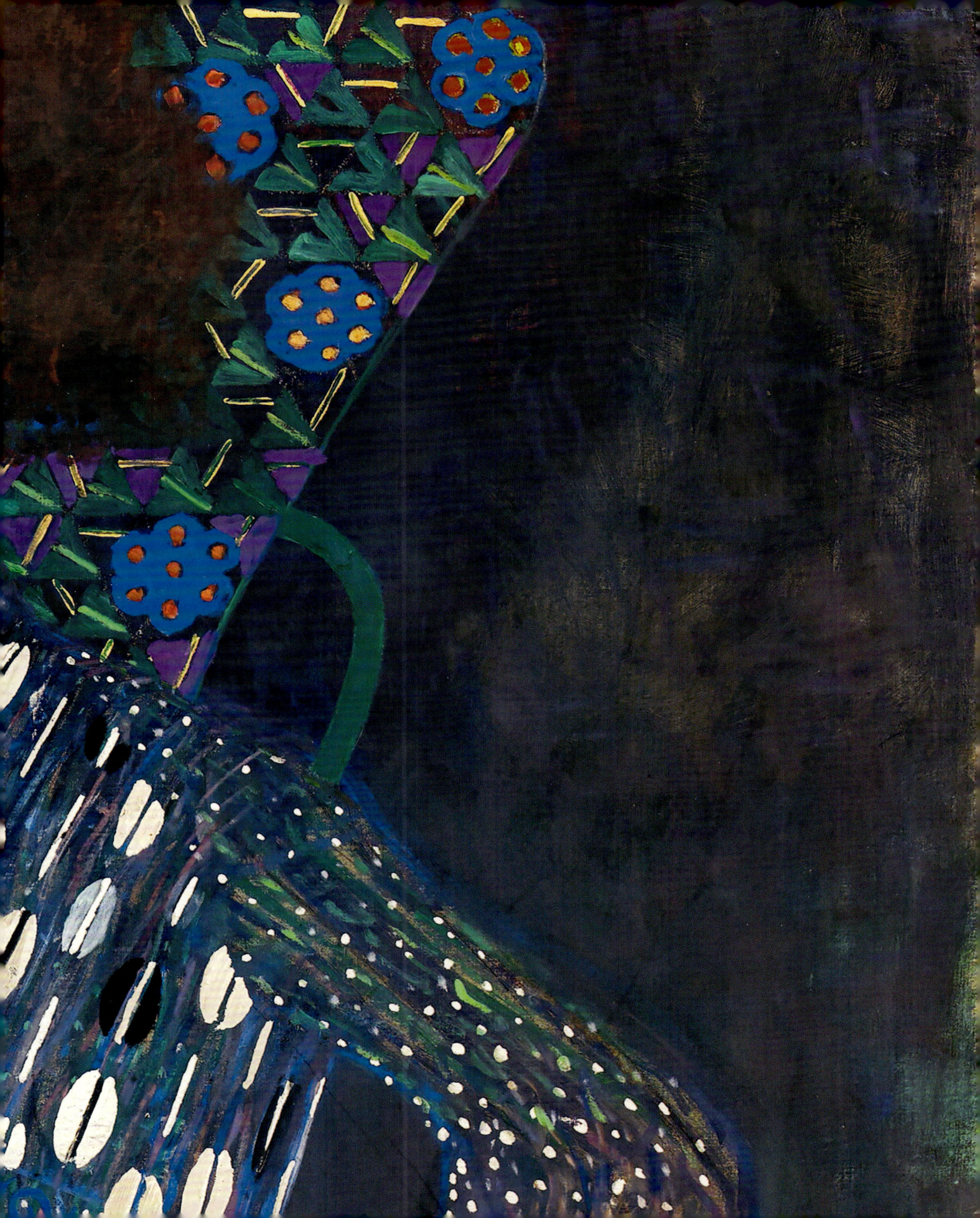

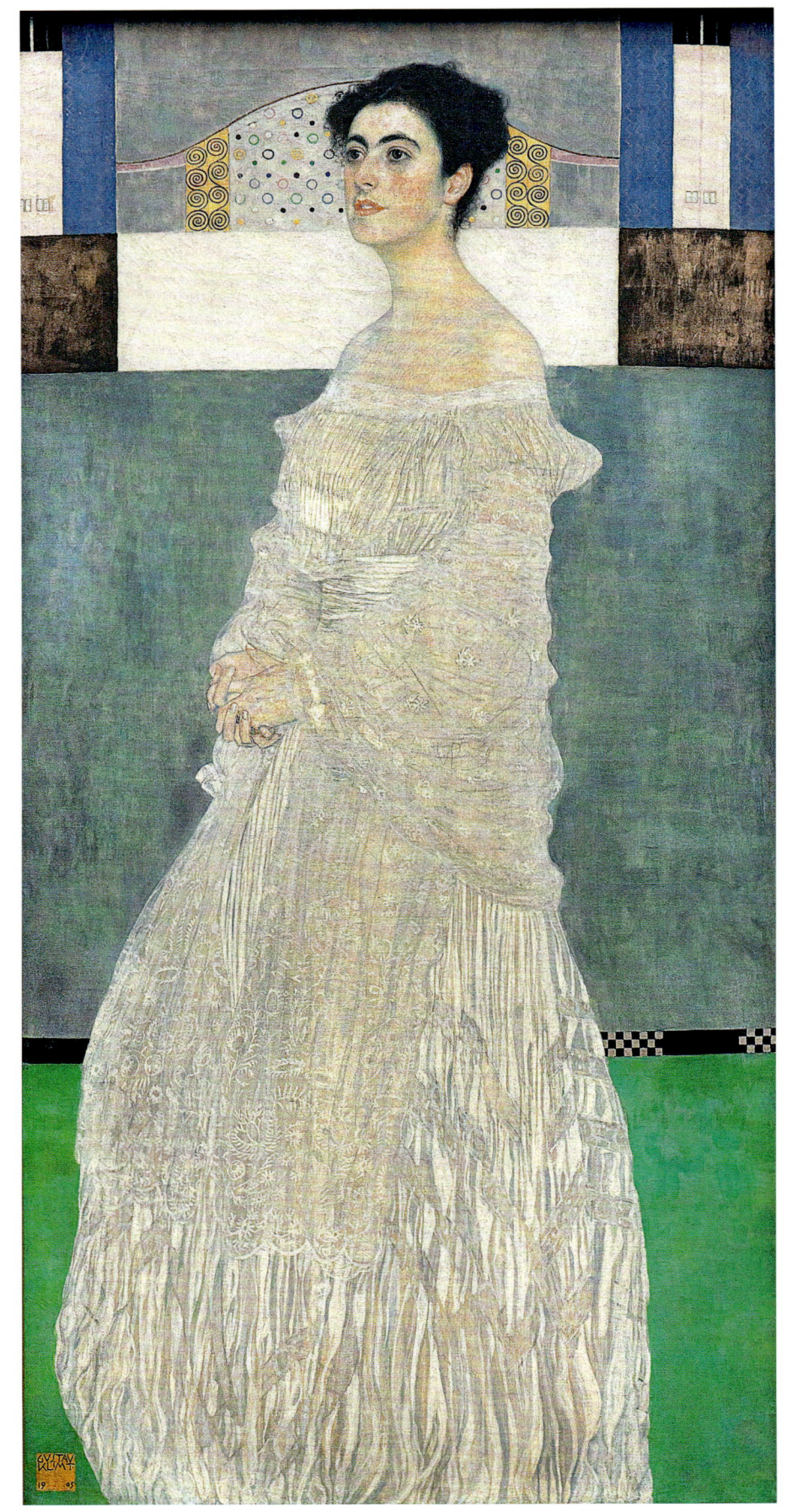

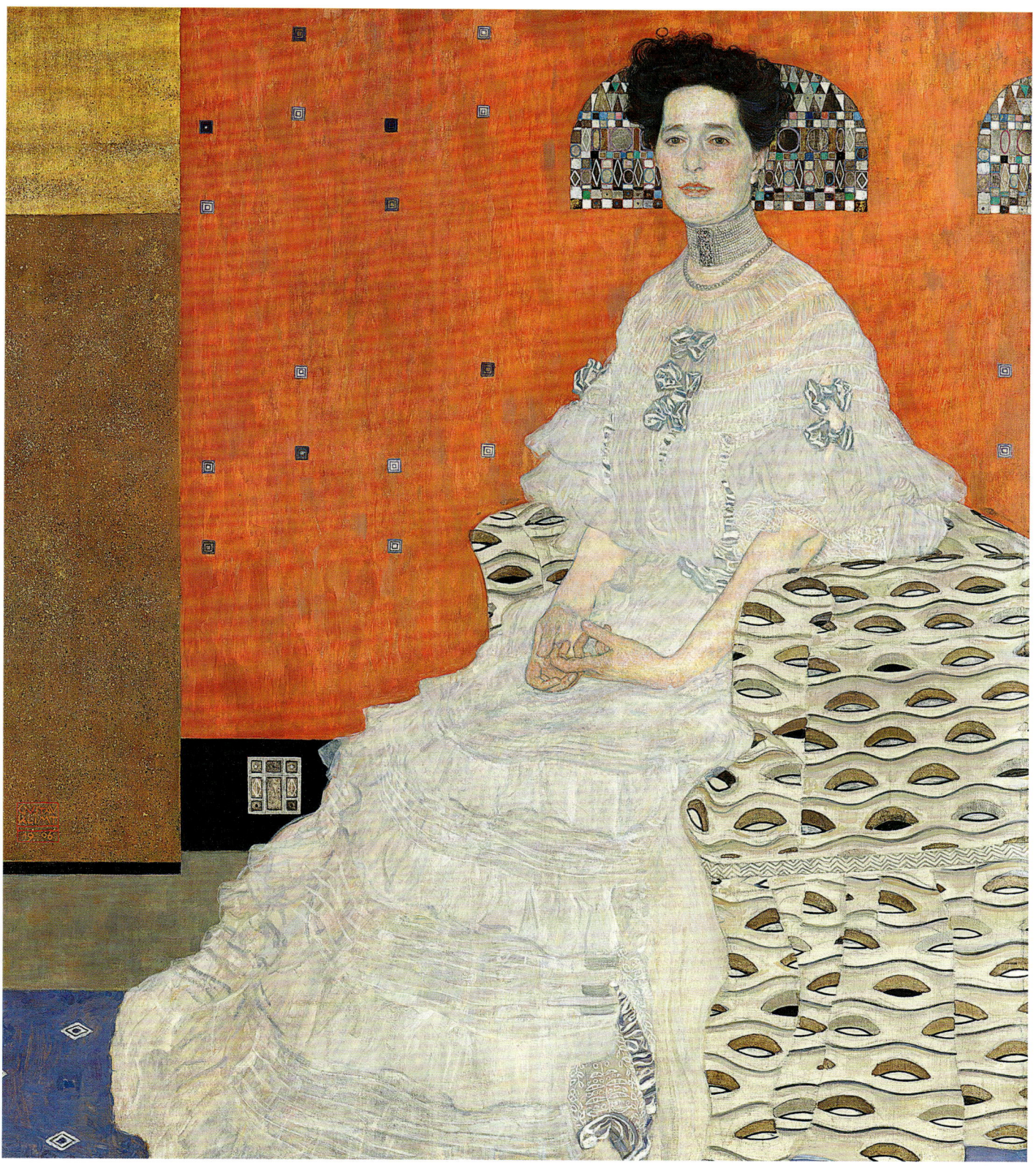

Portrait of Margaret Stonborough-Wittgenstein, 1905, oil on canvas, 180 × 90 cm,
Bayerische Staatsgemäldesammlungen – Neue Pinakothek, Munich (opposite)

Portrait of Fritza Riedler, 1906, oil on canvas, 153 × 133 cm,
Österreichische Galerie Belvedere, Vienna (above)

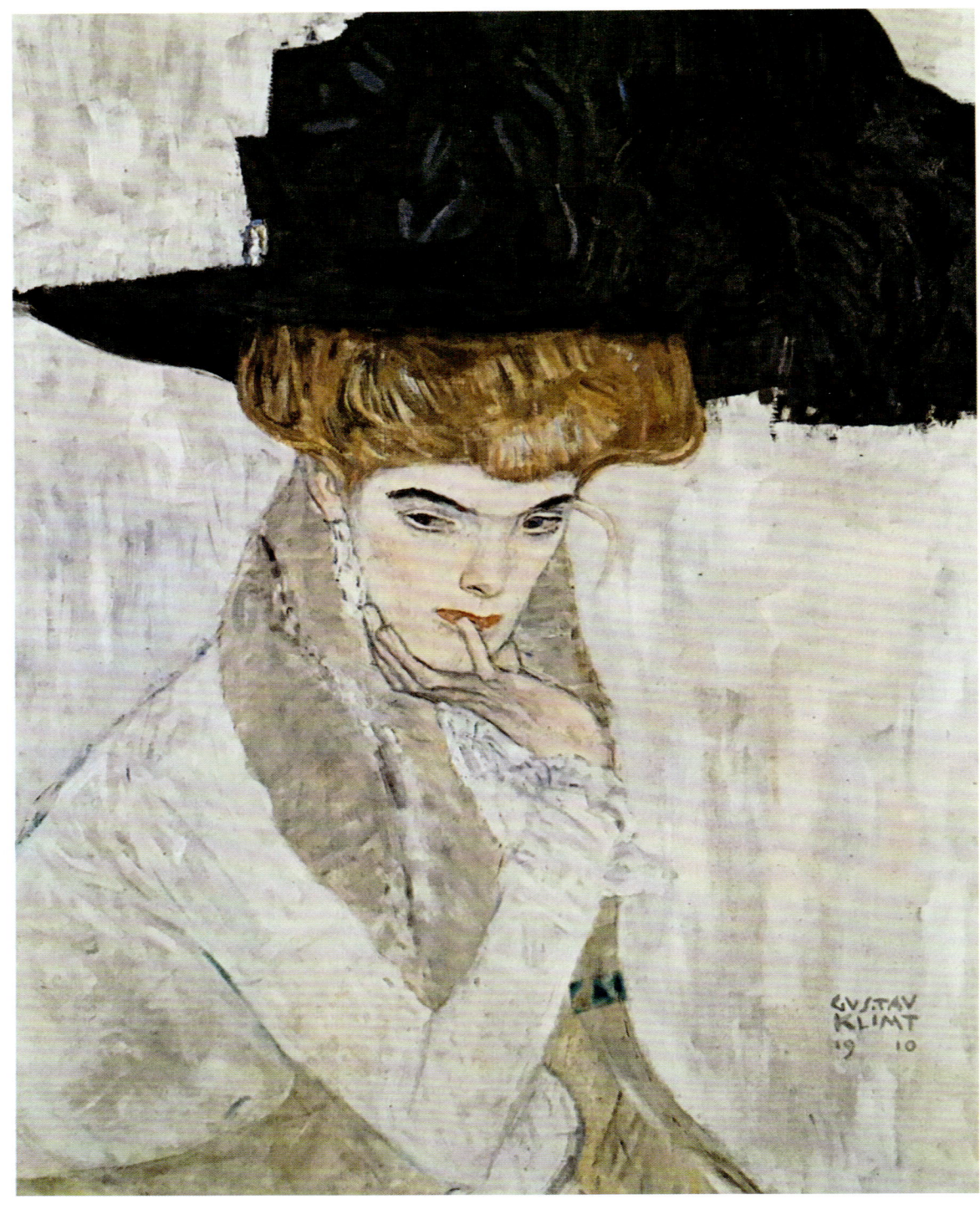

The Black Feathered Hat, 1910, oil on canvas, 79 × 63 cm, private collection, New York (above)

Lady with a Hat and Feather Boa, *c.* 1910, oil on canvas, 69 × 55 cm, private collection (opposite)

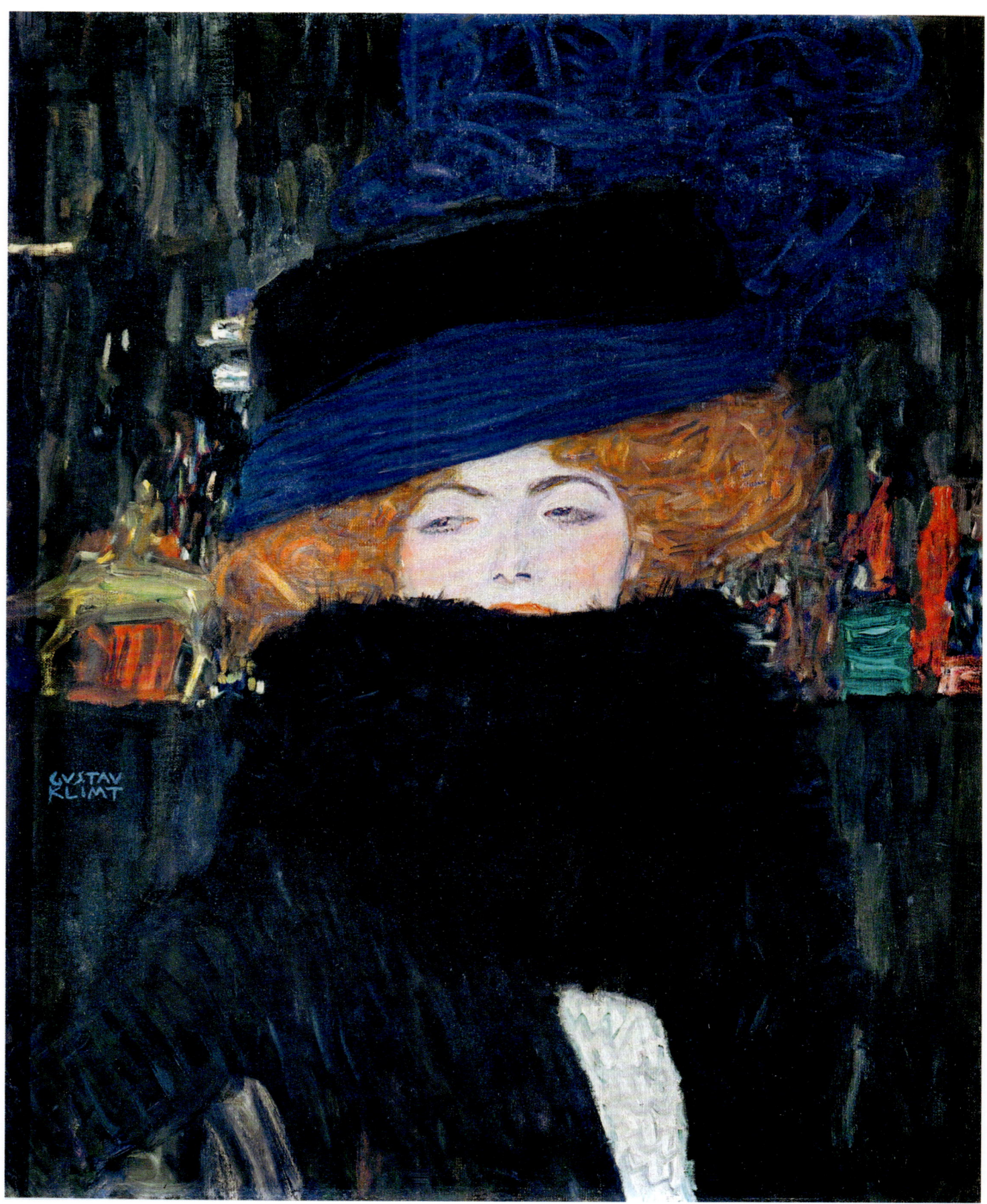

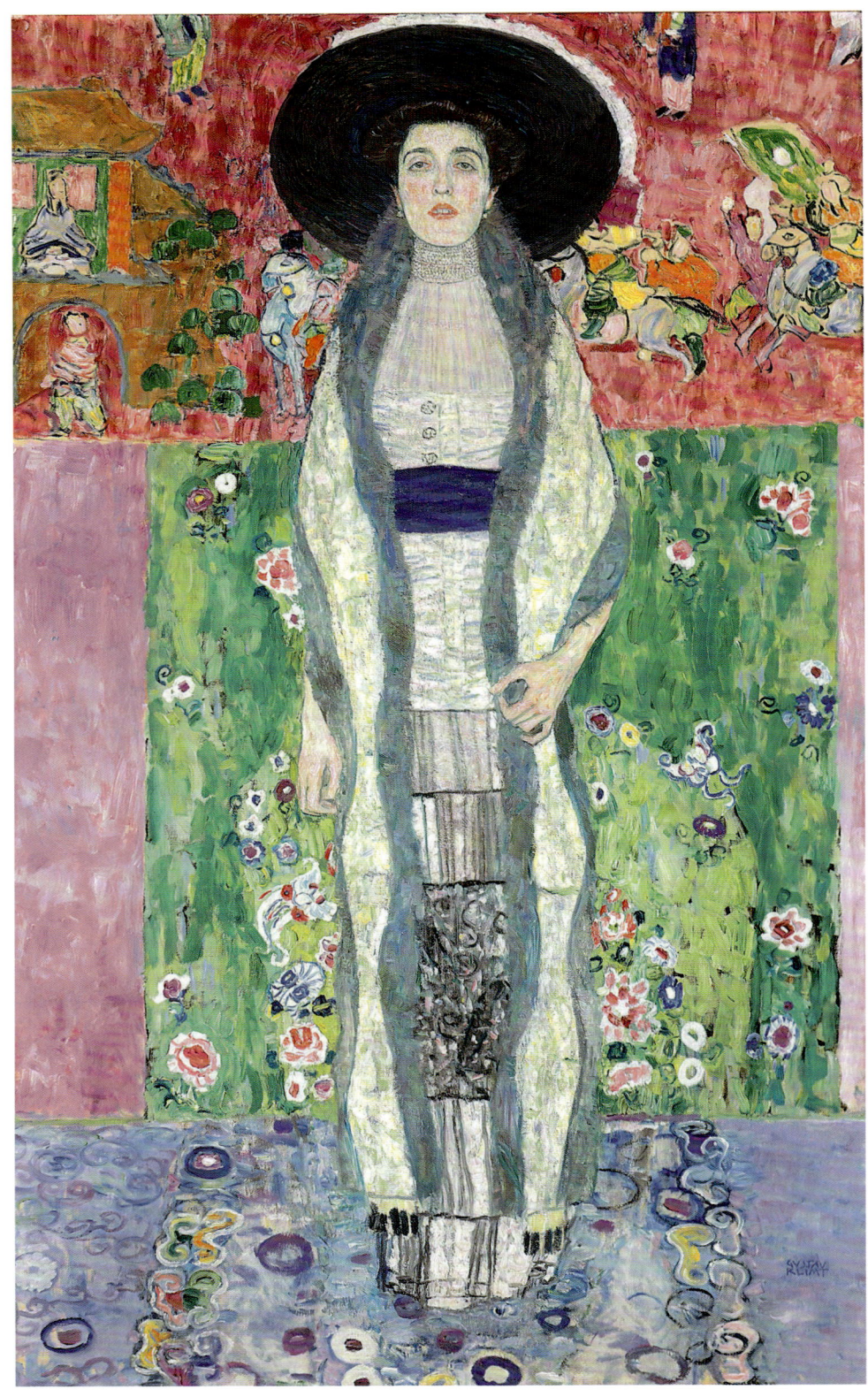

Portrait of Adele Bloch-Bauer II, 1912, oil on canvas, 190 × 120 cm,
private collection (above)

Portrait of Mäda Primavesi, 1913, oil on canvas, 150 × 110 cm,
The Metropolitan Museum of Art, New York (opposite, detail)

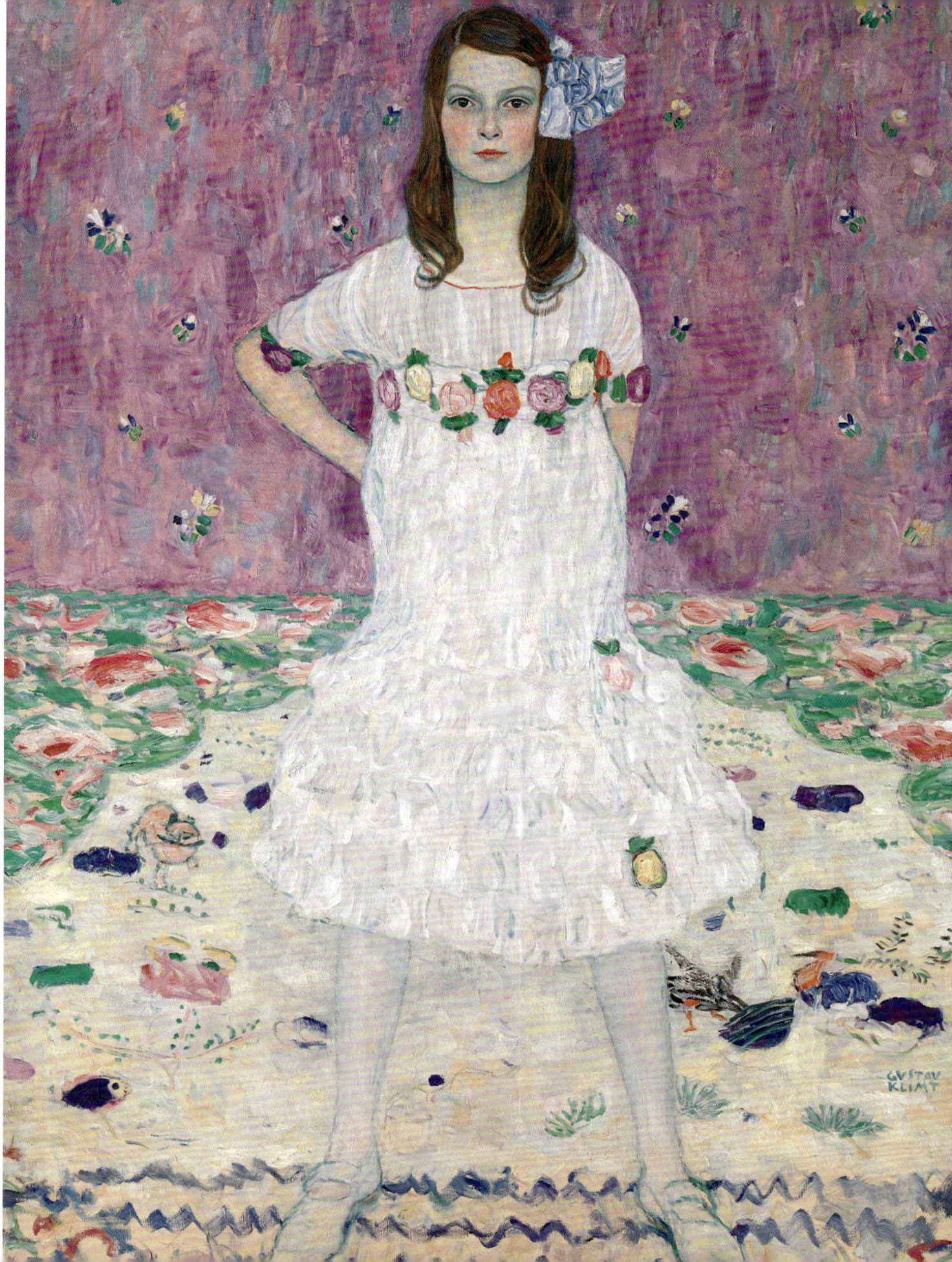

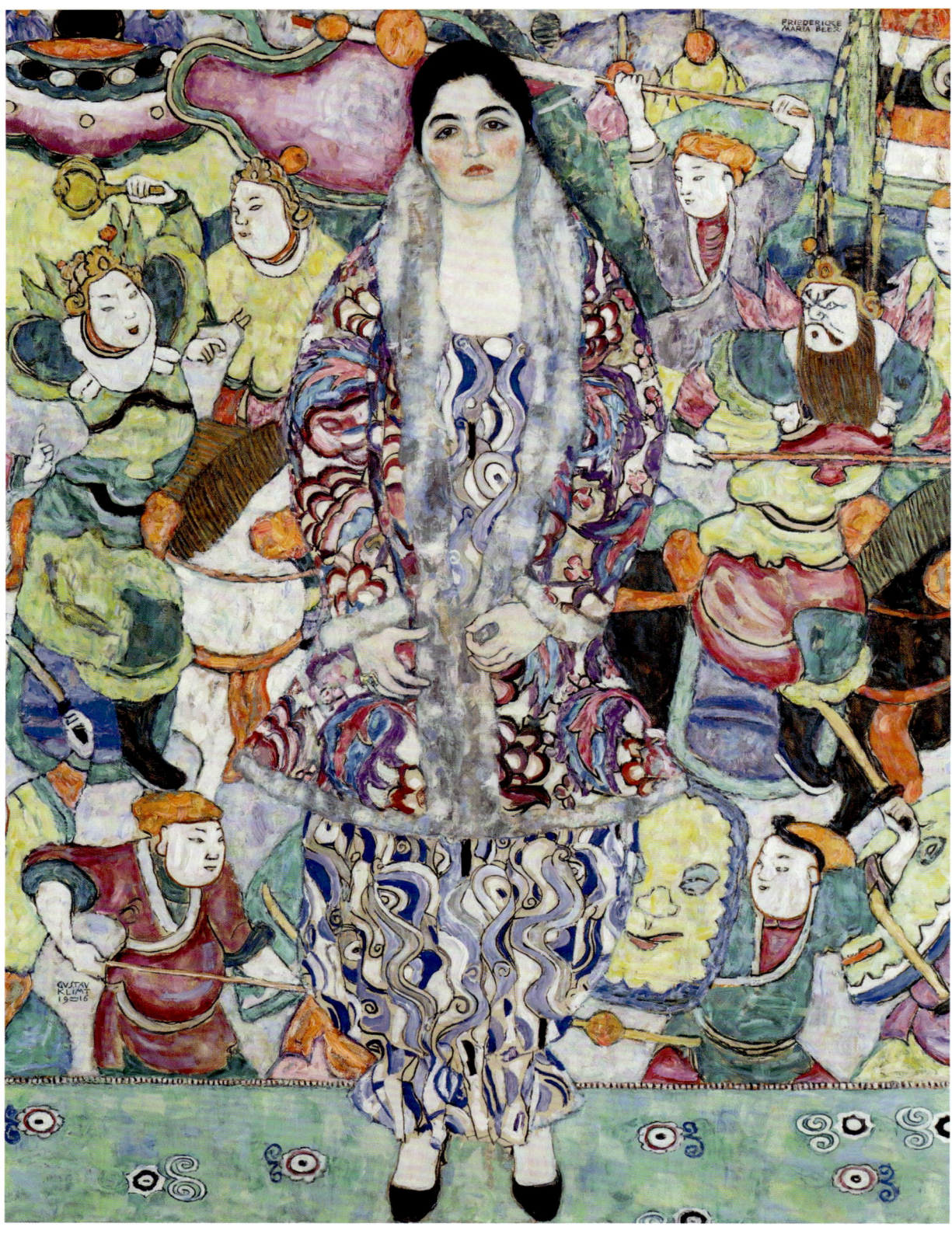

Portrait of Friederike Maria Beer, 1916, oil on canvas, 168 × 130 cm,
Museum of Art, Mizne-Blumenthal Collection, Tel Aviv (above)

Portrait of Elisabeth Lederer, 1914–1916, oil on canvas, 180 × 128 cm,
private collection, New York (opposite)

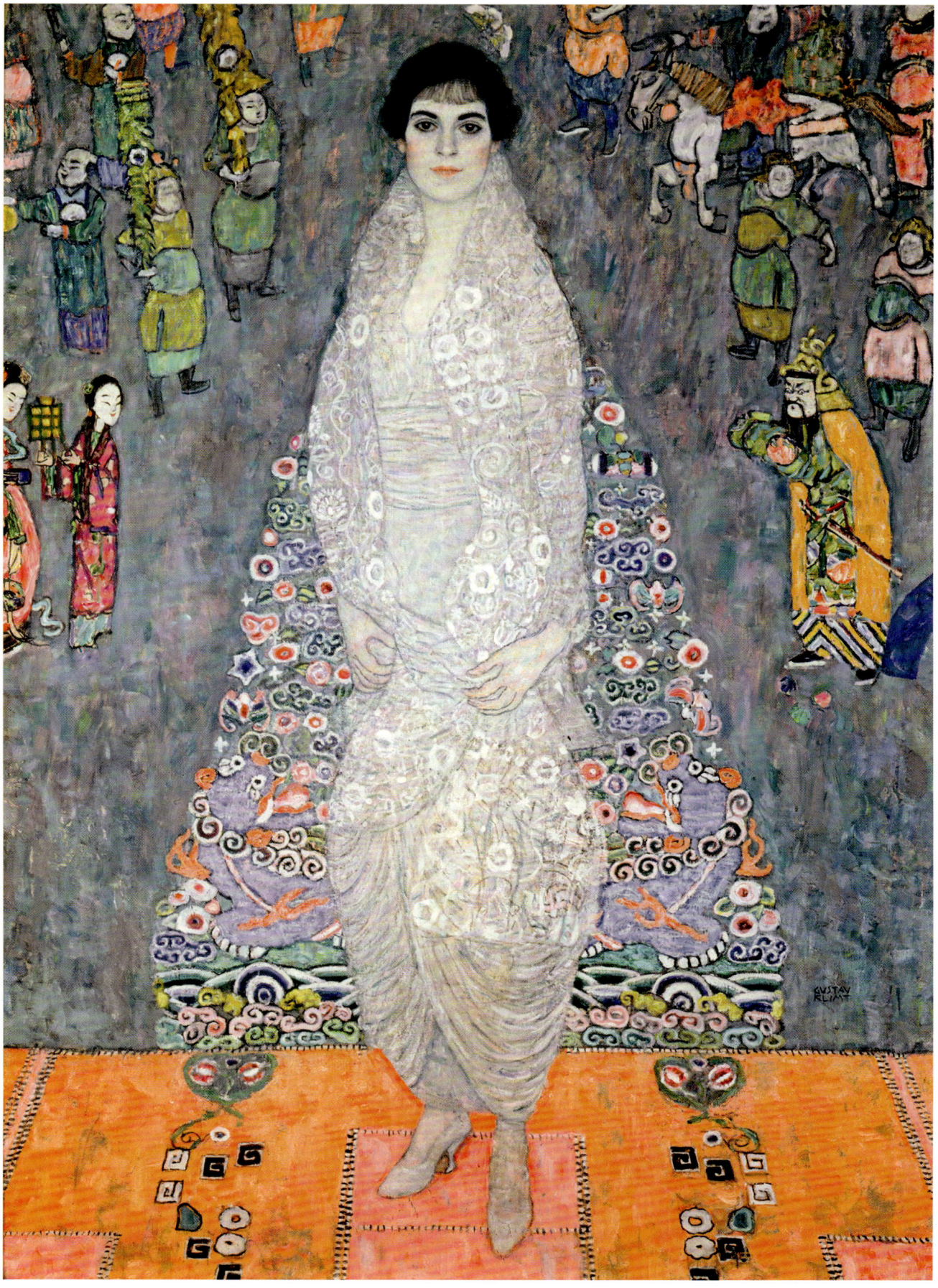

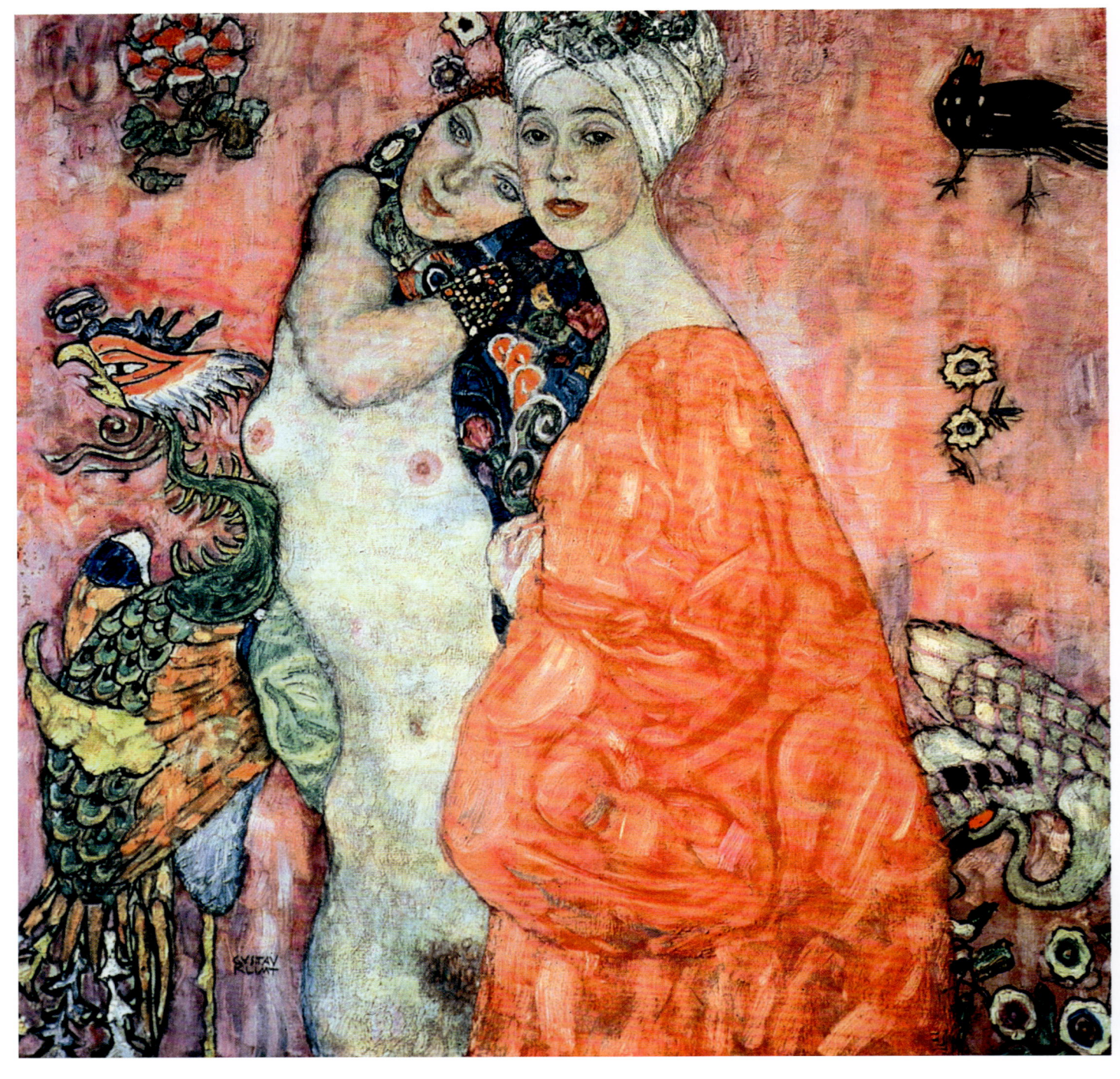

Friends II, 1916/1917, oil on canvas, 99 × 99 cm, destroyed in the 1945 fire at Schloss Immendorf (above)

The Dancer, 1916/1917, oil on canvas, 180 × 90 cm, private collection, New York (opposite)

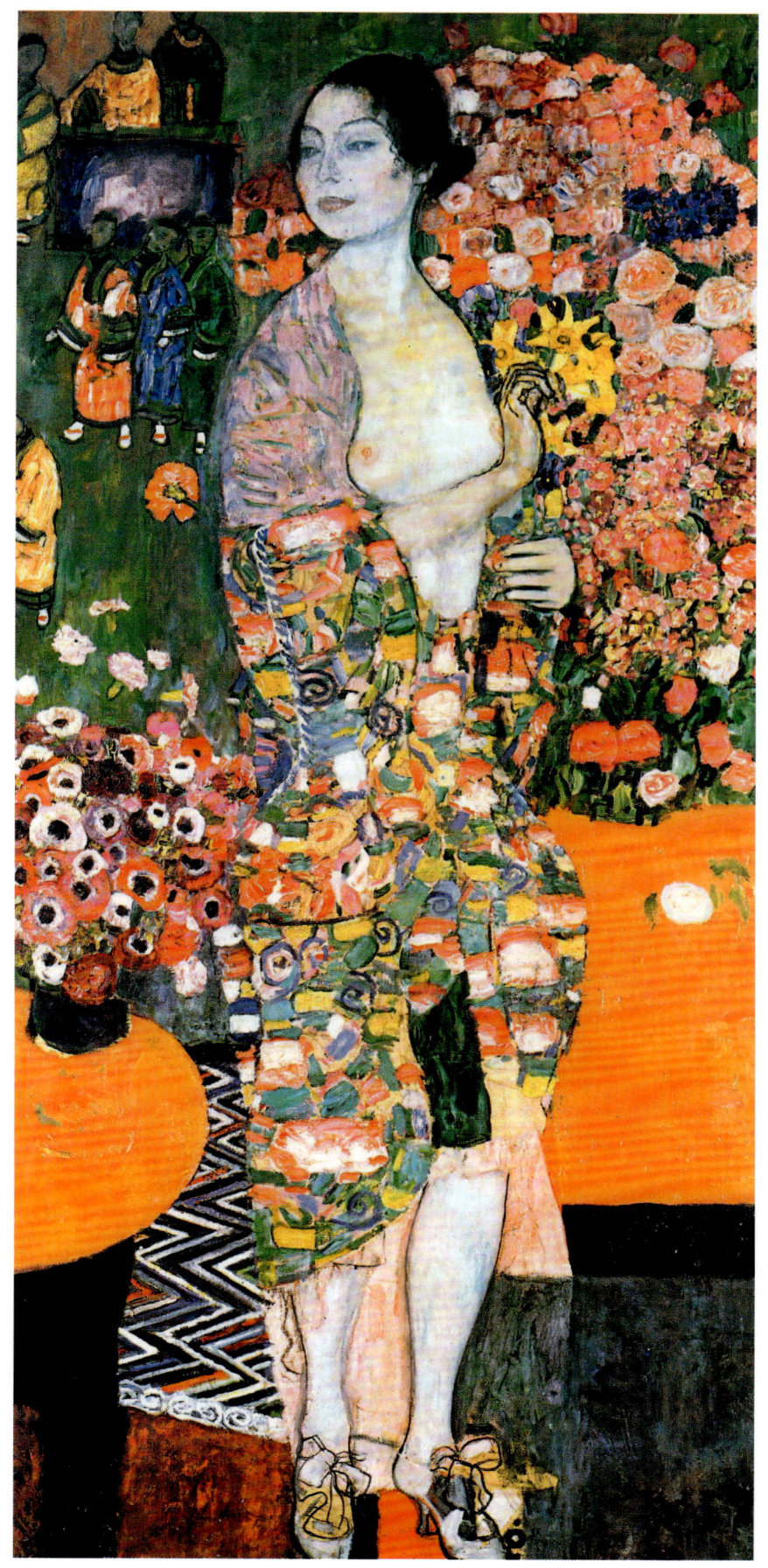

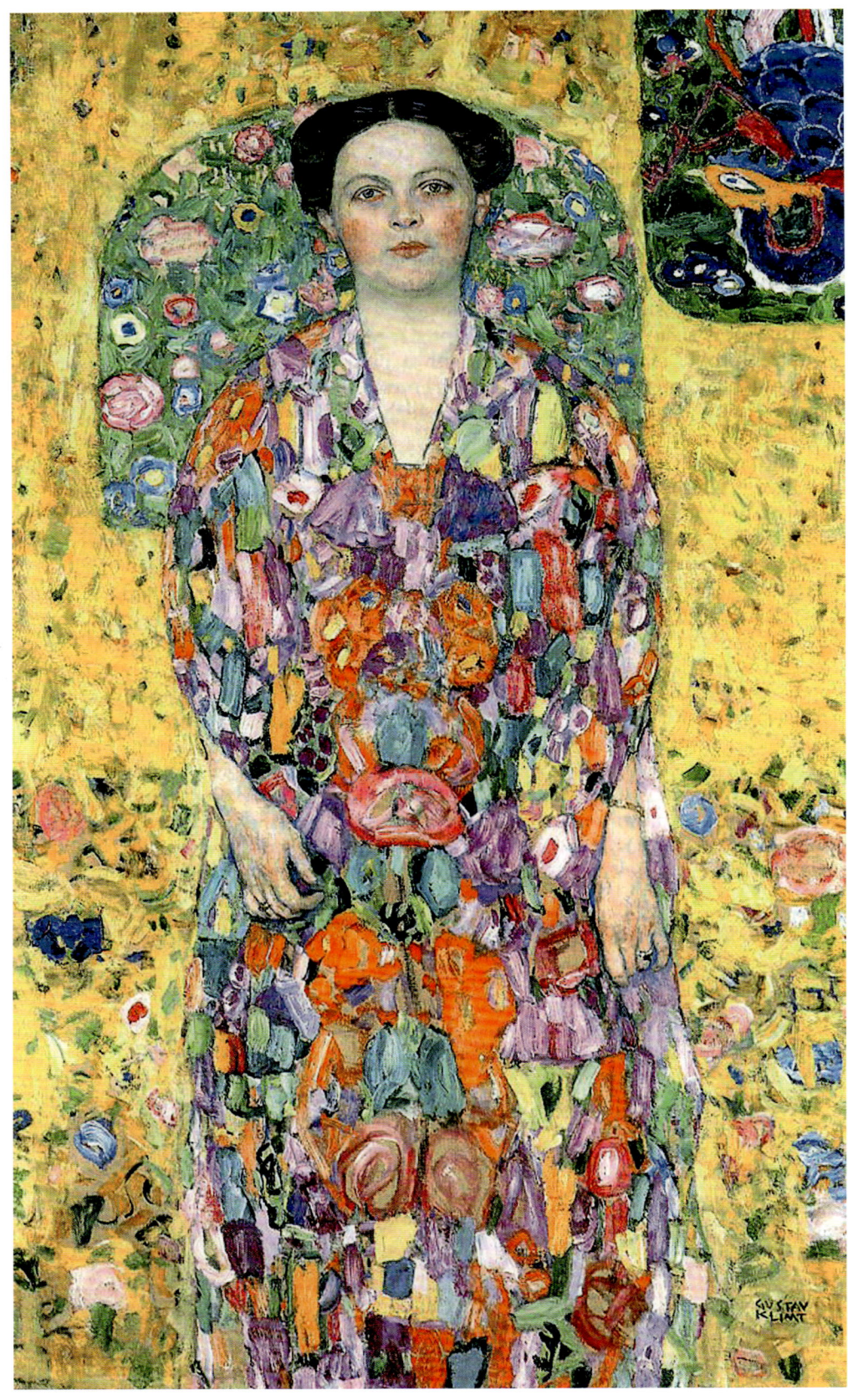

Portrait of Eugenia (Mäda) Primavesi, 1913/1914, oil on canvas, 140 × 84 cm, Municipal Museum of Art, Toyota (above)

Adele Bloch-Bauer I

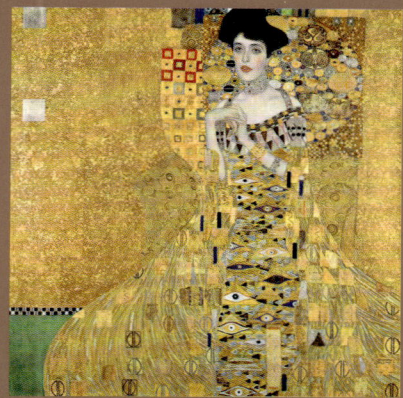

Adele Bloch-Bauer (1881–1925) was from an important Jewish Viennese family, and her husband was a sugar manufacturer and a director at a prestigious Protestant bank. A passionate lover of literature, she held a salon frequented by Gustav Klimt. Although the portrait was commissioned in 1903 for a fee of four thousand Austro-Hungarian crowns, it was not delivered until 1907. Using mixed media on the canvas—oil paint with gold and silver leaf—Klimt achieved decorative patterns in very light relief with a mixture of paint, gypsum and chalk. The subject leans against a chair, her body sheathed in a form-fitting dress, with her gaze fixed on the viewer. The composition is distinguished by a categorical denial of any spatial effect. Aside from the face and hands, whose treatment verges on photorealism, the entire painted area is treated as pure decoration. Various elements including spirals, arabesques, triangles, squares, eyes, ocelli and triskelions, are fitted closely together like the tesserae of a mosaic, with the abundance of gold lending a sacred quality to the work.

Adele Bloch-Bauer I, 1907, oil on canvas with gold and silver leaf, 140 × 140 cm, Neue Galerie New York

Lady with a Fan, 1917/1918, oil on canvas, 100 × 100 cm, private collection (p. 73, detail)

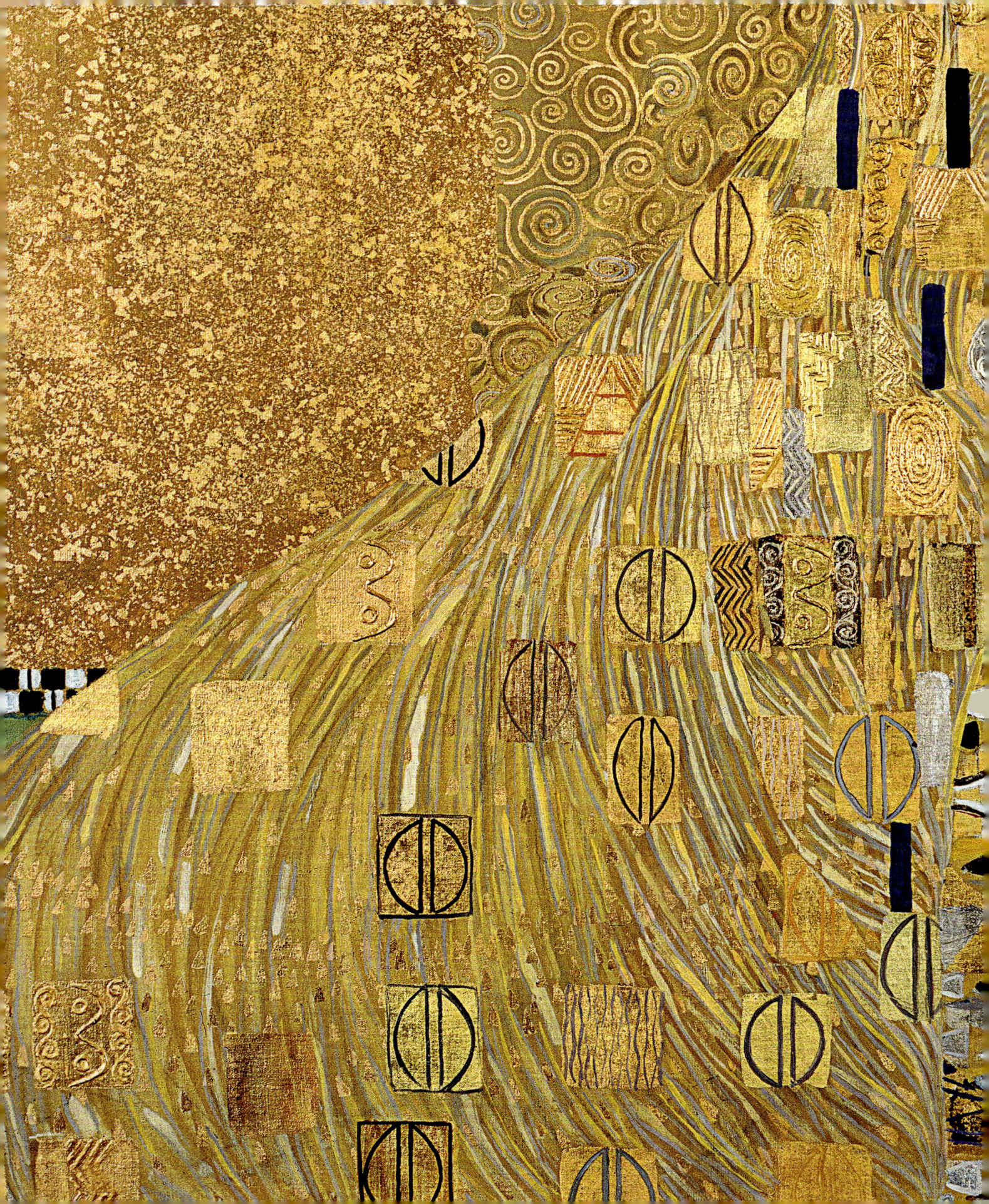

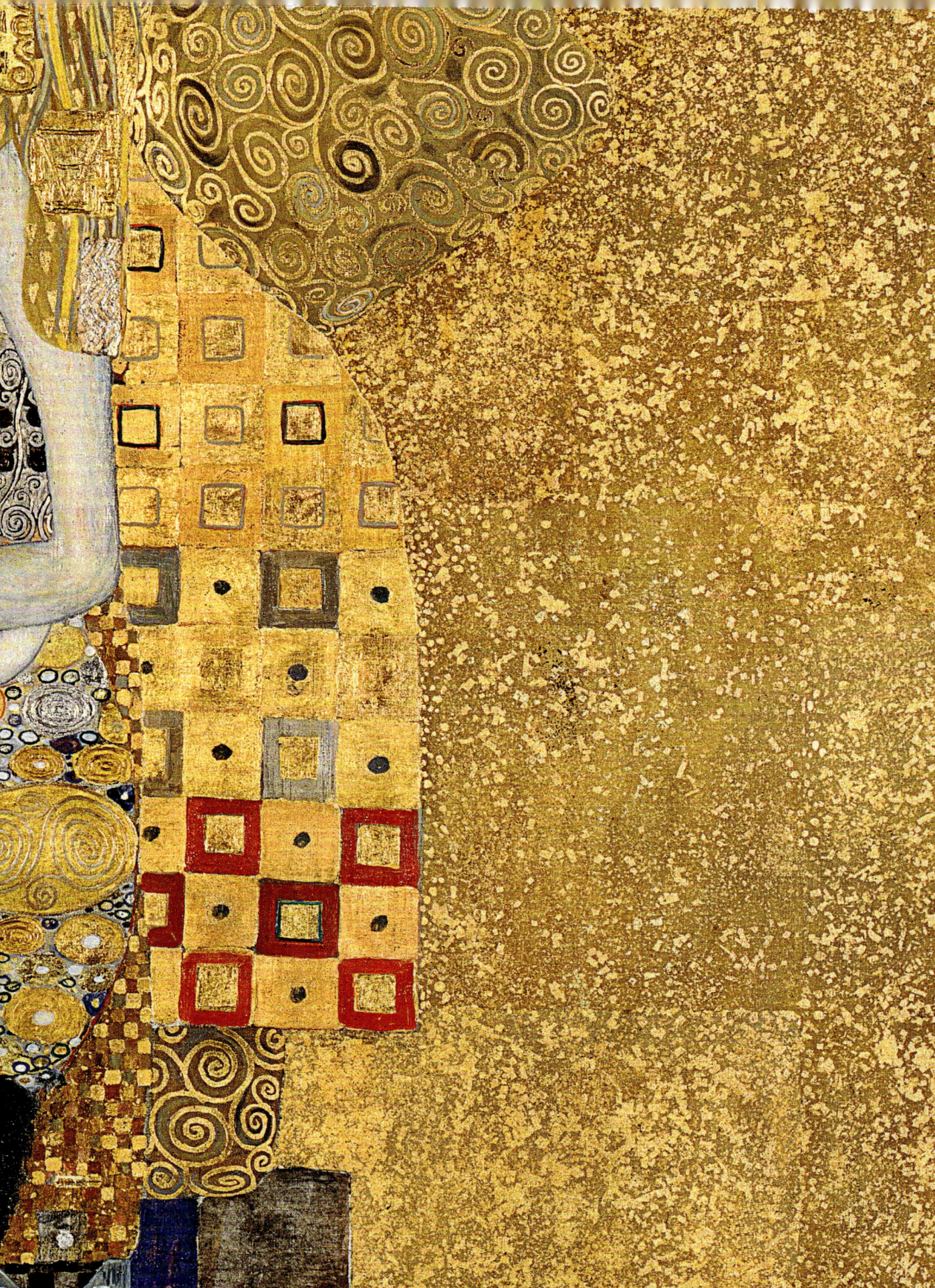

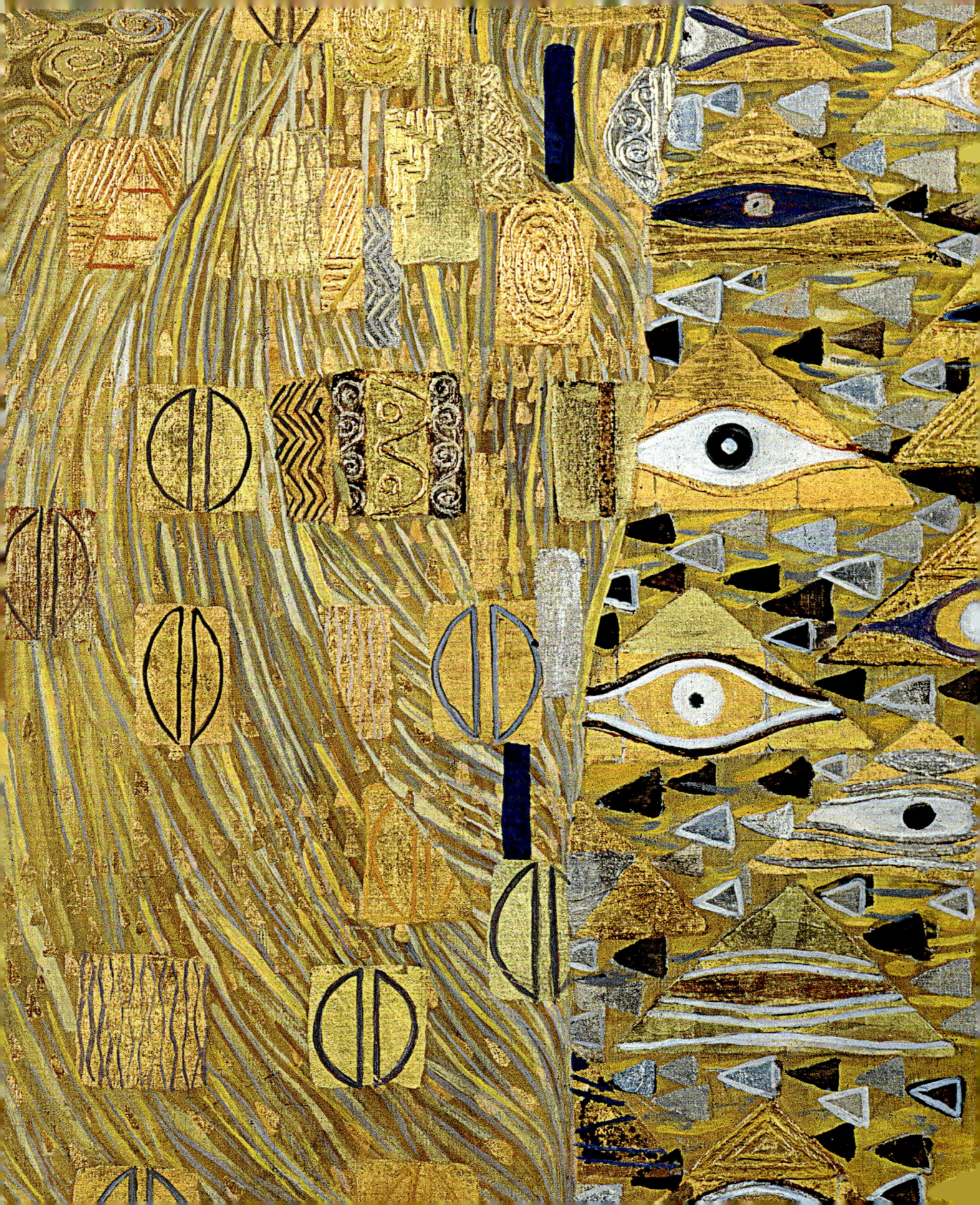

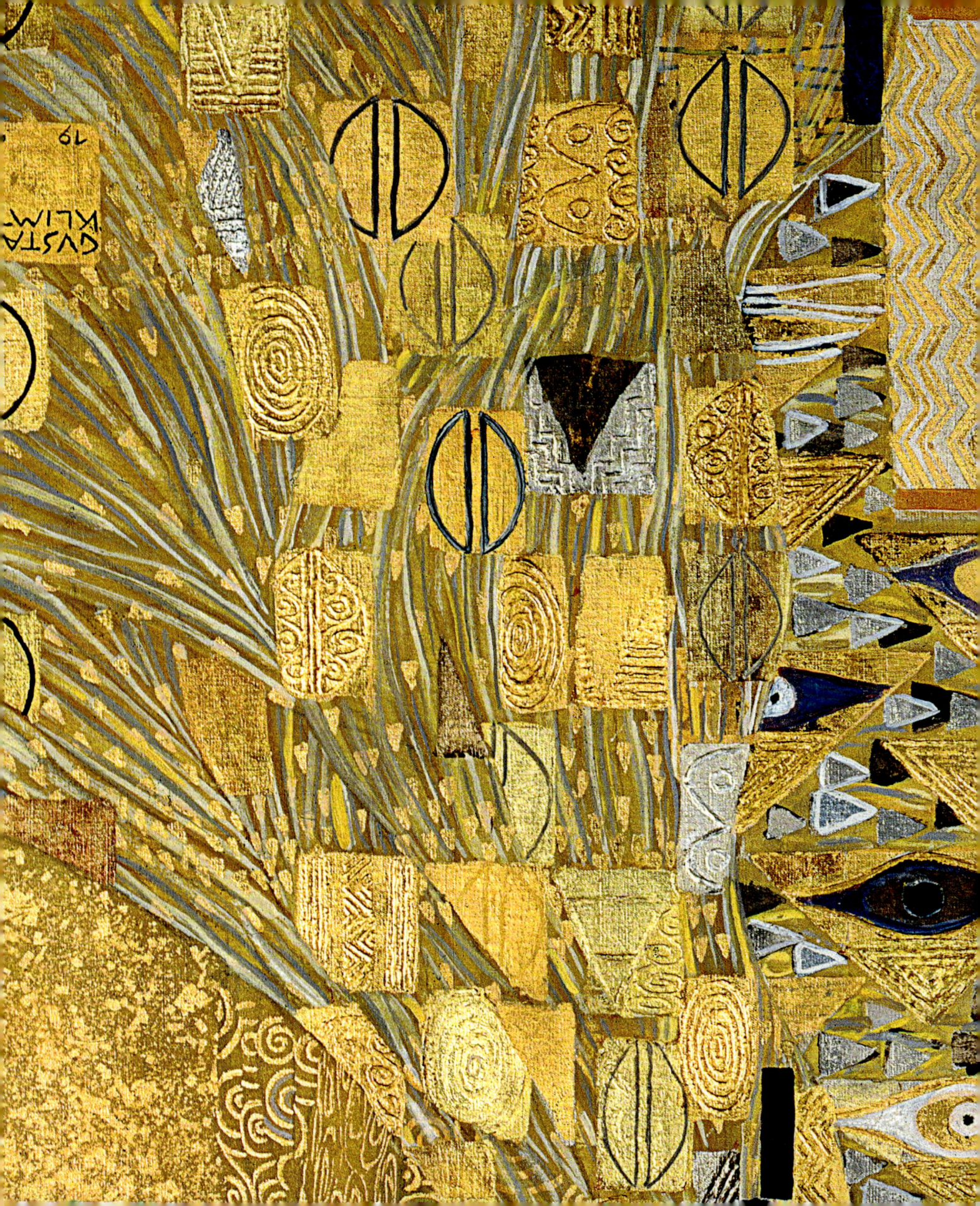

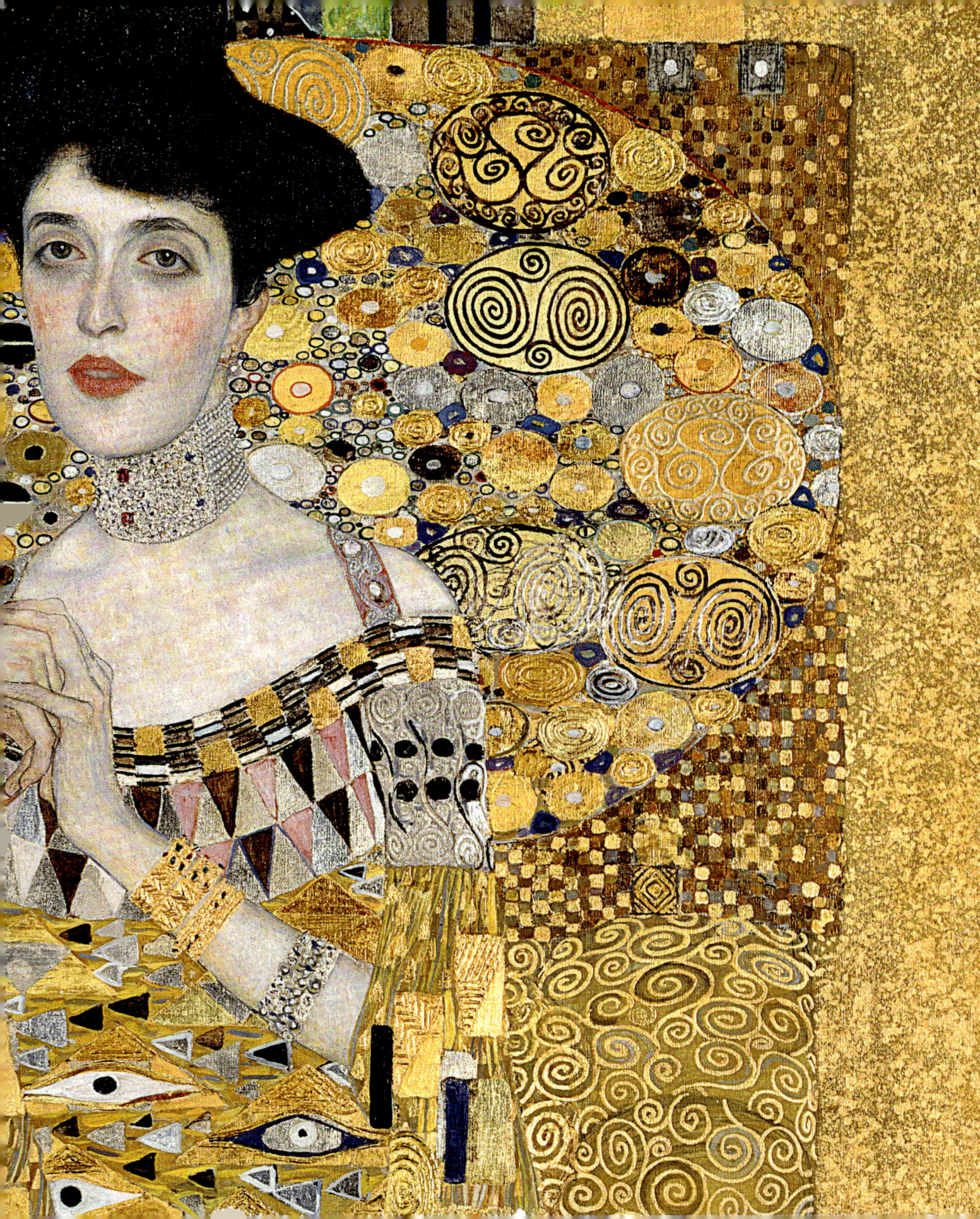

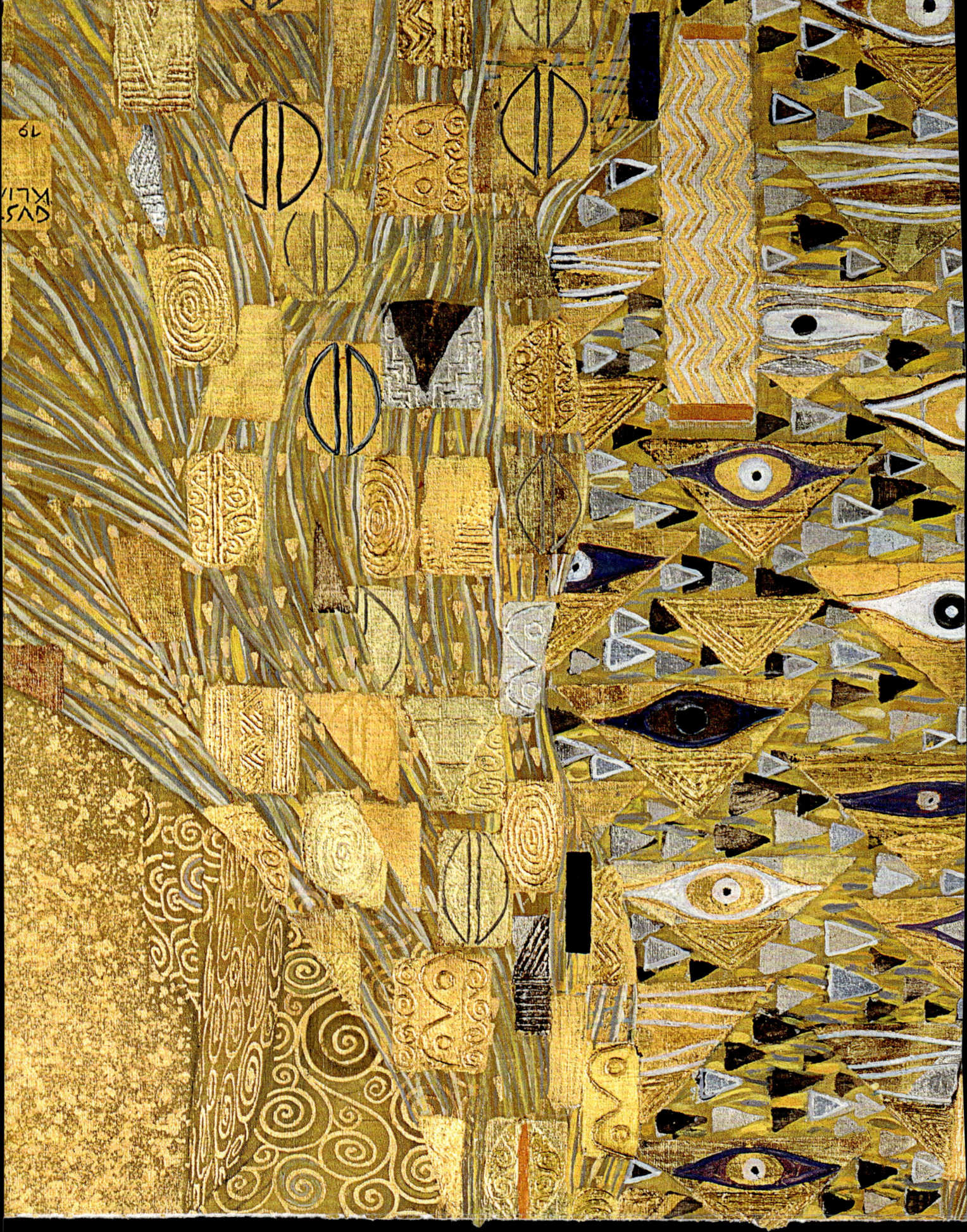

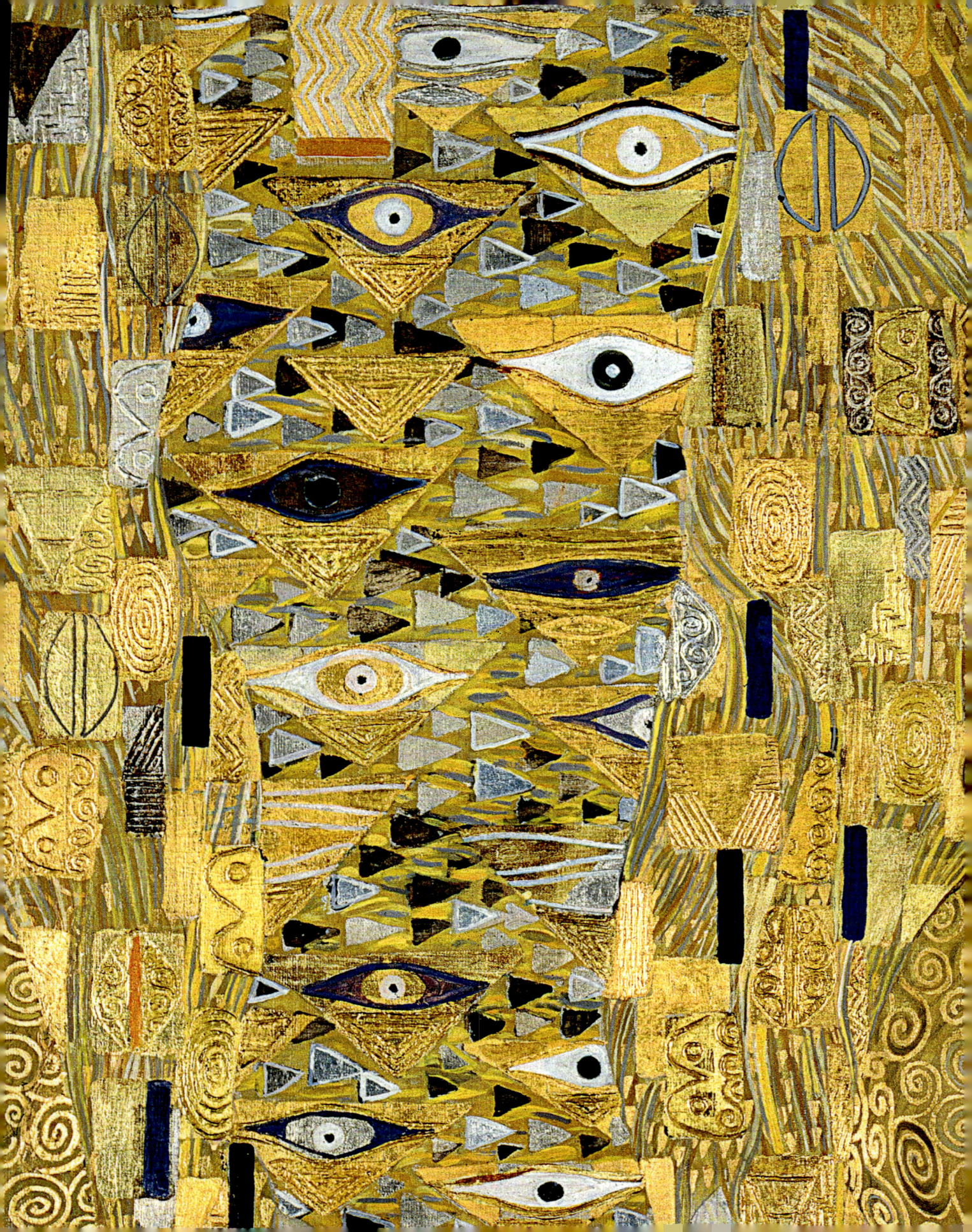

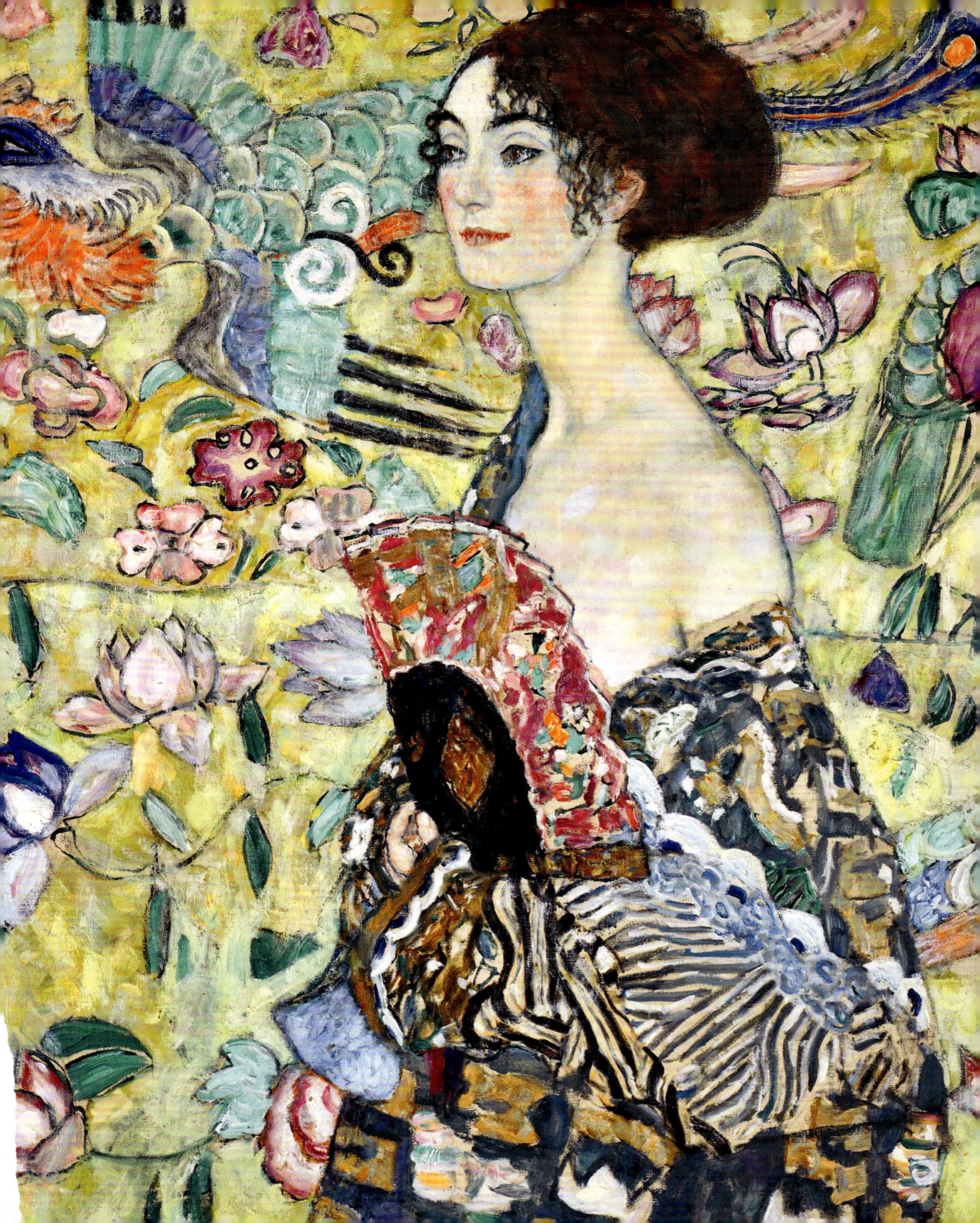

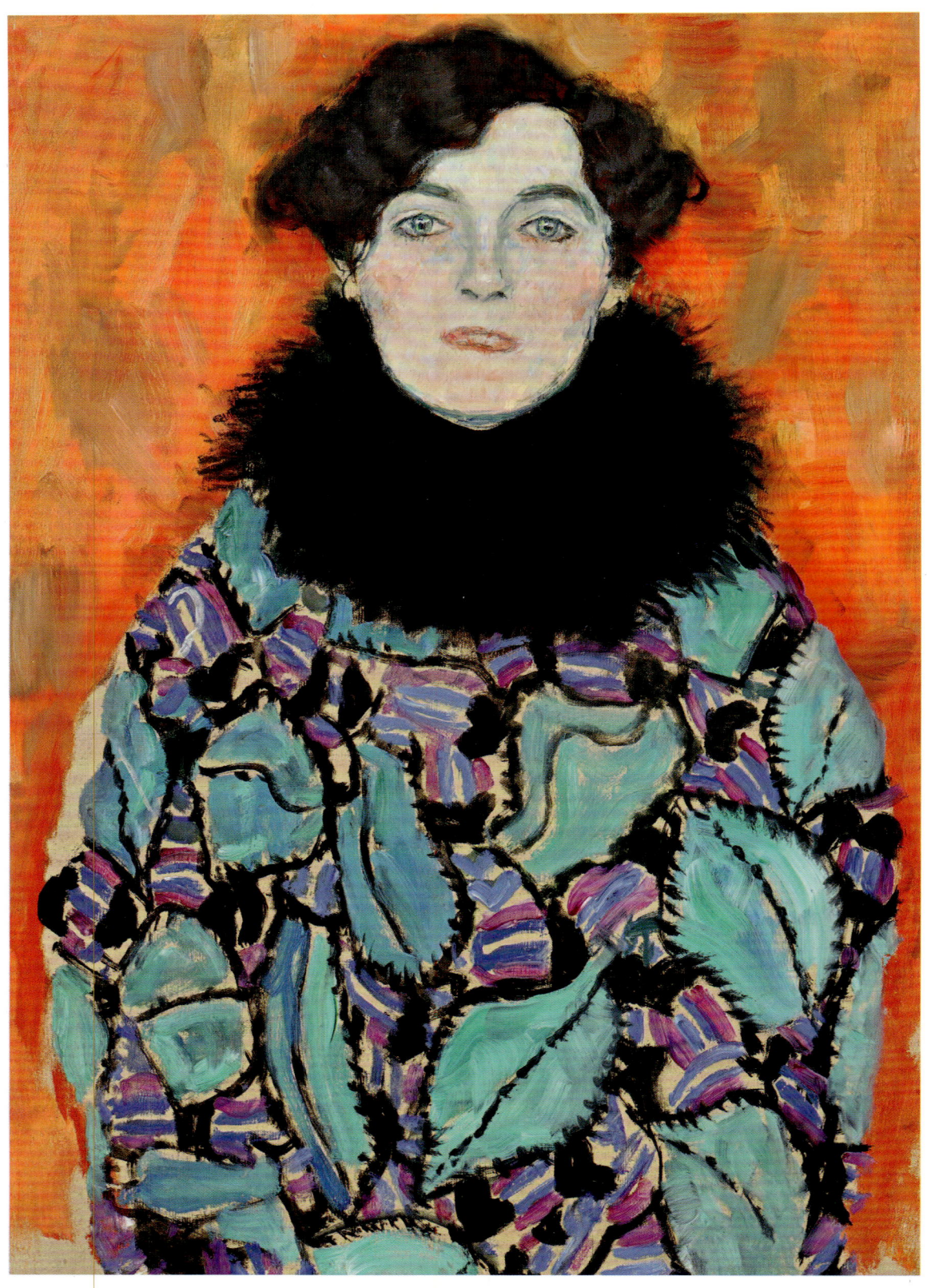

Portrait of Johanna Staude, 1917 (unfinished), oil on canvas, 70 × 50 cm,
Österreichische Galerie Belvedere, Vienna (above)

Portrait of a Young Woman, 1916/1917, oil on canvas, 68 × 55 cm,
Galleria d'Arte Moderna Ricci Oddi, Piacenza (opposite, detail)

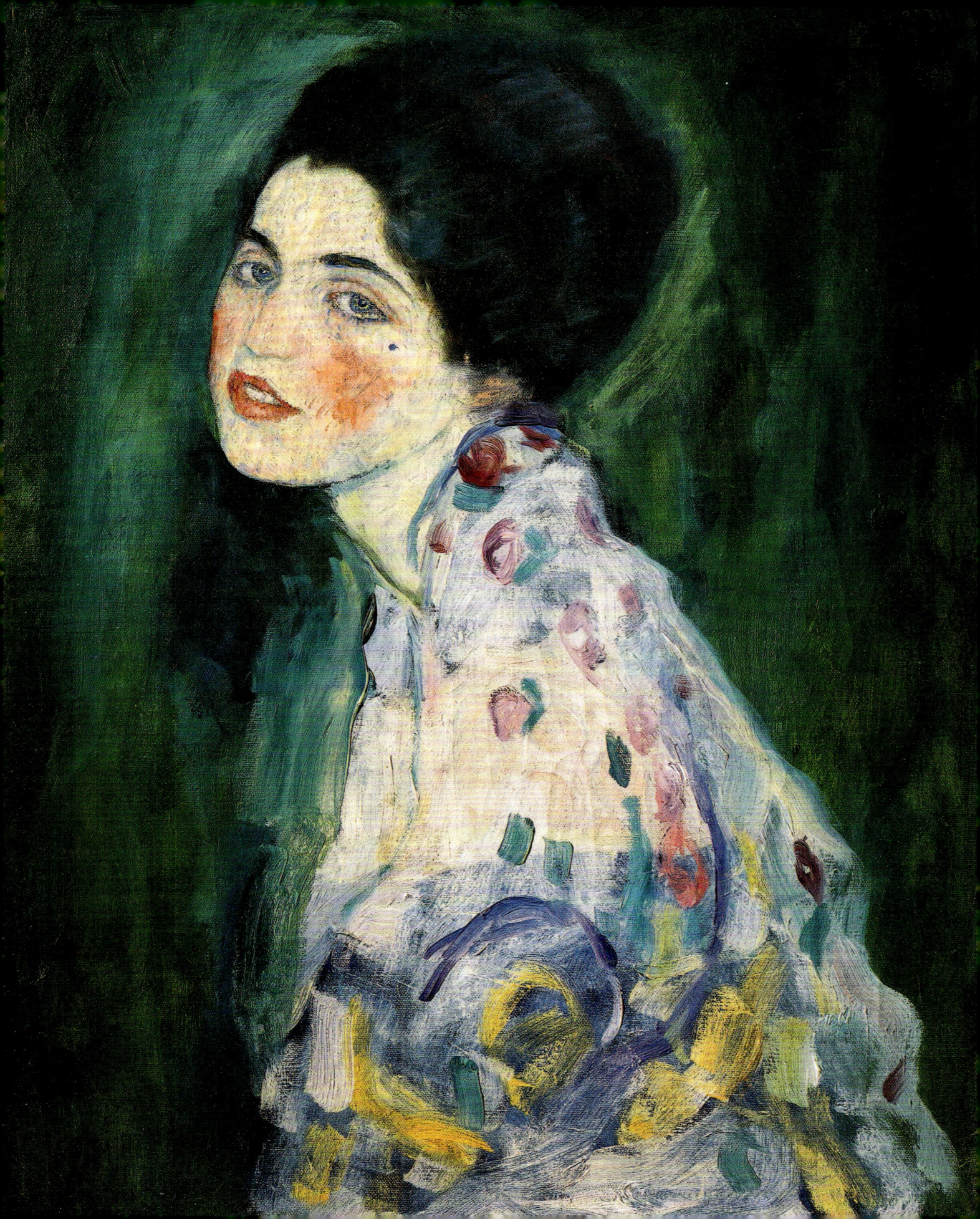

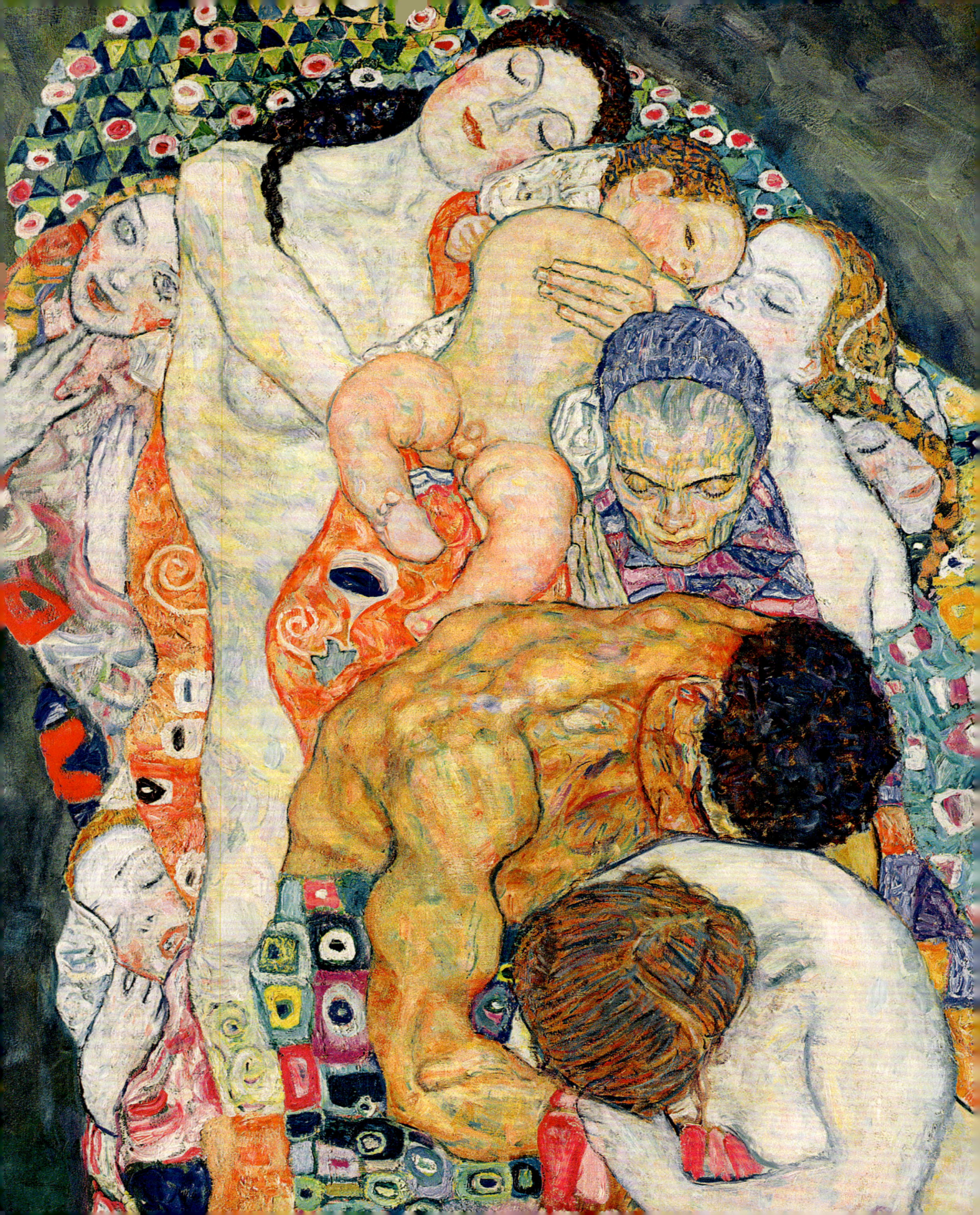

Life and Death

Although his training was in decorative and monumental painting, Gustav Klimt found himself faced with the task of depicting various historical cycles and allegories. His innate predispositions and his talent, well developed by a remarkable education, quickly earned him a reputation that led to the opportunity to contribute to the interior decoration of the most prestigious buildings of the Ringstrasse. Although his predilection for allegory persisted for his entire career, it underwent changes that led him to distance himself from tradition and convention in favour of renewing the genre. On the one hand, he stripped it of obsolete historical references, replacing them with a form of universal expression, in the manner of Symbolism. On the other hand, he inserted his figures into an ornamental framework, bringing him closer to the principles of the new art movement. Finally, he explicitly introduced eroticism, which was central to Viennese culture.

In 1886, the German-Austrian psychiatrist Richard von Krafft-Ebing had upended popular thought about sex with his work *Psychopathia Sexualis*. This compelled a German critic to refer to the doctor's writings in his discussion of the central section of the *Beethoven Frieze*: "Klimt's frescoes could pass for a temple to Krafft-Ebing. ... The representations of lust on the central wall are some of the most extreme examples of obscene art ever produced." In 1902, the Viennese philosopher Otto Weininger published *Geschlecht und Charakter* (Sex and Character), a profound and unblushing investigation in which Sigmund Freud outlined a set of anxieties linked to modernity. But as we know, it was up to Freud to demonstrate that the sex drive was a powerful force that generated all sorts of behaviour and interacted with the death wish; this was seemingly proven by a contemporary event, the Mayerling Affair, in which the sexual act was followed immediately by death. The duo of Eros and Thanatos was surely a preoccupation of the Viennese culture of the time. Outside the world of scientific research, it was manifested in literature and art, particularly in the work of Arthur Schnitzler and Gustav Klimt.

In Klimt's work, the duality of Eros and Thanatos is often associated with the evocation of mankind's distress and precarity. The grand allegories designed for the Great Hall of the University of Vienna – works that have since been destroyed – were a vehicle for the artist's inventiveness, as he desired to express his vision of the human condition. In them, humanity was represented as a mass of suffering bodies floating in space and drawn into an inevitable, fatal plunge; in the face of this, Jurisprudence, Philosophy and Medicine are forced to admit that they are powerless. The glorious nudes of traditional allegories are absent; there are only emaciated, skeletal bodies, and when a beautiful female body appears, its erotic charge is such that it seems provocatively immodest.

In Klimt's oeuvre, death affirms its presence from the moment of conception. In *Hope I* (pp. 84–85), the pregnant, nude young woman, who seems serene and confident of the future precisely because of the hope that inhabits her womb, is dominated by a frieze of lugubrious, menacing faces and encircled by a sea monster and by Death enrobed in a sort of blue cape. It differs to a fair degree from the initial plan, which is documented in preparatory drawings: a nude couple, the man encircling his pregnant companion's shoulders in his arms. In *Hope II* (pp. 86–87), created four years later, in 1907–1908, the young pregnant woman is also shown in profile, but her lower body is enveloped in a red fabric adorned with gilded patterns. The face, with its closed eyes, its sunken cheeks and its tight lips, is less peaceful than that of the young woman from 1903, as death is always present, lying in wait among the folds of the dress where three of the floating creatures so dear to Klimt are lurking. While maternity seems joyful in *The Three Ages of Woman* (pp. 88–89), the presence of an emaciated, barren female body alongside the young woman cuddling her young child reminds the viewer that this joy can only be ephemeral.

The subject of the ages of woman would reappear some years later in a more complex composition whose centre is occupied by the well-muscled figure of a man that contrasts starkly with the various pale-skinned figures of women of various ages who encircle him (pp. 90–91). The shimmering colours that envelop and isolate the group suggest a happy, protected world. But, again, this *joie de vivre* – also present in *The Virgin* (fold-out p. 94), whose subject is carried away in a carefree whirl – will only be fleeting, because Death, hidden in the nocturnal cosmos, awaits the moment to brandish his cudgel and reduce this passing happiness to nothing.

The young child – usually asleep – has a place in every one of these allegorical compositions: the embodiment of innocence and the beginning of life, in opposition to death. Klimt would revisit the subject in a later painting, dated 1917–1918. Stripped of all allegorical meaning, the work consists of a carefully developed, multi-coloured decorative arrangement (pp. 92–93). The head of this baby, in apparent good health and seen from an oblique angle, emerges at the summit of a triangular mountain of various fabrics that hide its body from view. In contrast to the portraits of women from the same period, in which the strong presence of textiles is an expression of modern elegance, here the joyful abundance of cloth plunges the viewer into the world of childhood reveries.

Death and Life, 1910/1911 and 1915/1916,
oil on canvas, 180.5 × 200.5 cm, Leopold Museum, Vienna (p. 76, detail; see pp. 90–91)

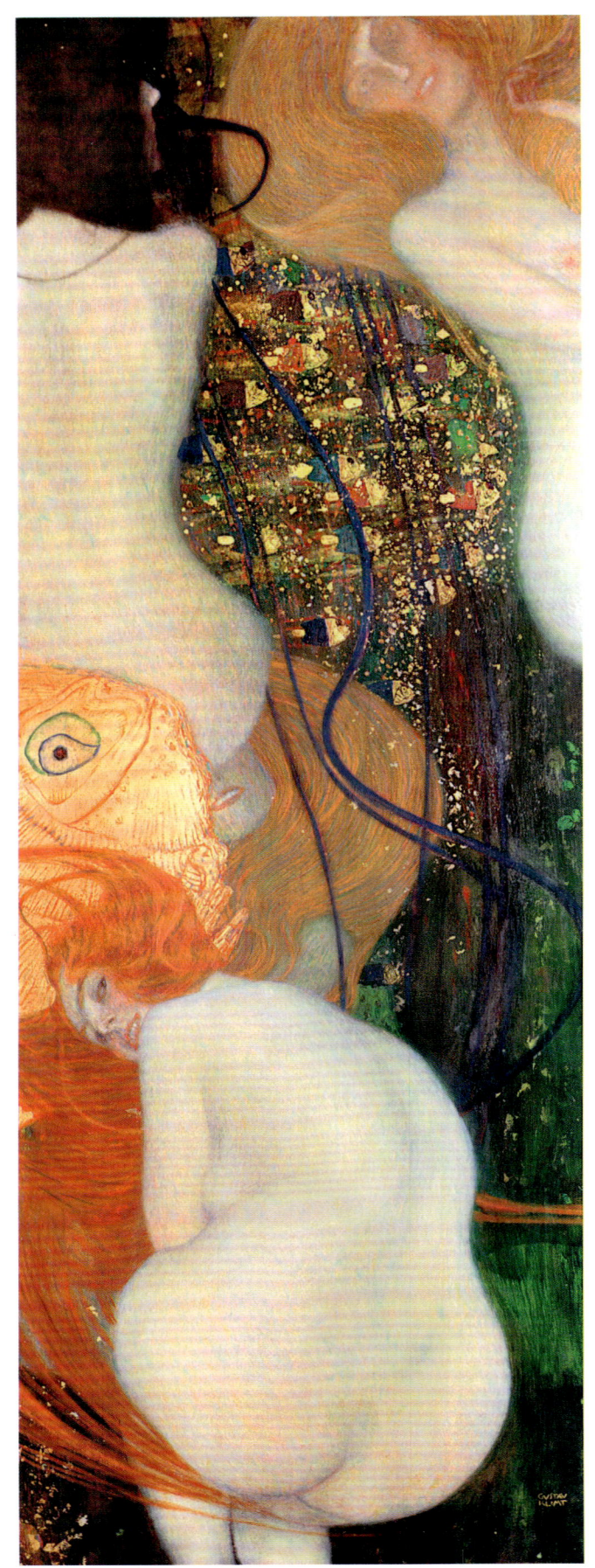

Goldfish,
1901/1902, oil on canvas,
181 × 67 cm,
Kunstmuseum Solothurn

Water Snakes I and II

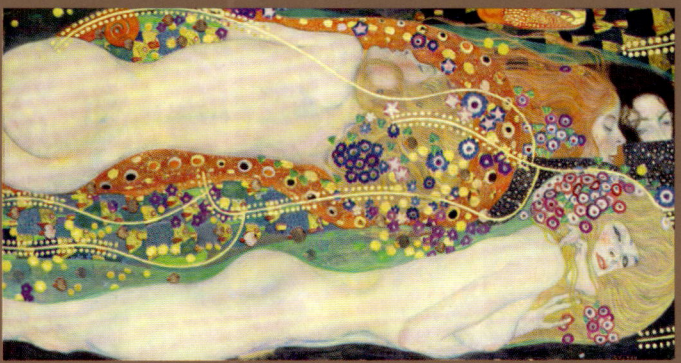

Water sprites were popular in nineteenth-century German culture, culminating in Richard Wagner's *Das Rheingold,* the opera that begins with the aquatic games of the Rhinemaidens, the guardians of the gold on the riverbed. They are frequently a subject in Symbolist painting, and Klimt depicted them in several works, including the two versions of *Water Snakes*. He emphasizes the fusion of the slim bodies with their long, slender legs and loose hair flowing in the rapid water into a single malleable mass. In addition, the closeness of the bodies that glide by one another in the liquid surroundings clearly evokes Sapphic love, an omnipresent theme in Klimt's oeuvre. In a speech delivered in September 1917, the Viennese poet Peter Altenberg said of Klimt's creatures, which float both in water and air, as in the *Beethoven Frieze,* that "the nude bodies of all these ascetic women – thin – tender – delicate – the fingers, the hands, the arms, the legs of these graces born, as it were, of the evil and afflicted matter that only undermines the spirit and the soul." For Altenberg, these works were the manifestation of the "fantastic naturalism of the most authentic ideal of modern beauty."

Water Snakes II, 1904 and 1906/1907, oil on canvas, 80 × 145 cm, private collection

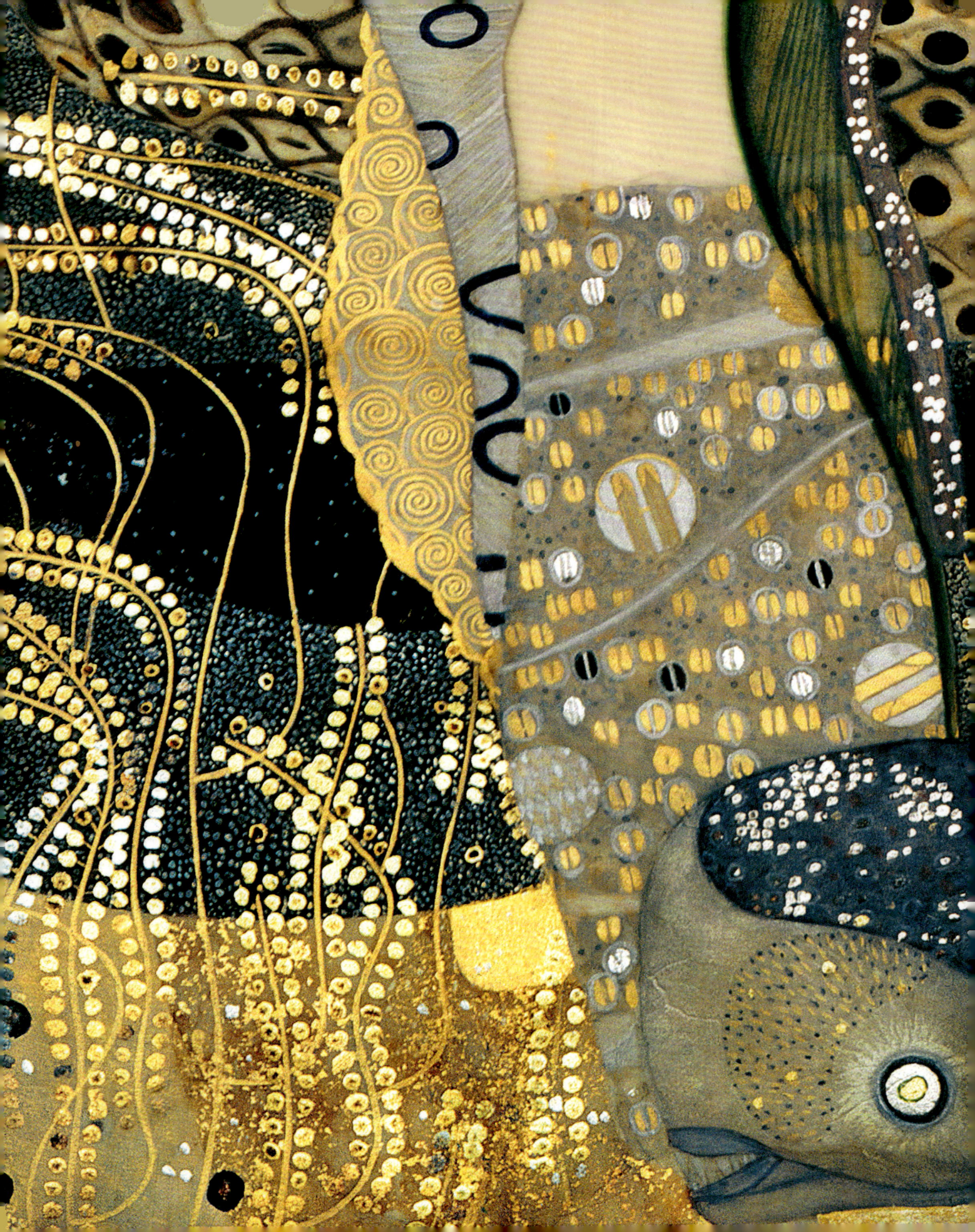

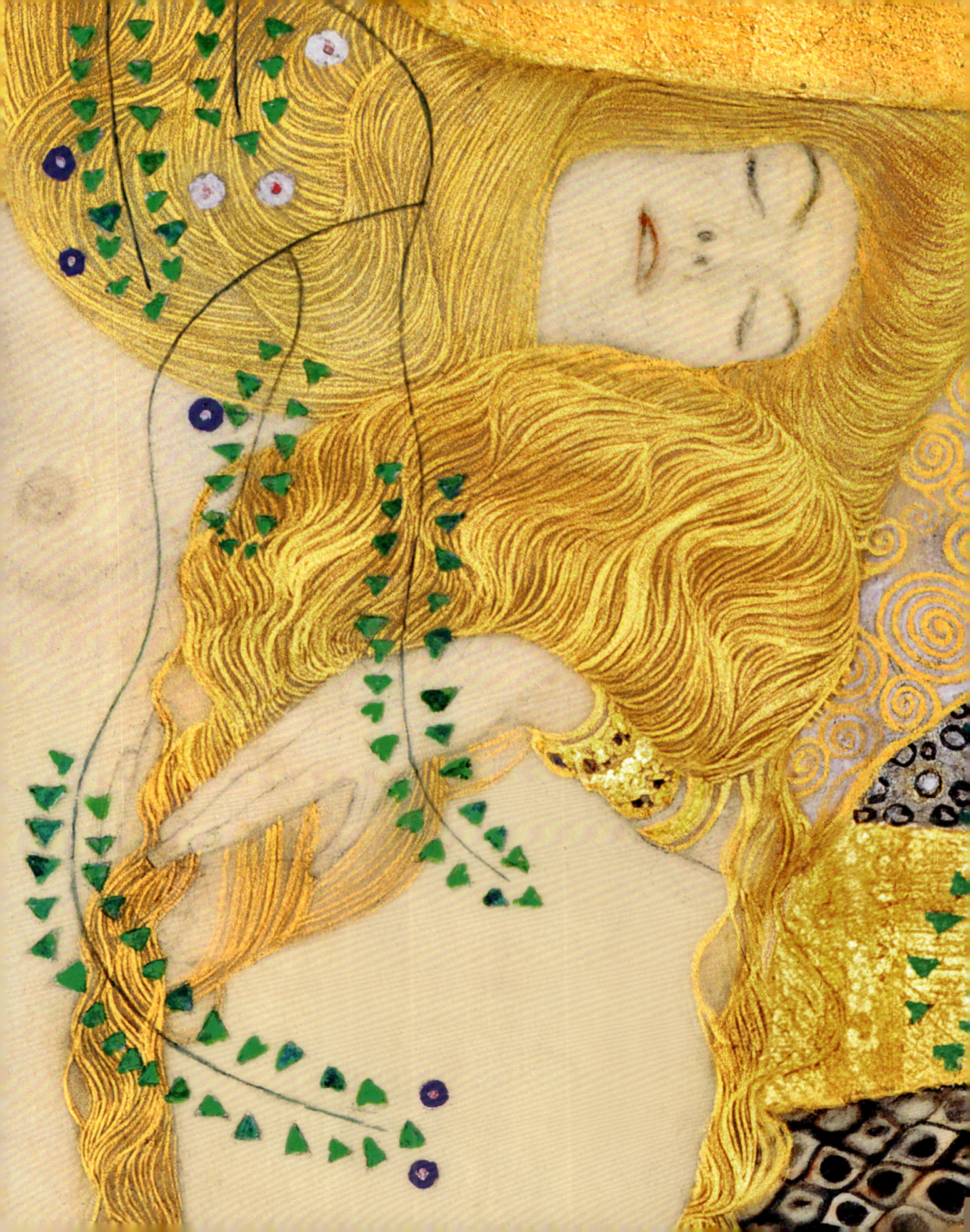

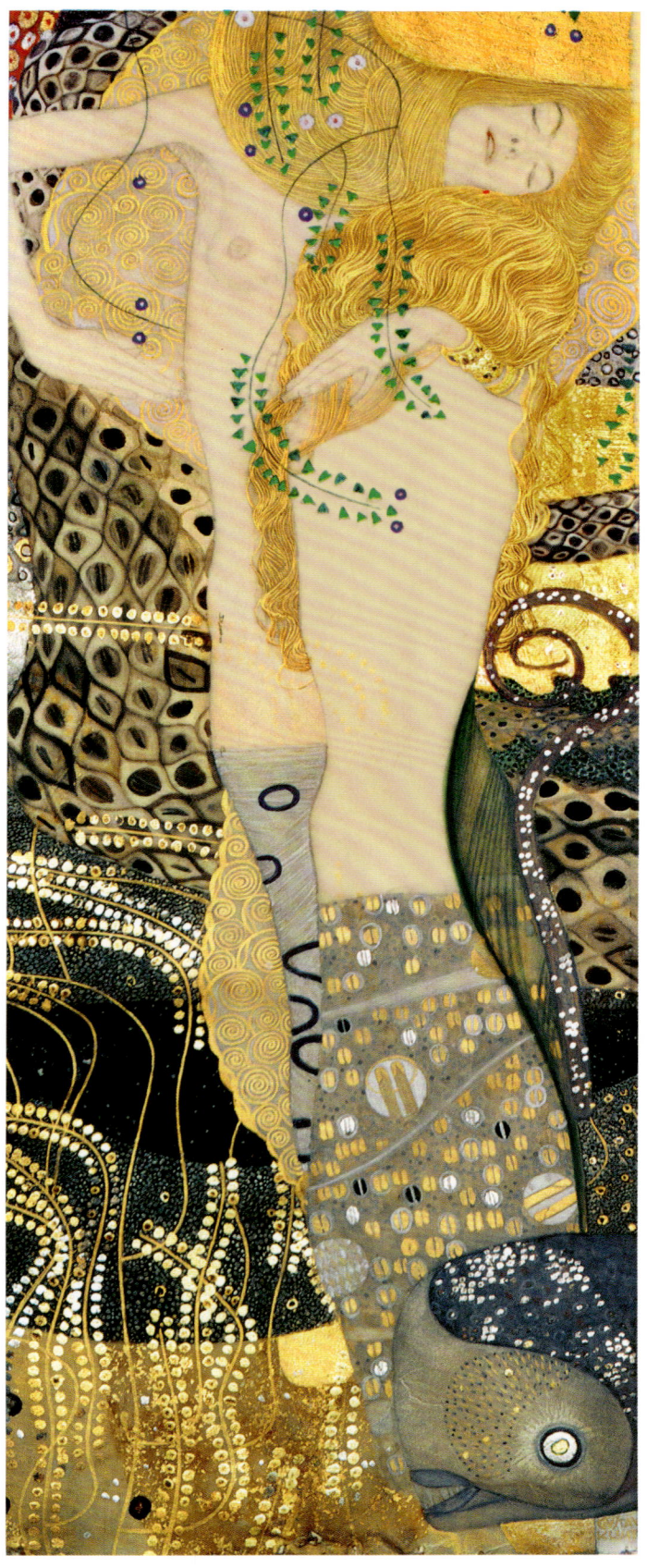

Water Snakes I, 1904–1907, pencil on parchment with watercolour and gouache, with brass, silver, gold and platinum, 50 × 20 cm, Österreichische Galerie Belvedere, Vienna (details on fold-outs)

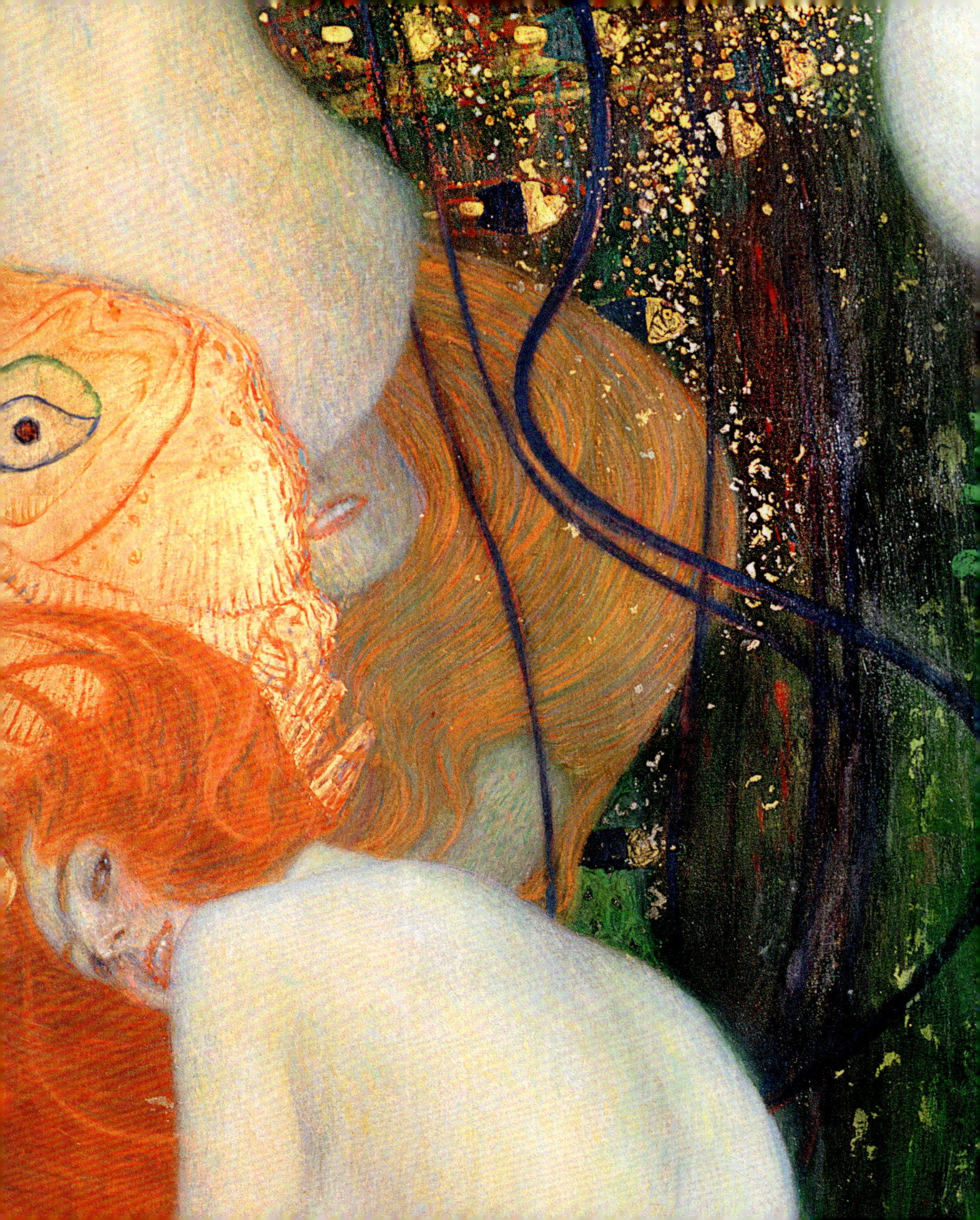

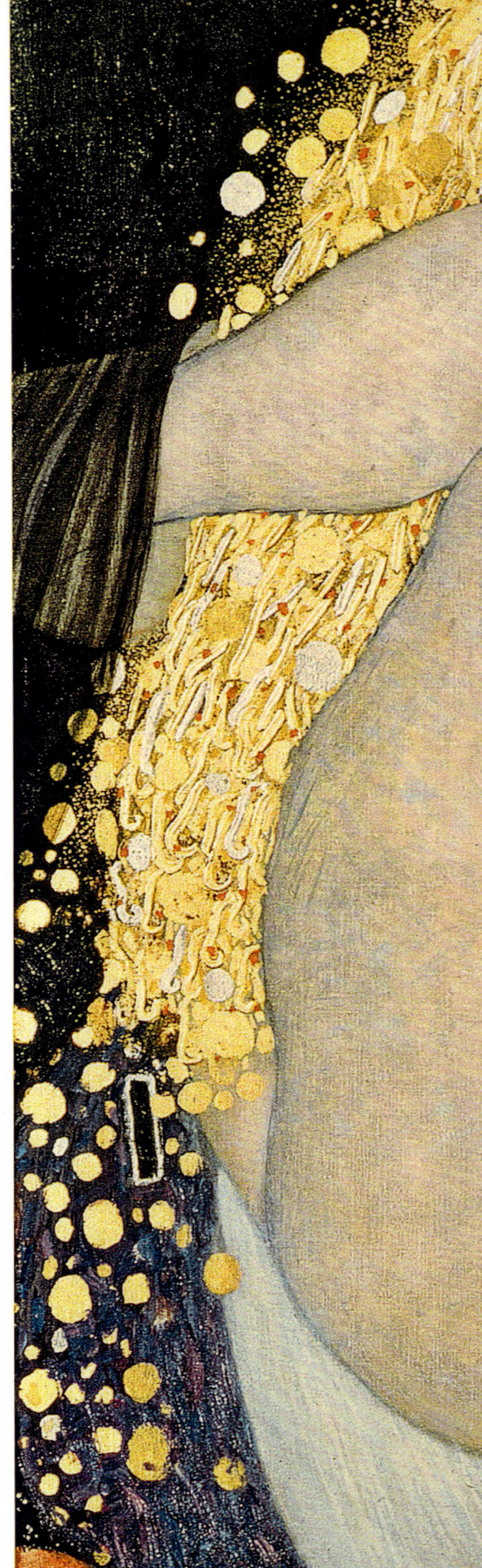

Danaë,
1907/1908, oil on canvas,
77 × 83 cm,
Dichand family, Vienna
(detail)

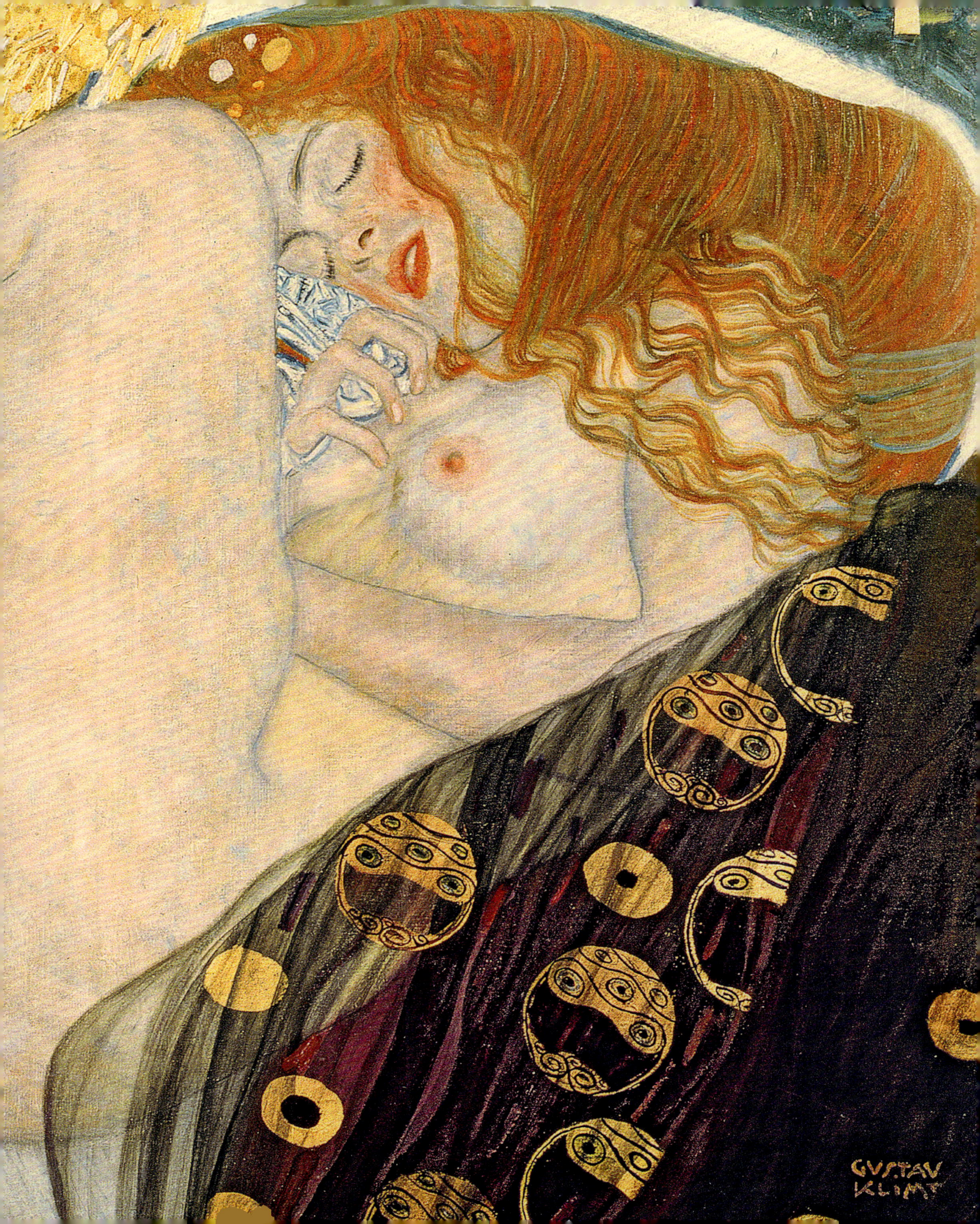

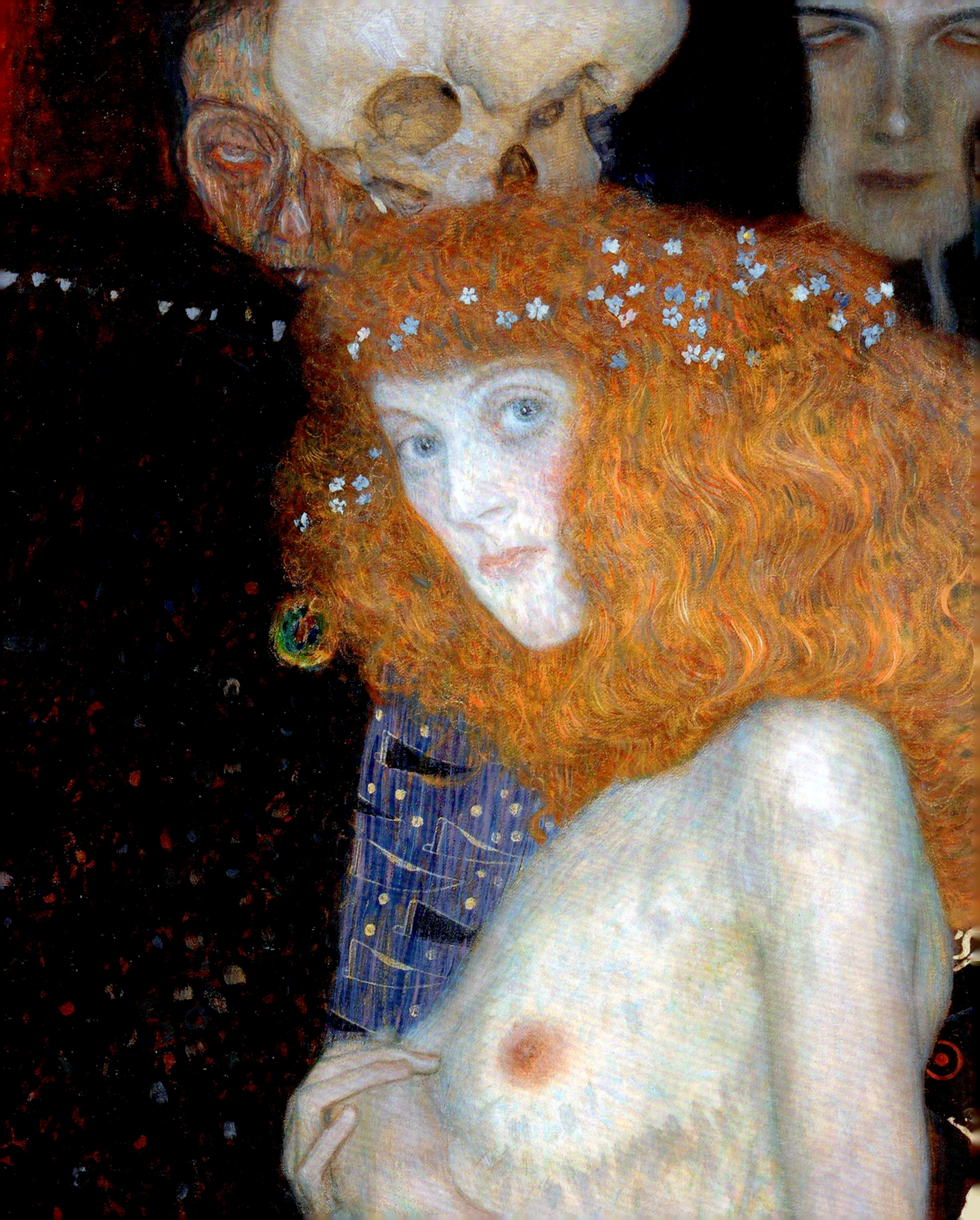

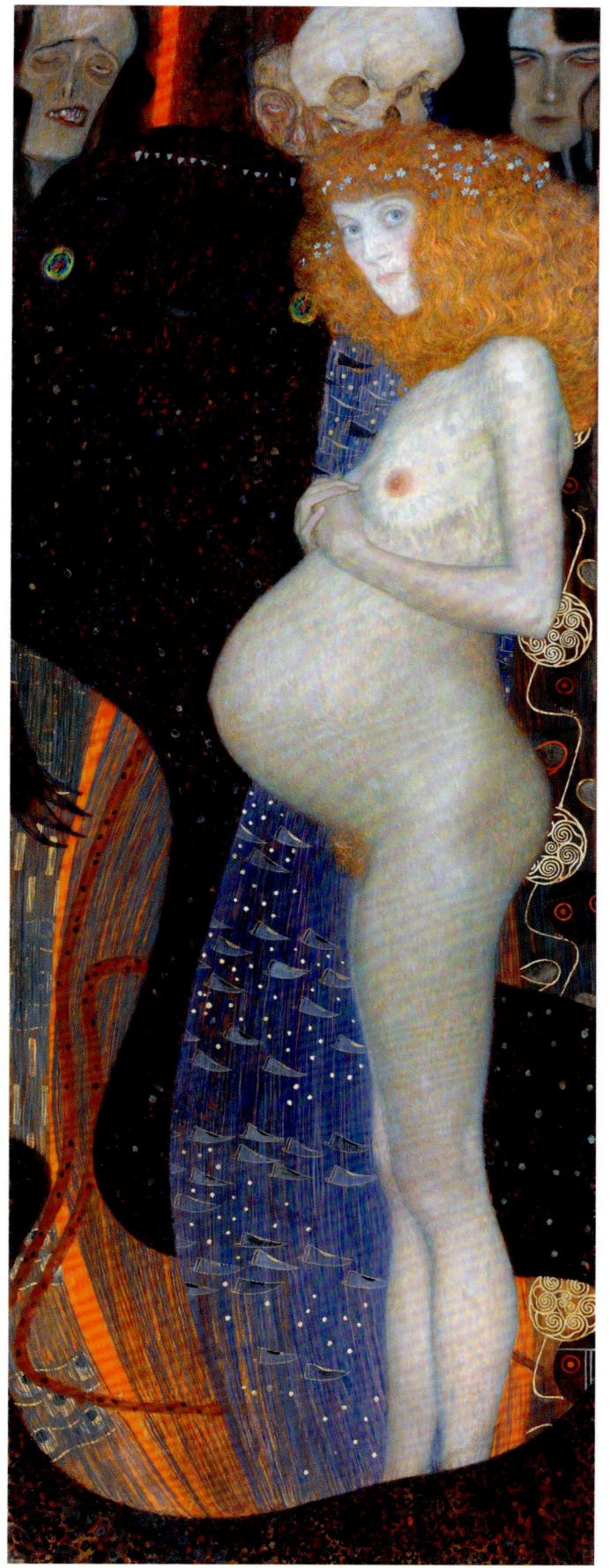

Hope I,
1903/1904, oil on canvas,
189.2 × 67 cm,
National Gallery of Canada, Ottawa

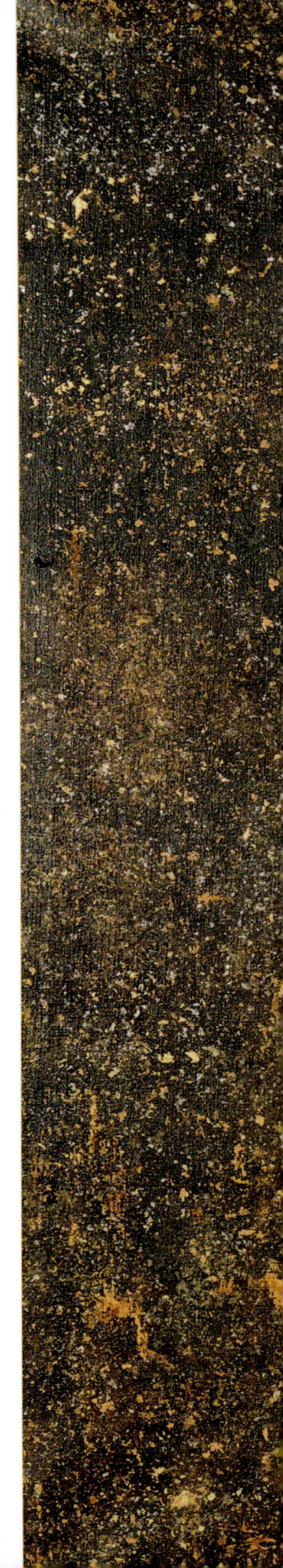

Hope II (Vision),
1907/1908, oil on canvas with gold and platinum,
110.5 × 110.5 cm,
Museum of Modern Art, New York

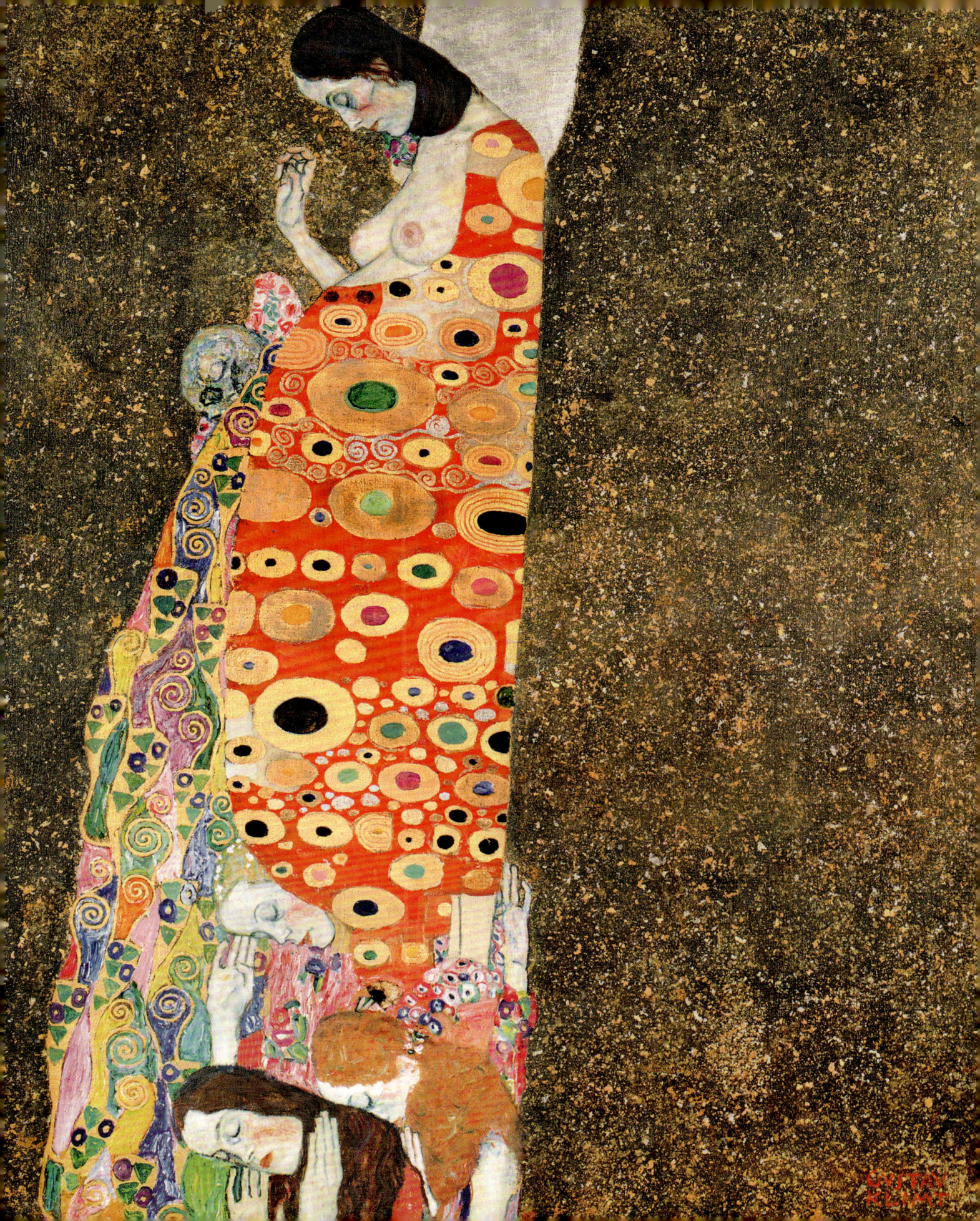

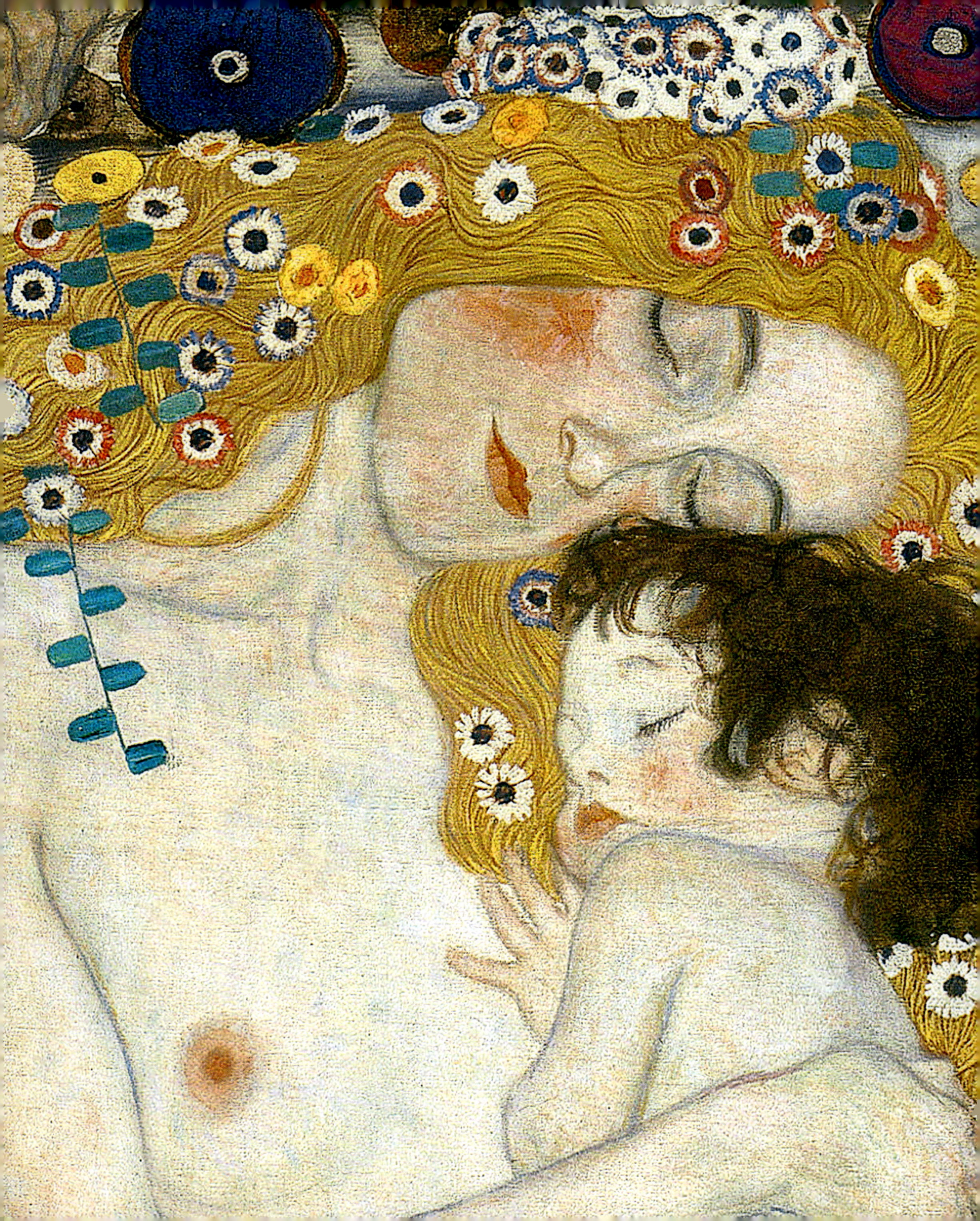

The Kiss

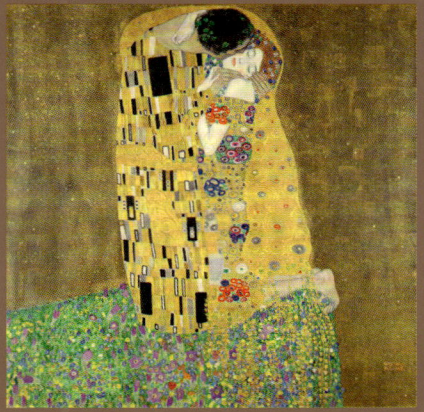

The couple in love is a theme that first appears in Klimt's 1895 work *Allegory of Love* (pp. 14 and 31). The subjects hold each other at a certain distance, and they wear contemporary clothing. Their bodies are not intertwined, nor are they embracing. The theme becomes more urgently passionate in the 1902 *Beethoven Frieze* (fold-out p. 50), in which two nude bodies fuse together, with the woman disappearing in the man's embrace. Equally passionate is the ecstatic embrace of the couple in the Palais Stoclet dining room mosaics (fold-out, pp. 120 and 123), perceived as the fulfilment of feminine desire. The man, literally inhaling the woman (of whom we see only the face), is clad in a sumptuous coat. Similarly extravagant are the clothes that envelop the two entwined bodies of *The Kiss,* another masterpiece of Klimt's Golden Period. Their decorative motifs—rectangles on the man and eye-like spirals on the woman—heighten the disconcertment of the seduction already conveyed by the woman's kneeling position.

The Kiss was acquired by the Austrian Gallery for the substantial sum of twenty-five thousand gold crowns following the painting's presentation at the Kunstschau exhibition in spring 1908. That same year, the Historical Museum purchased the *Portrait of Emilie Flöge* (pp. 59–61) for the price of twelve thousand gold crowns.

The Kiss, 1907/1908, oil and gold and silver leaf on canvas, 180 × 180 cm, Österreichische Galerie Belvedere, Vienna

The Three Ages, 1905, oil on canvas, 180 × 180 cm, Galleria Nazionale d'Arte Moderna e Contemporanea, Rome (left page, detail)

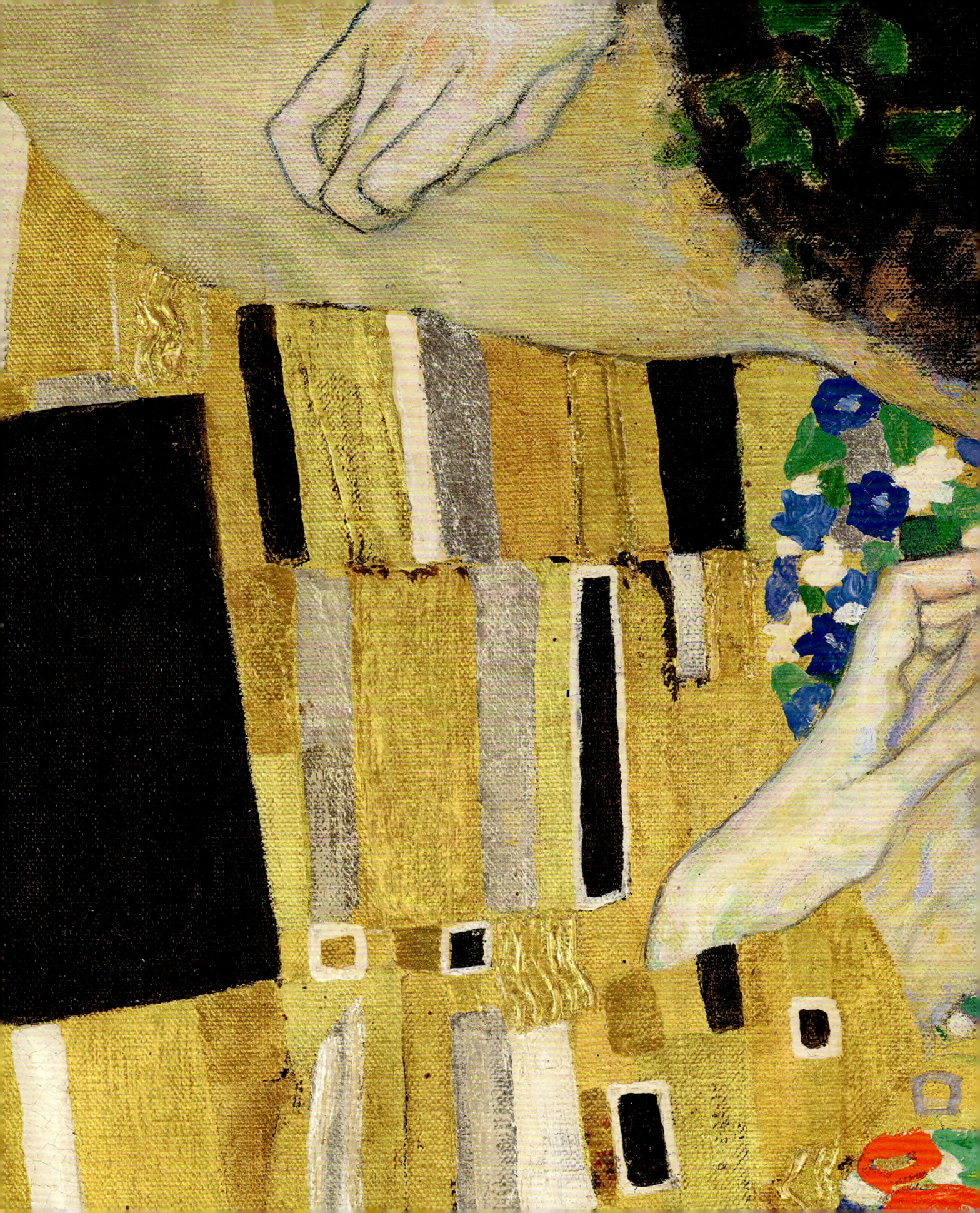

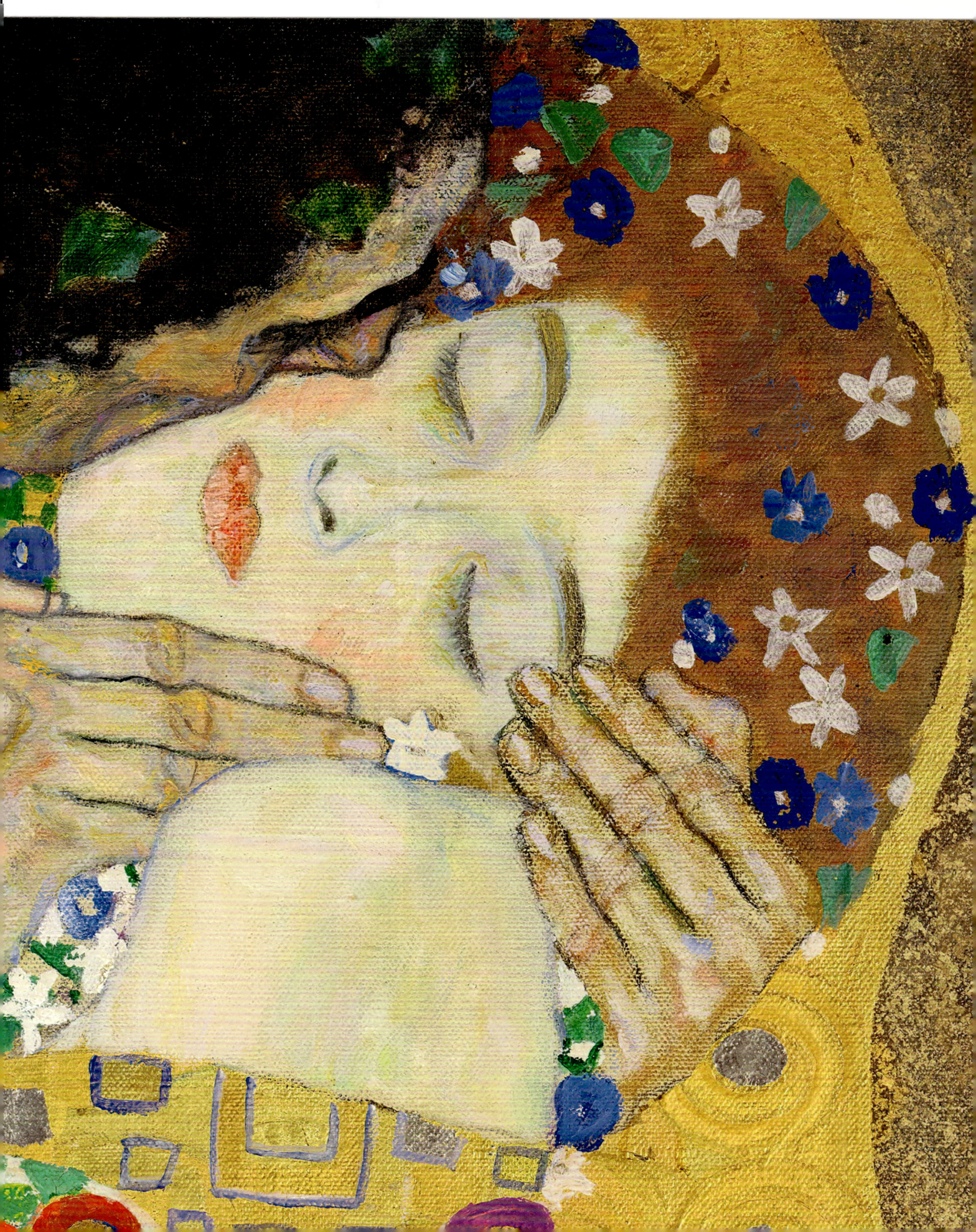

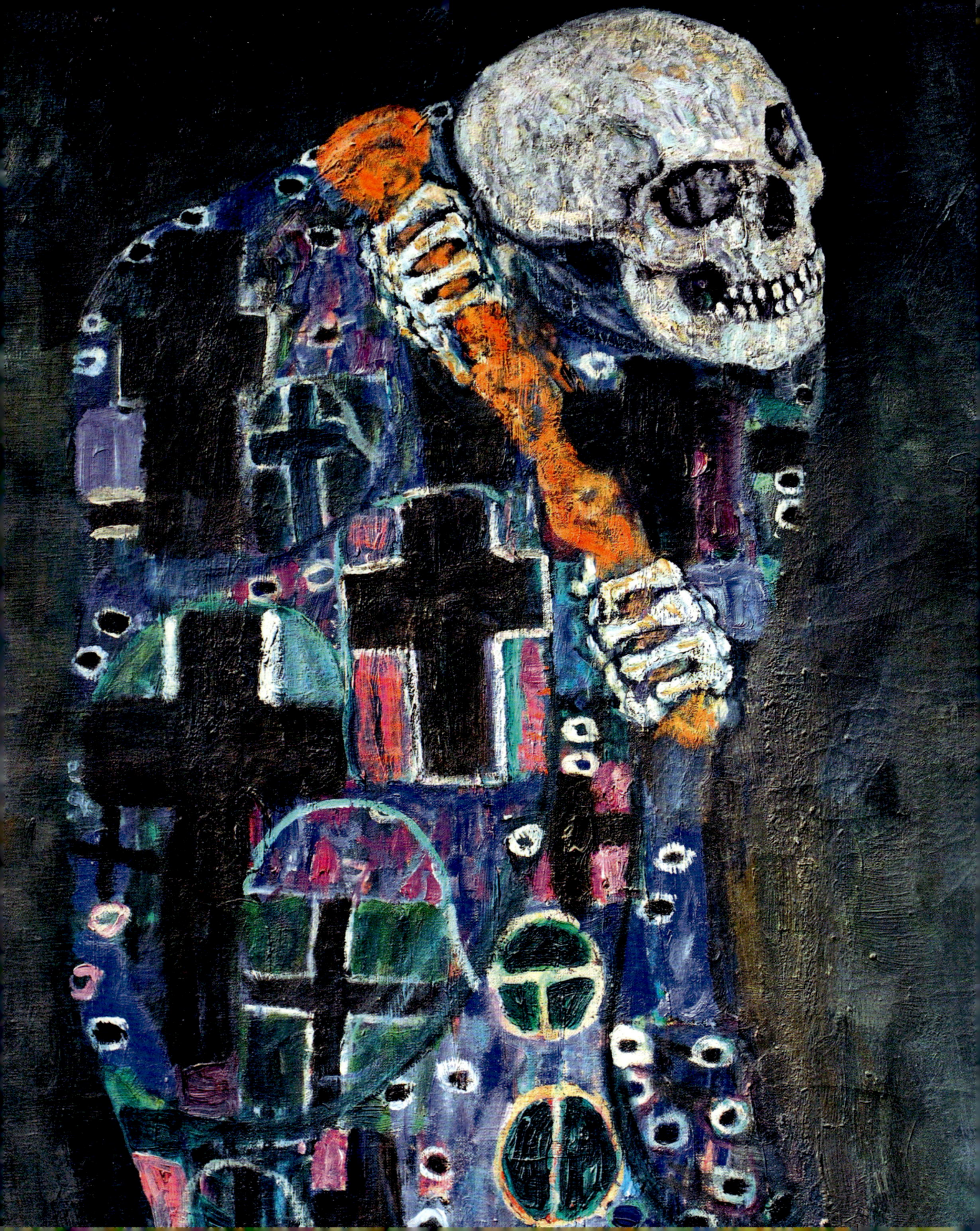

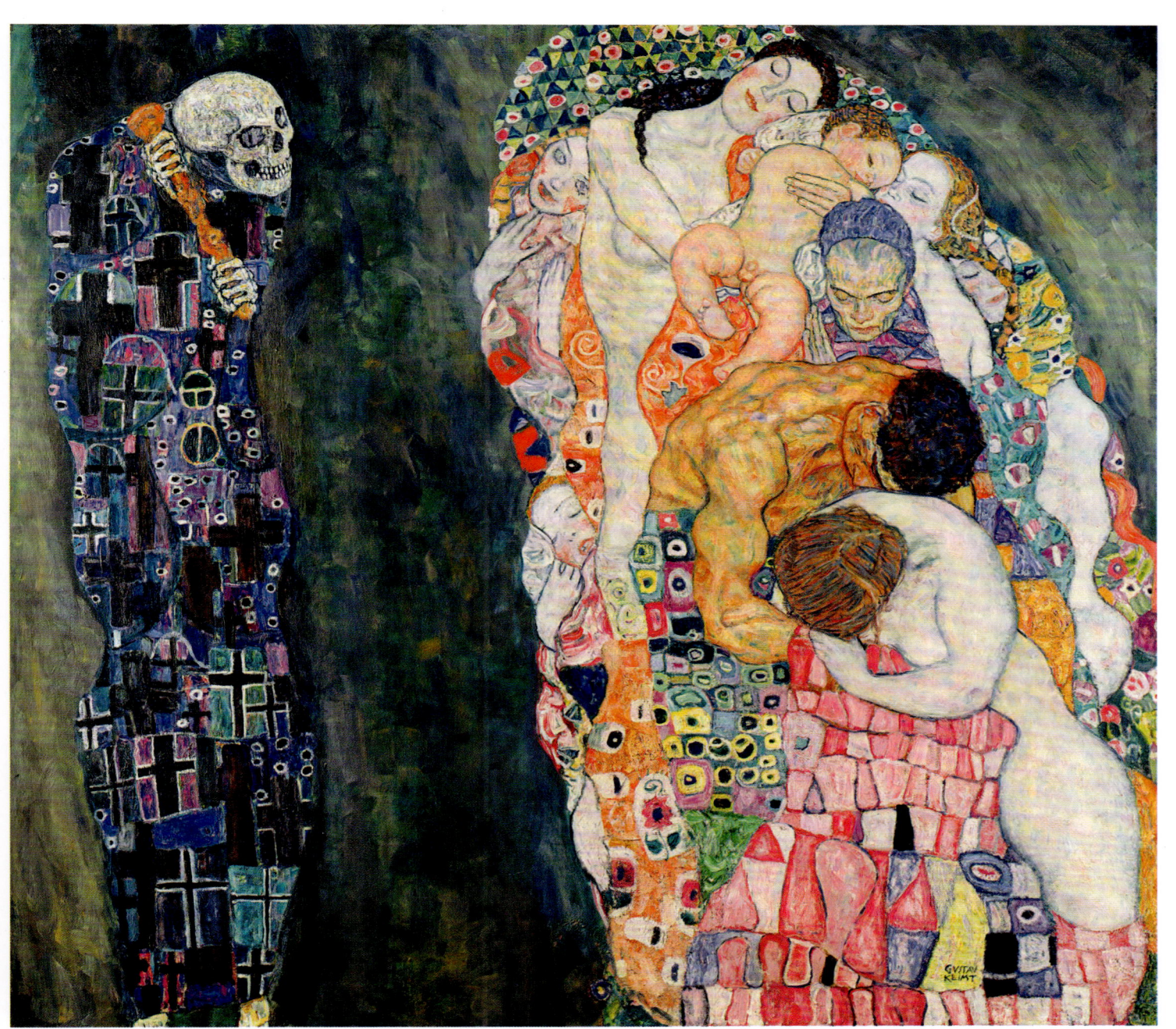

Death and Life,
1910/1911 and 1915/1916, oil on canvas, 180.5 × 200.5 cm, Leopold Museum, Vienna

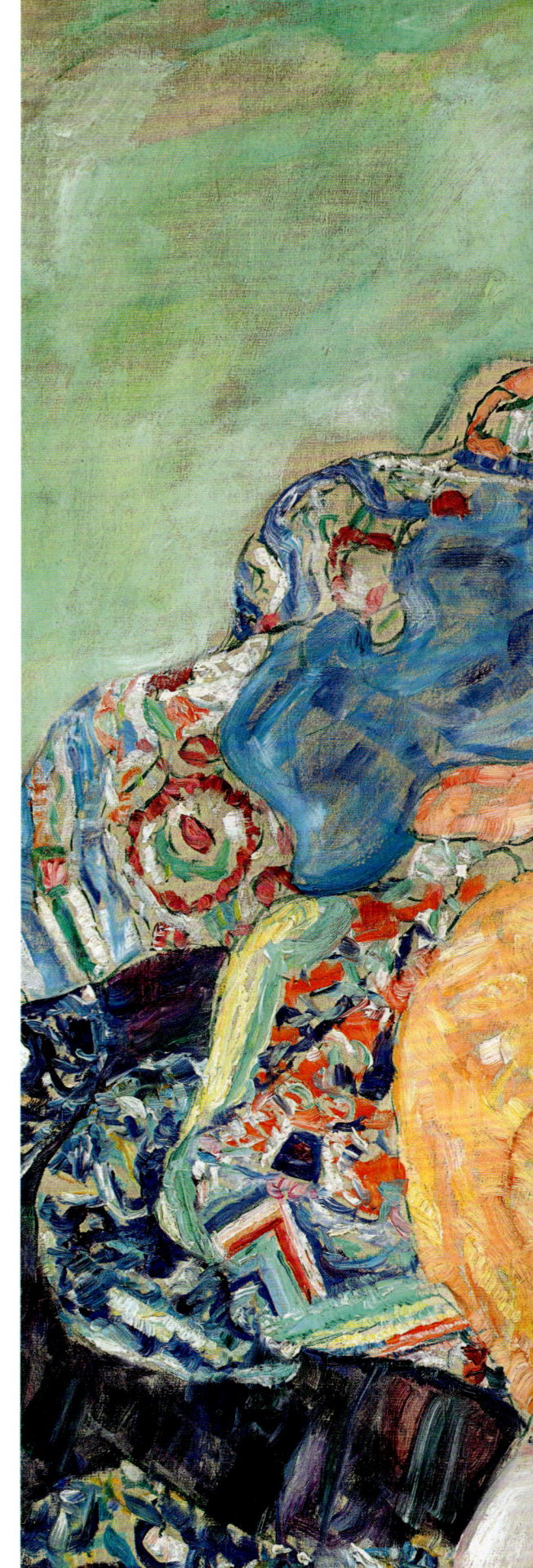

Baby,
1917, oil on canvas,
110 × 110 cm,
National Gallery of Art,
Washington, DC (detail)

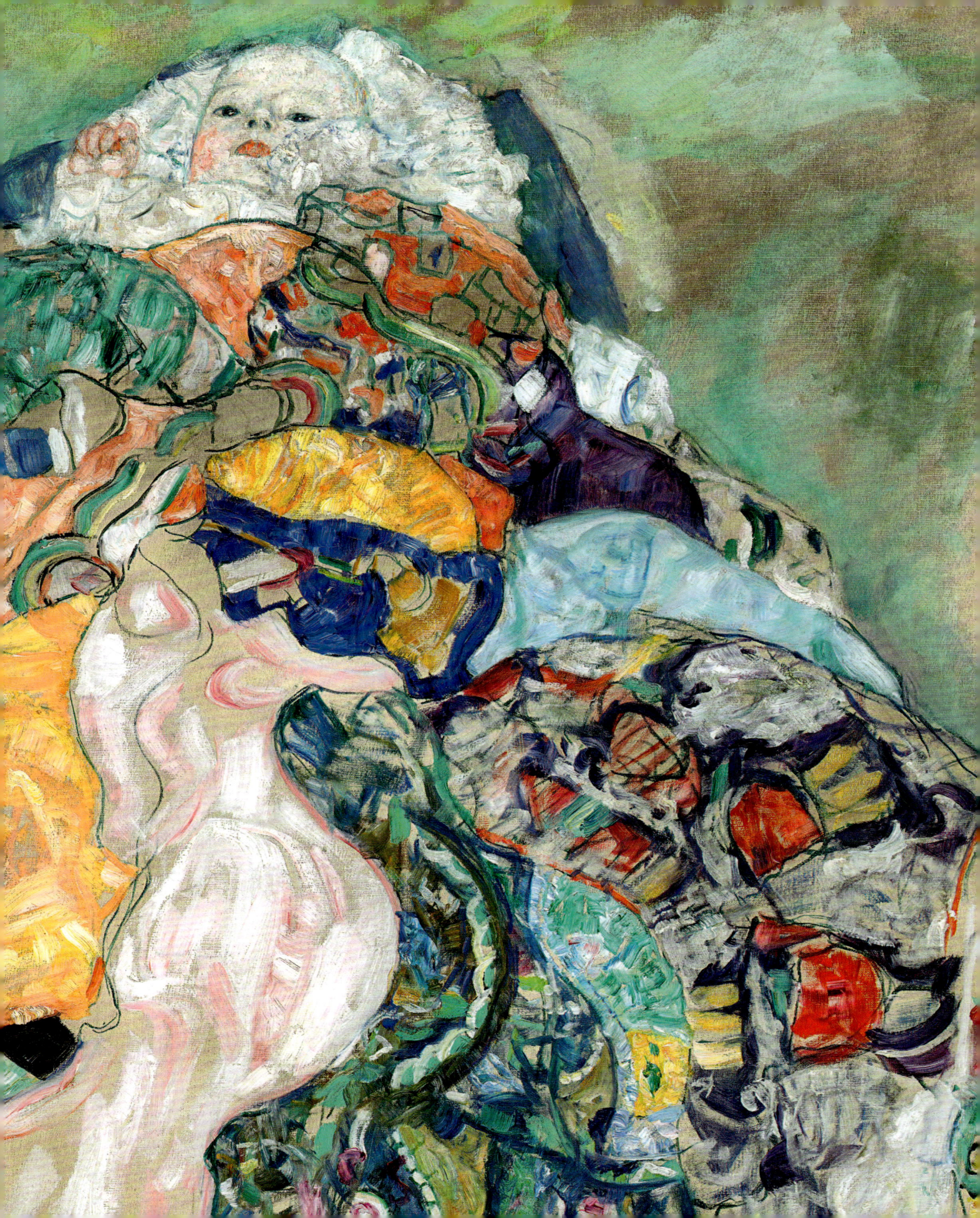

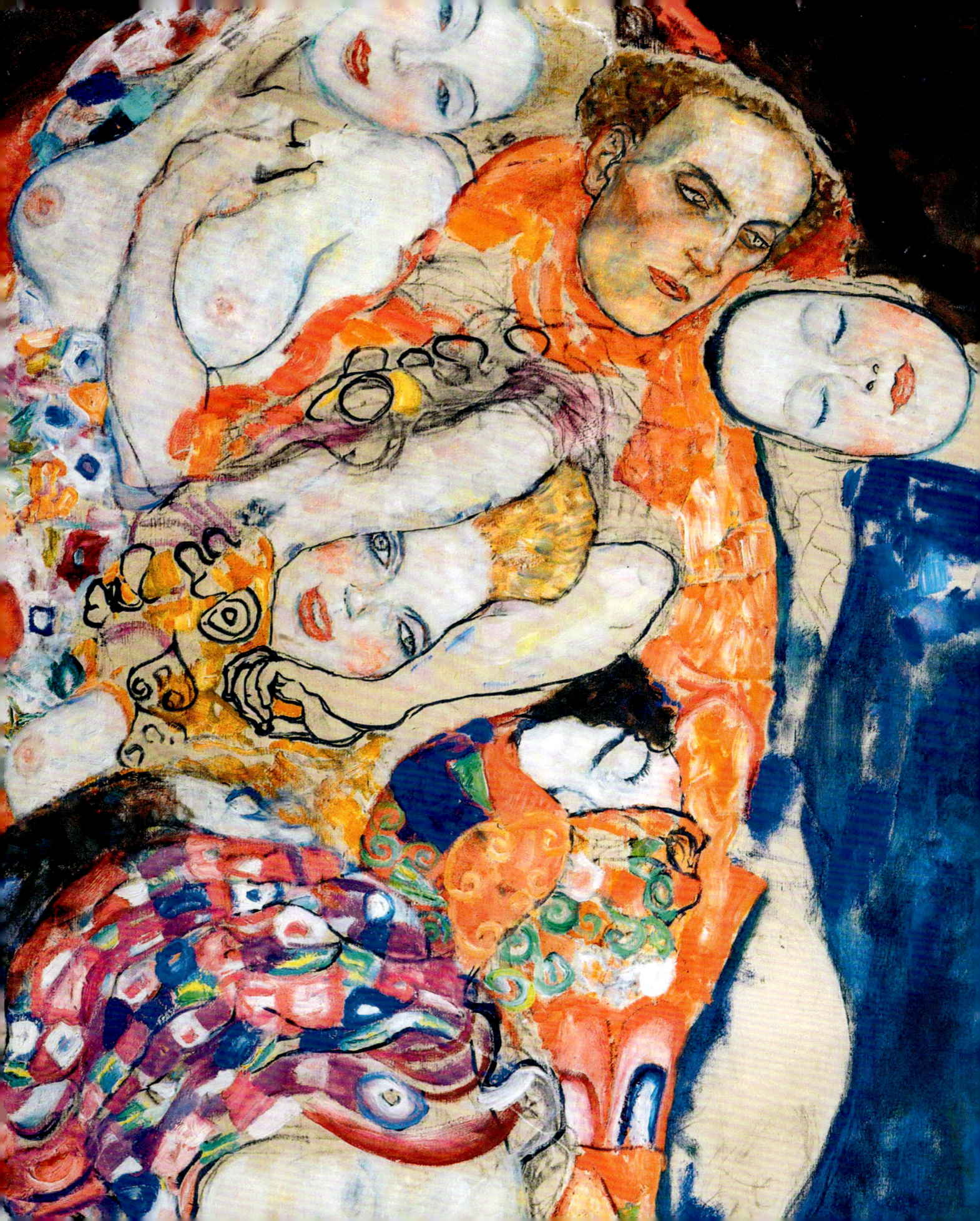

The Virgin

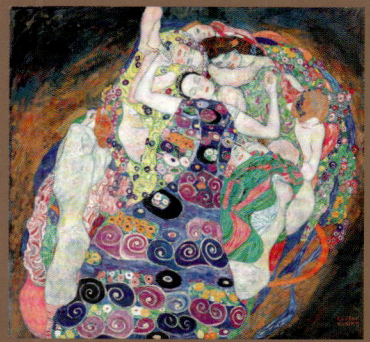

Girls are rare subjects in Klimt's oeuvre. None are depicted in *Allegory of Love* (pp. 14 and 31), nor do any appear in *The Three Ages* (pp. 88–89). In Klimt's portraits, Mäda Primavesi was a little girl aged only nine when she posed for the artist in 1913 (p. 67). However, in Klimt's final allegorical creations, at a time when he was focussing on landscapes and portraiture, his attention turned to nubile young women, which he made the subject of a painting. Dozing or dreaming, a young woman wearing a dress adorned with spiral patterns – which in Klimt's oeuvre are associated with femininity – occupies the centre of a circle of figures. Other young, nude women suggest the erotic character of the images taking shape behind the closed eyes of the central figure. This woman reappears in an unfinished painting, *The Bride* (pp. 94–95), but there she is detached from the circle, where the groom's face has been inserted. The partially undressed female body is depicted with bent and spread legs, a frequent pose in the artist's compulsive erotic drawings. An outline of a coloured garment veils the lower body yet does not conceal the pelvic region. This suggests that bodies in Klimt's figural compositions were sometimes first drawn in the nude and their nudity was then covered partly or fully by garments.

The Virgin, 1913, oil on canvas, 190 × 200 cm, Národní galerie, Prague

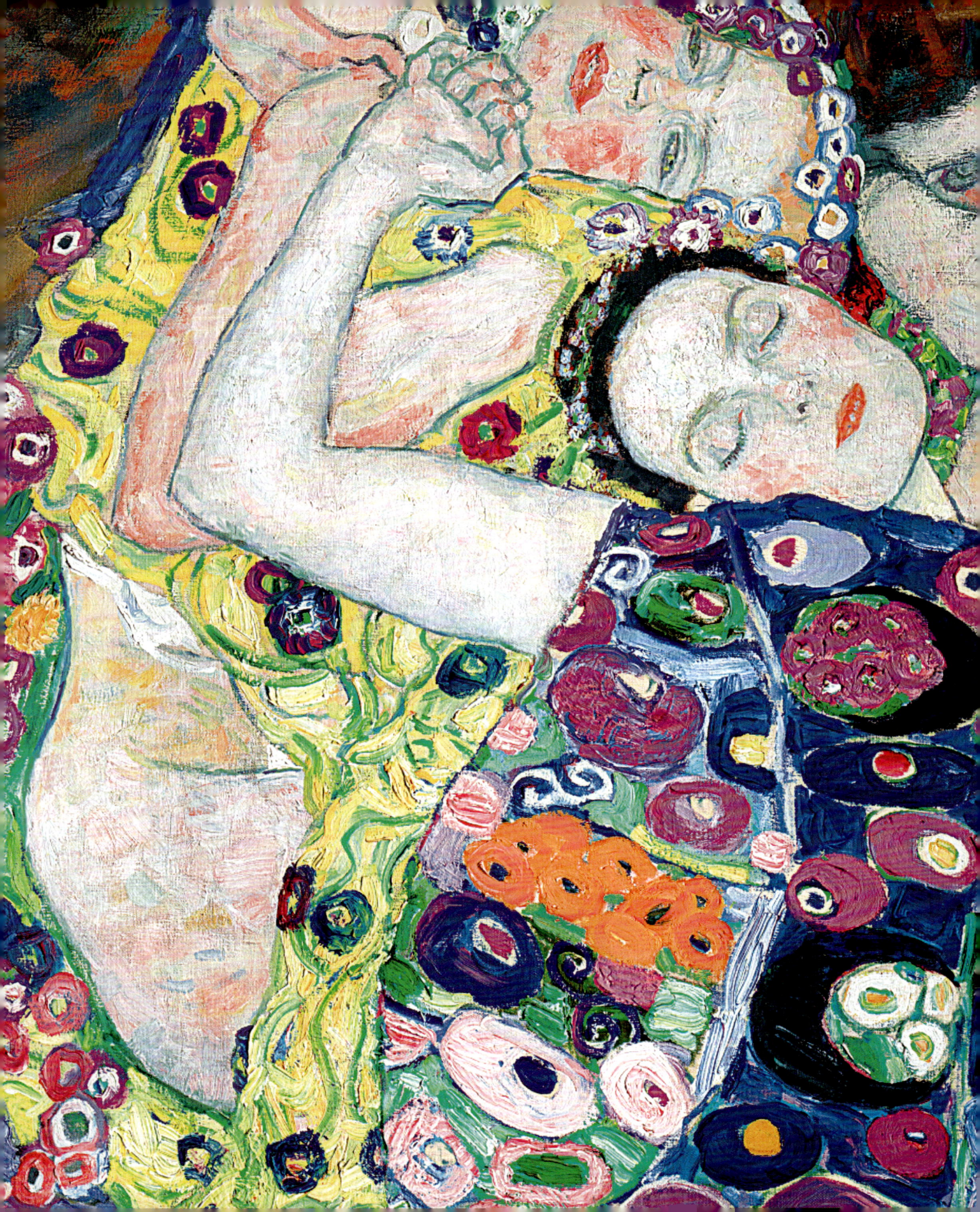

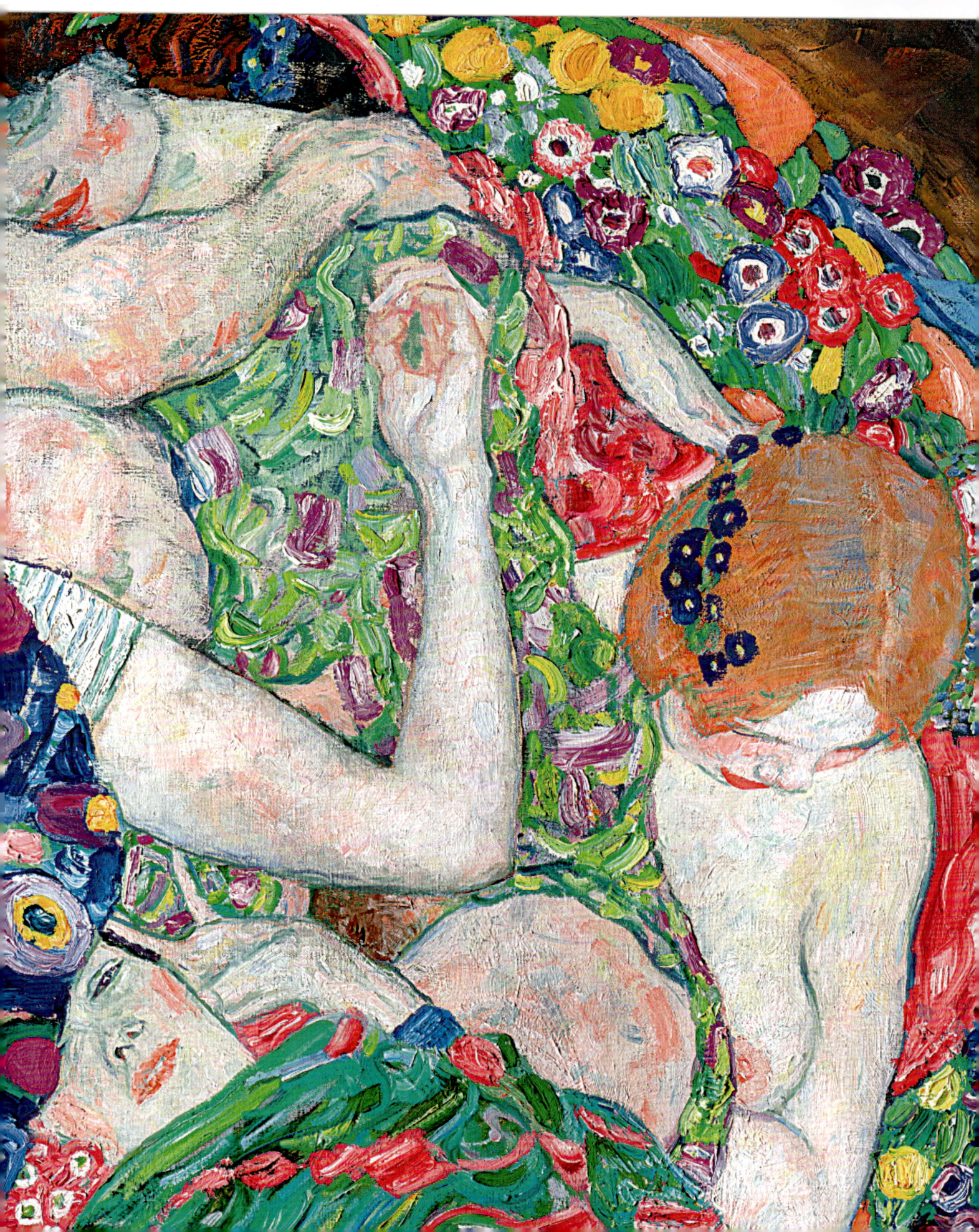

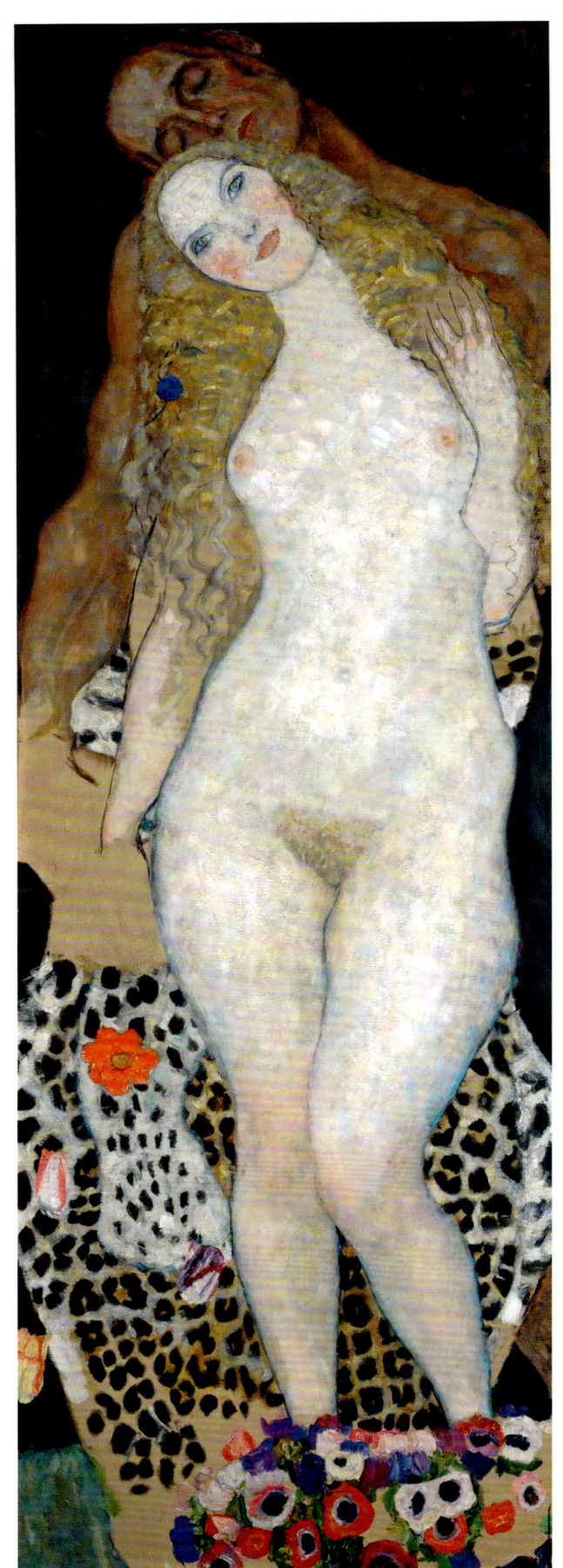

Adam and Eve,
1917/1918 (unfinished),
oil on canvas,
173 × 60 cm,
Österreichische Galerie Belvedere,
Vienna

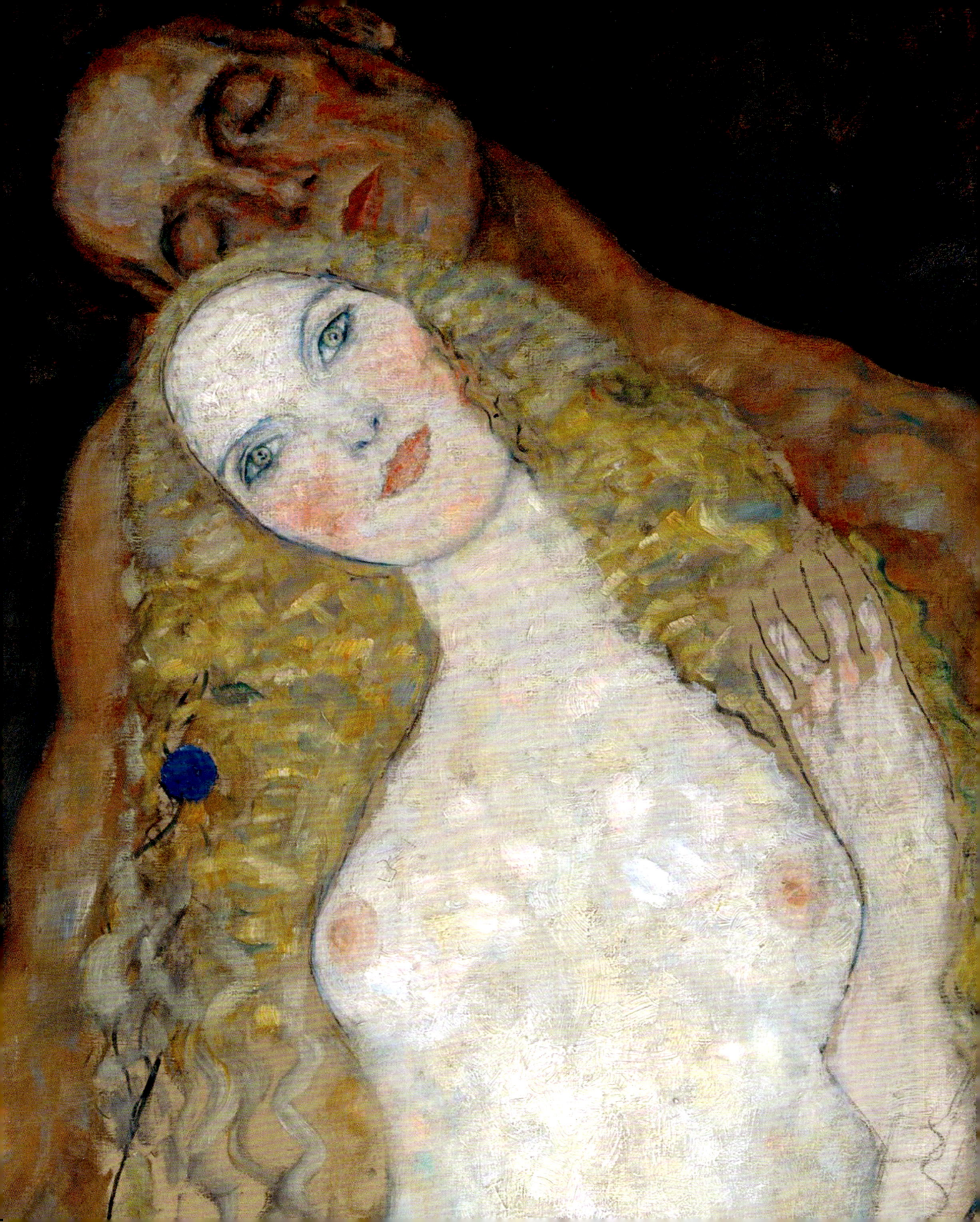

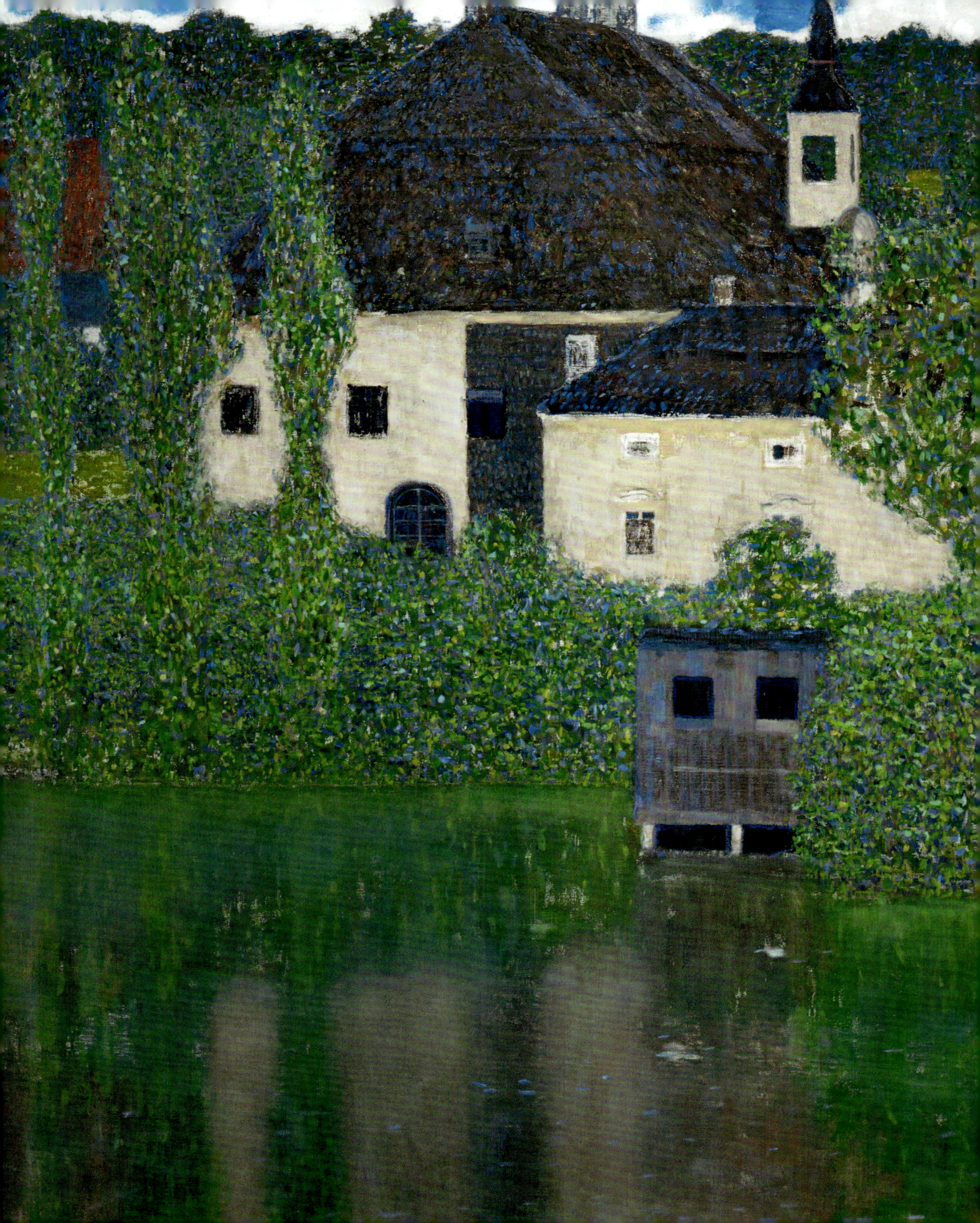

Landscapes

Although landscape painting was not taught at the School of Arts and Crafts, beginning in 1900, Klimt increasingly focussed on the genre. Klimt was aware of the studies conducted by other artists in this area, particularly in other countries; nevertheless, his landscapes show a very individual approach. They have little in common with the other genres that Klimt engaged in: allegory and portraiture. They are devoid of human presence; not even the hint of a silhouette is to be found.

Nearly all the landscapes were executed in the summer, in the south of the forested region bordering the north-western banks of the Atter-see, a lake in Upper Austria located near Salzburg, an area where Klimt spent a large part of his vacation time with the Flöge family. A letter addressed in August 1902 to Marie Zimmermann – a model, nicknamed Mizzi, with whom he had two children – gives an idea of what a day in the life of Klimt the landscape painter was like. He wrote, "I get up early, usually around six o'clock. After breakfast, I have a dip in the lake, which I then draw a bit if the weather is nice. If the weather is bad, I draw the landscape from my window. Sometimes, instead of painting, I get comfortable outside and immerse myself in one of my Japanese books. By then it's midday. After lunch I have a siesta or read until the evening meal. Shortly before or after that, I take another dip in the lake. After the meal I start painting again."

Klimt's first landscapes are oriented more on Symbolism than Impressionism. Of course, with its foreground showing the play of light on the water's surface (which is partly covered with lily pads and the reflections of the sky in the water), *The Marshy Pond* (pp. 104–105) is reminiscent of paintings by Claude Monet. Nevertheless, the perspective from above the stagnant water, the suggestion of forest (of which

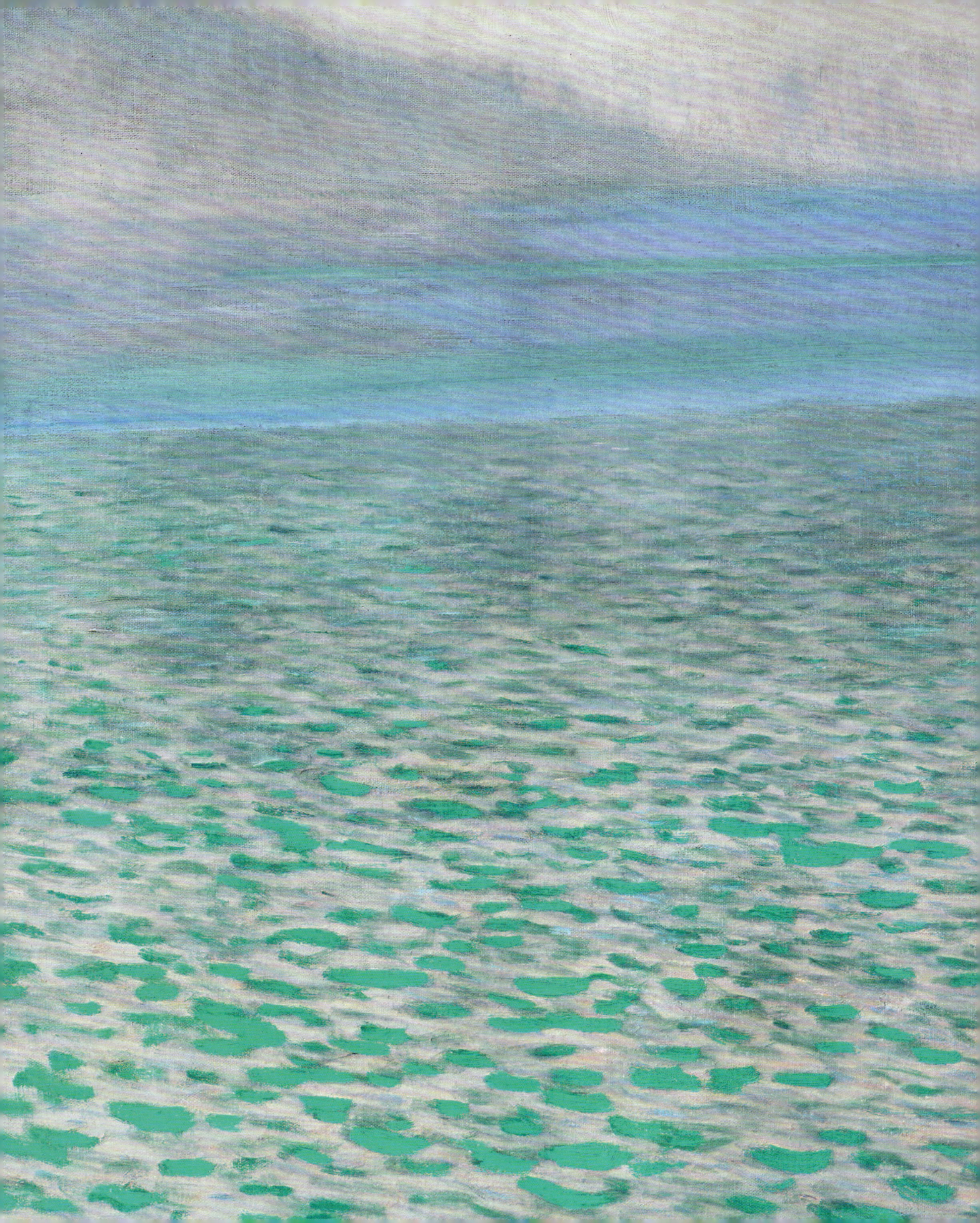

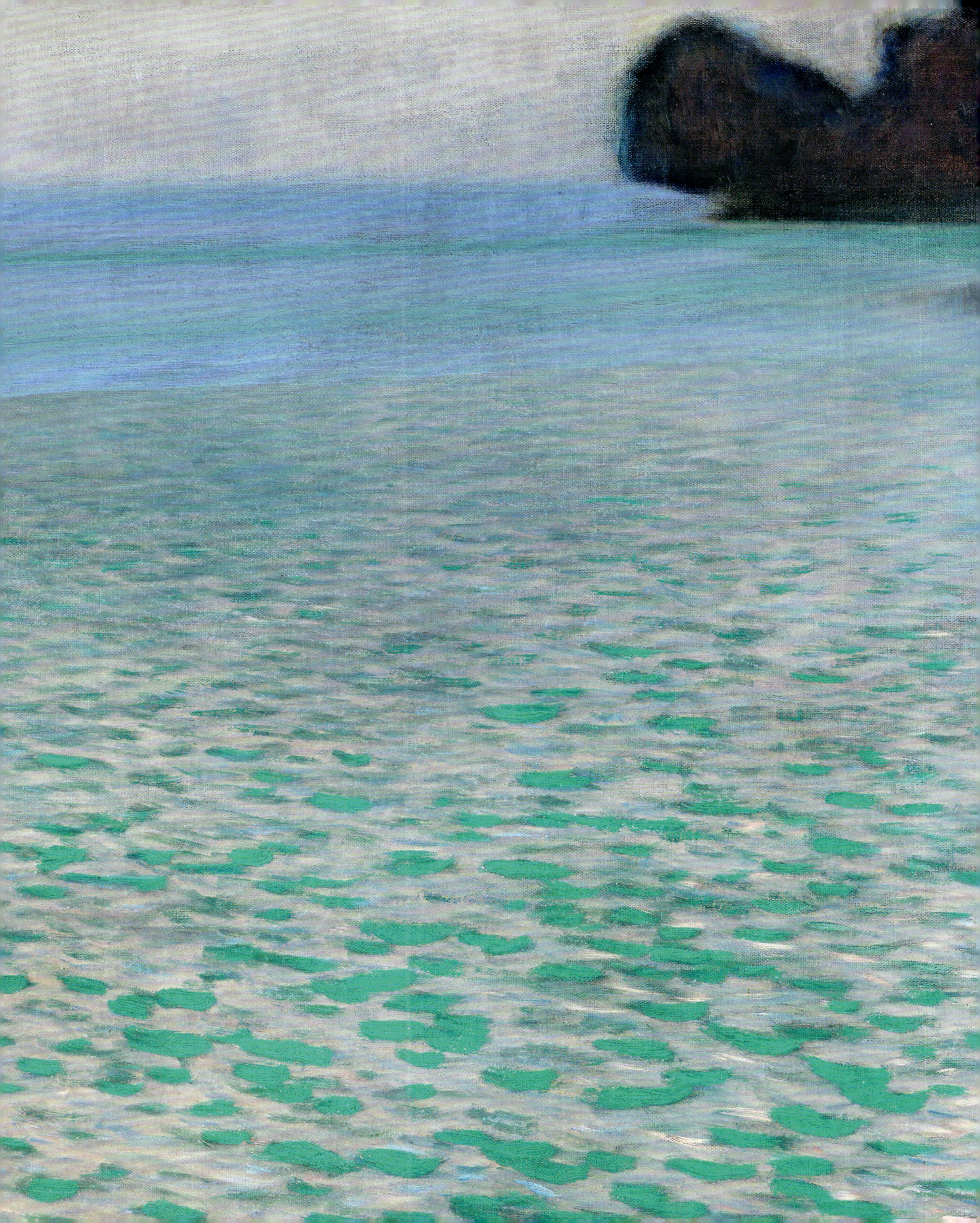

only the tree trunks are visible) and the mystery-tinged calm that emanate from this composition express melancholy more than awestruck admiration of nature's beauty. Similar affinities to Symbolism are even more evident in the series of underbrush scenes, including stands of beech trees (p. 106) and birches (p. 107), completed in 1902 and 1903. Here, all points of spatial reference have disappeared; not even a path is indicated. A horizon line is discernable between the straight trunks, but their foliage is not visible. The artist's aim was to express the silence that reigns in this closed-off world as well as the resulting feeling of impenetrability.

In contrast, Klimt would focus his attention on the luxuriant foliage in parks and orchards in subsequent years. The branches become tangled, forming vaults and compact, colourful masses that sometimes reveal a bit of blue sky or a sunbeam on the lake. These unusual compositions and his predilection for the square format result from Klimt's use of what he called a *Sucher,* or viewfinder, a simple piece of cardboard with a square-shaped hole in the middle, which he used to limit the field of vision and practically eliminate the middle and background planes. His technique, which consisted of hatching of various sizes, also contributed to the reduction of volume and perspective.

According to Ludwig Hevesi, Klimt's landscapes after 1903 were influenced by his knowledge of Neo-Impressionism, to which the Secession had dedicated several exhibitions: Théo van Rysselberghe was featured in January 1899, followed by Paul Signac in March 1900. In 1903, works by these artists and other Neo-Impressionists, as well as by Paul Gauguin, Félix Vallotton, Pierre Bonnard, Édouard Vuillard, Henri Matisse and Vincent van Gogh, were exhibited. Since Galerie Miethke also exhibited around forty works by Vincent van Gogh in January 1903, his influence on Klimt, who abandoned the Pointillist technique for a more fluid stroke when he painted the flowerbeds in the gardens of local farms, should be mentioned. Klimt had an affinity for gardens, starting with those at his various studios, which are documented in photographs and eyewitness descriptions. Egon Schiele, for example, relates, "When I visited Klimt for the first time in 1907, he appeared sturdy, tough and tanned. It was at Josefstädter Strasse 21, in a garden, one of these old, hidden gardens that are still so numerous in Josefstadt. … When this block of houses was demolished in 1911, Klimt had to leave his hidden house and moved to Feldmühlgasse in Hietzing. … Every year, Klimt planted beds of flowers to embellish the garden." This final garden, in Hietzing, is the one that Klimt referred to in spring 1916 in a letter to Emilie Flöge: "The sun beats down, and the weather is unbelievably beautiful. The crocuses are in bloom in the garden, and the ground resembles a star-spangled sky."

The comparison with a starry night sky is interesting, because it indicates the extent to which Klimt remained a decorator, even in his representations of nature. While he painted flowers – poppies, sunflowers, zinnias – for their own sake, with an exuberance and verve reminiscent of Van Gogh, the arrangement of the surrounding space, often strewn with smaller flowers, is not at all understandable but forms a kind of ornamental background. In 1906–1907, the sunflower motif takes on a well-defined pyramidal form that contrasts against a carpet of greenery conceived not as a natural environment but as a decoration (pp. 108–109). The principal motif is taken from its natural setting and inserted into an architectural structure – an unusual procedure having to do with the rivalry between naturalism and abstraction, which, according to Hugo Haberfeld, the proprietor of Galerie Miethke, generates "optical poetry".

Kammer Castle on Lake Attersee I (Castle in the Lake),
1908, oil on canvas, 110 × 110 cm, Národní galerie, Prague (p. 98, detail)

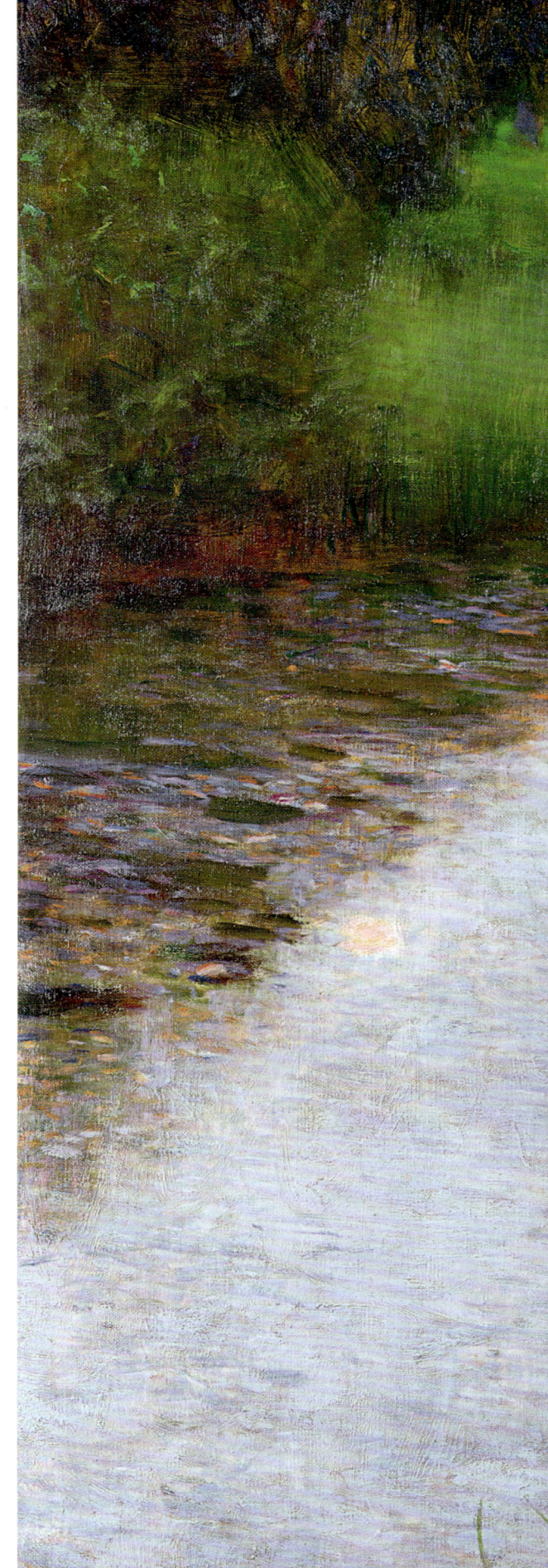

On Lake Attersee,
1900, oil on canvas,
80.2 × 80.2 cm,
Leopold Museum, Vienna
(pp. 100–101, detail)

The Marshy Pond,
1900, oil on canvas,
80 × 80 cm,
private collection
(opposite, detail)

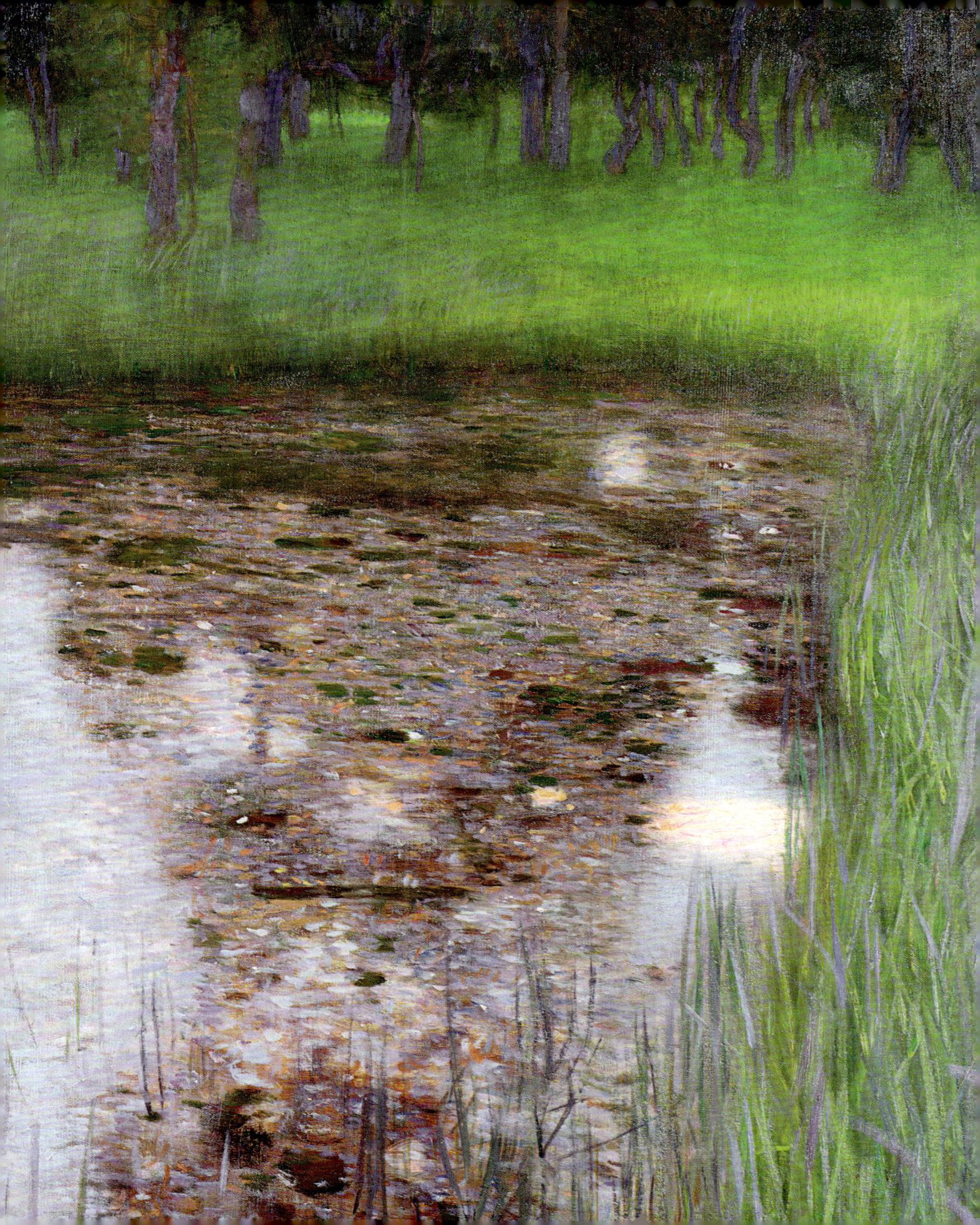

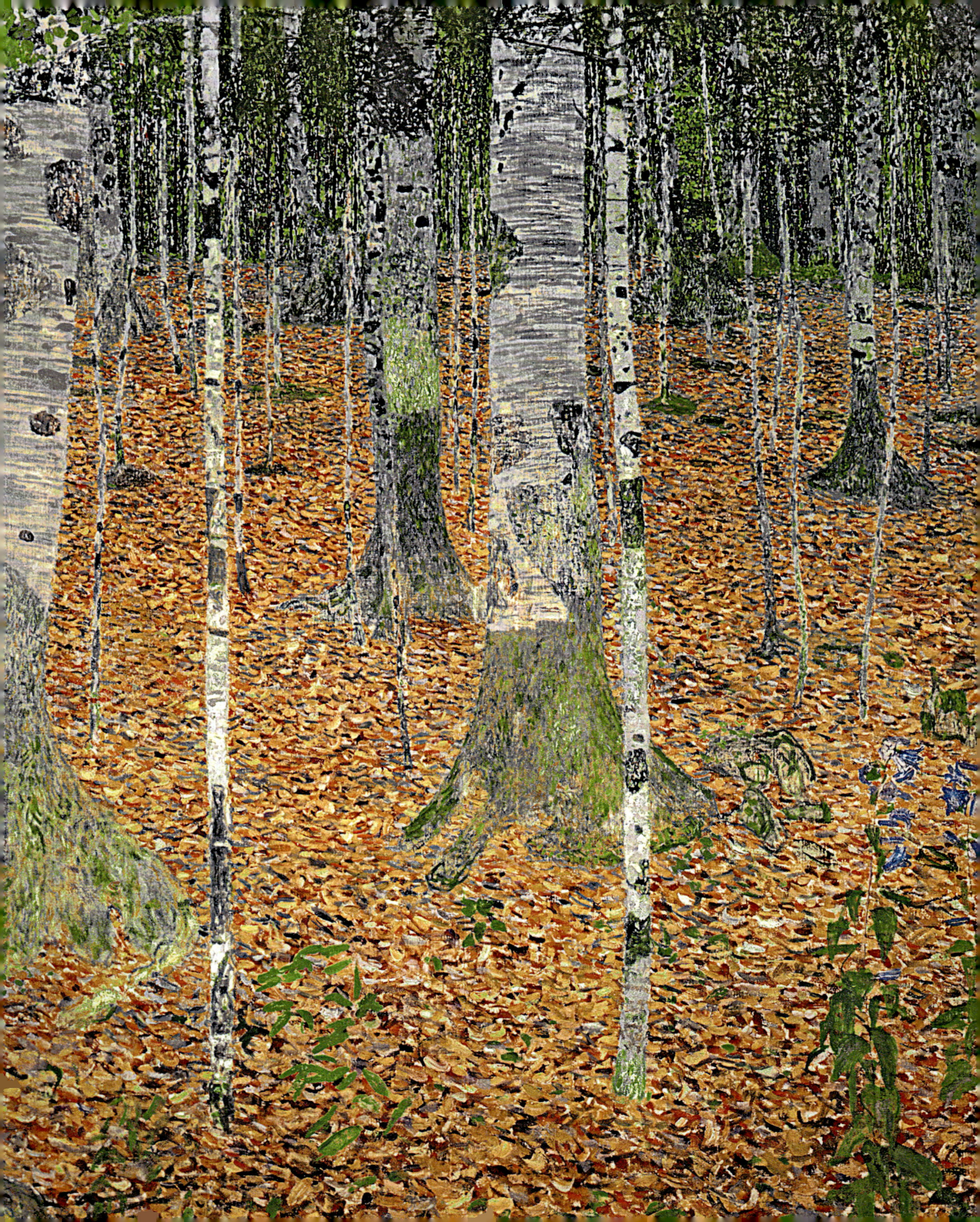

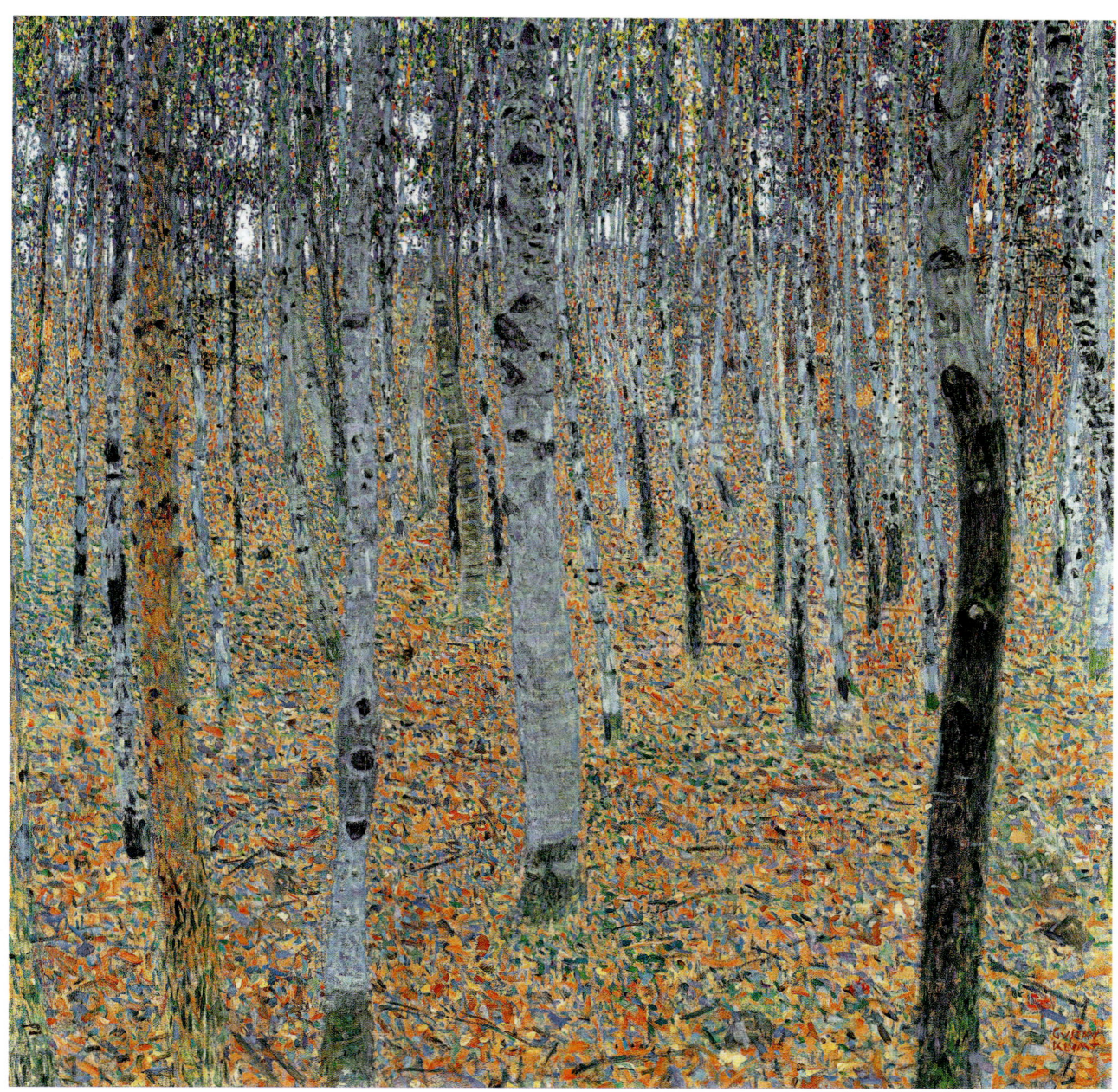

Birch Forest (Beech Forest), 1903, oil on canvas, 110 × 110 cm, private collection (opposite, detail)

Beech Forest II, *c.* 1902, oil on canvas, 100 × 100 cm, Galerie Neue Meister, Dresden (above)

The Sunflower, 1907, oil on canvas, 110 × 110 cm,
Österreichische Galerie Belvedere, Vienna (following spread on left, detail)

Cottage Garden with Sunflowers, 1908, oil on canvas, 110 × 110 cm,
Österreichische Galerie Belvedere, Vienna (following spread on right, detail)

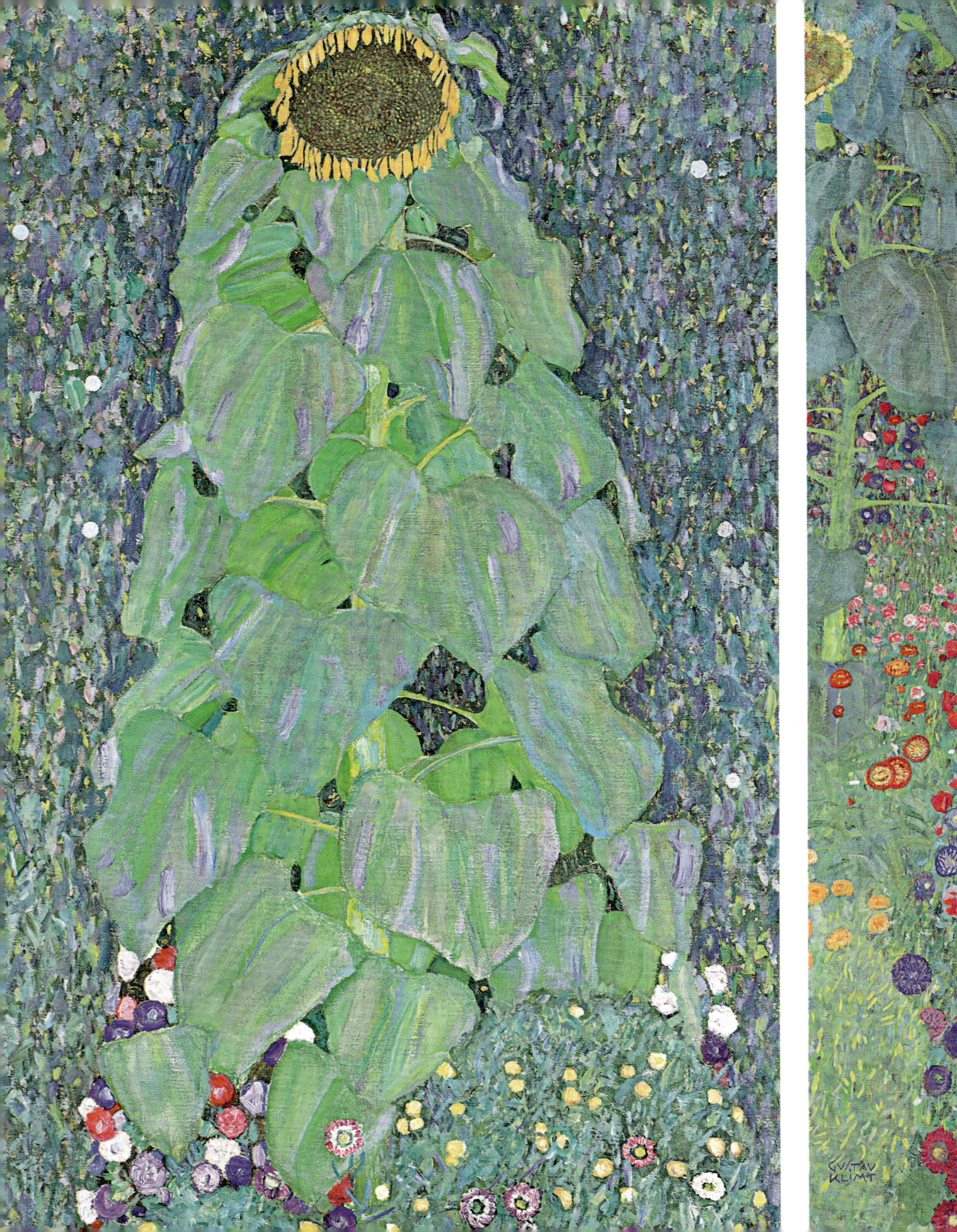

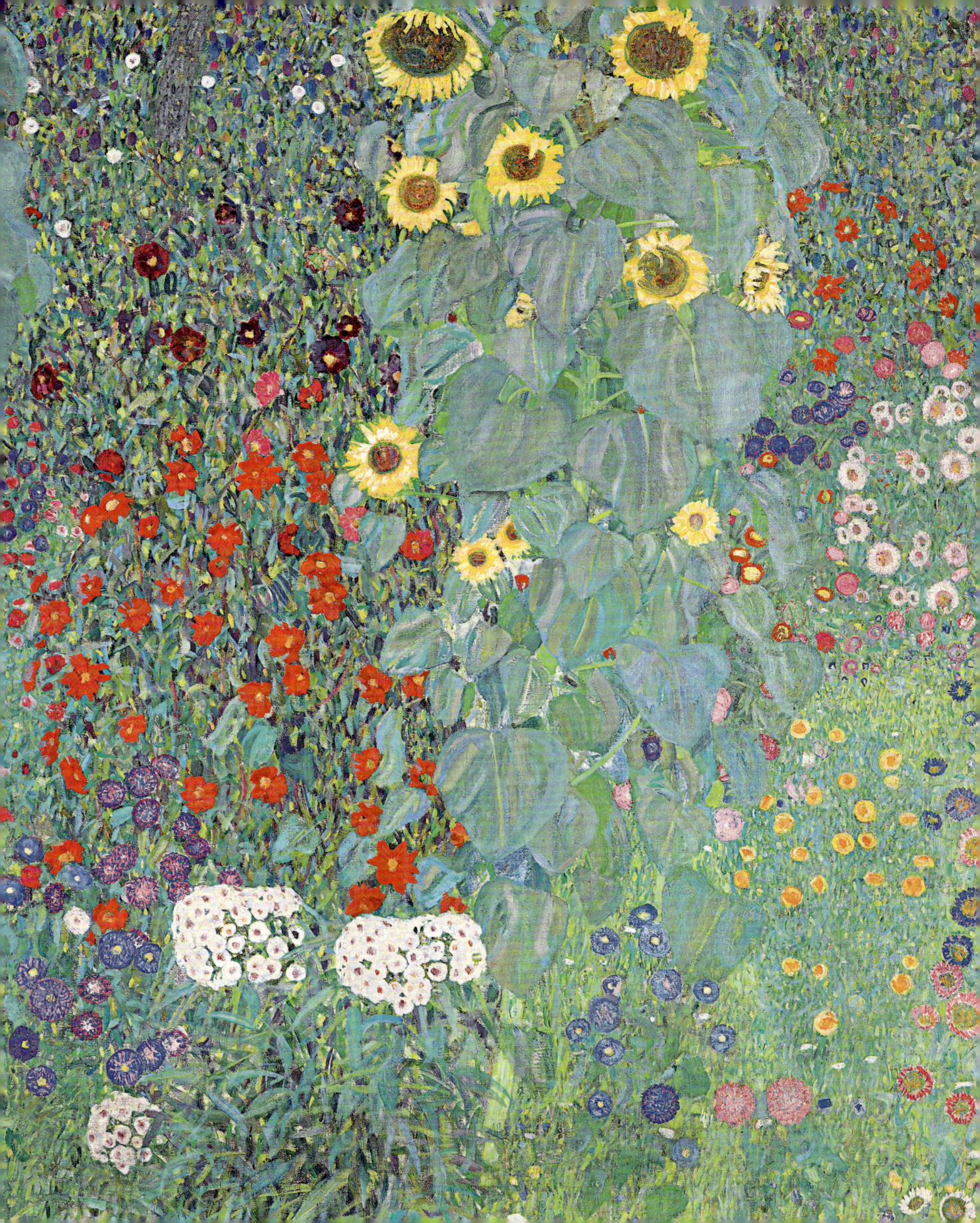

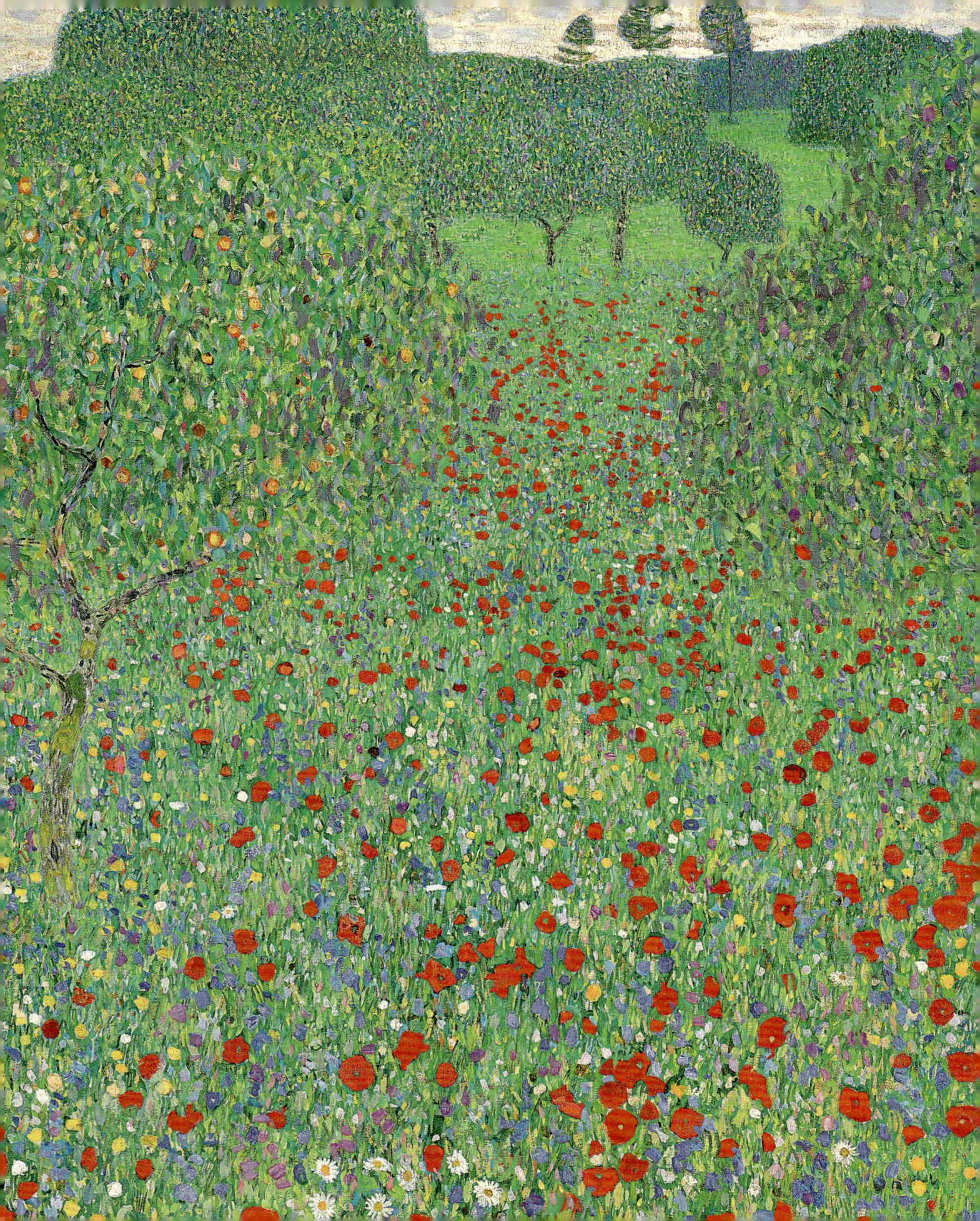

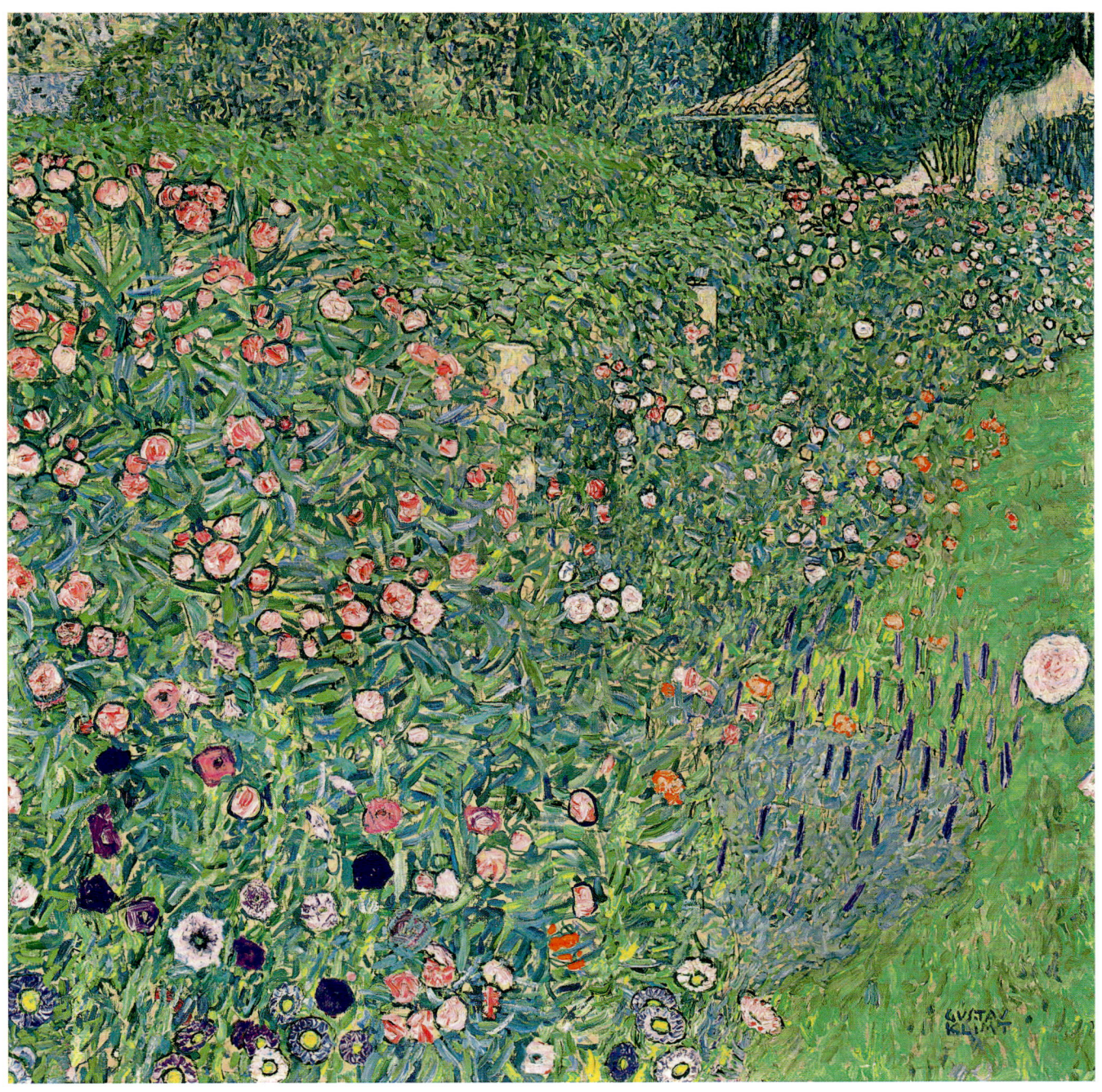

Poppy Field (Poppies in Bloom), 1907, oil on canvas, 110 × 110 cm,
Österreichische Galerie Belvedere, Vienna (opposite, detail)

Italian Garden Landscape, 1913, oil on canvas, 110 × 110 cm,
Kunsthaus Zug, Zug (above)

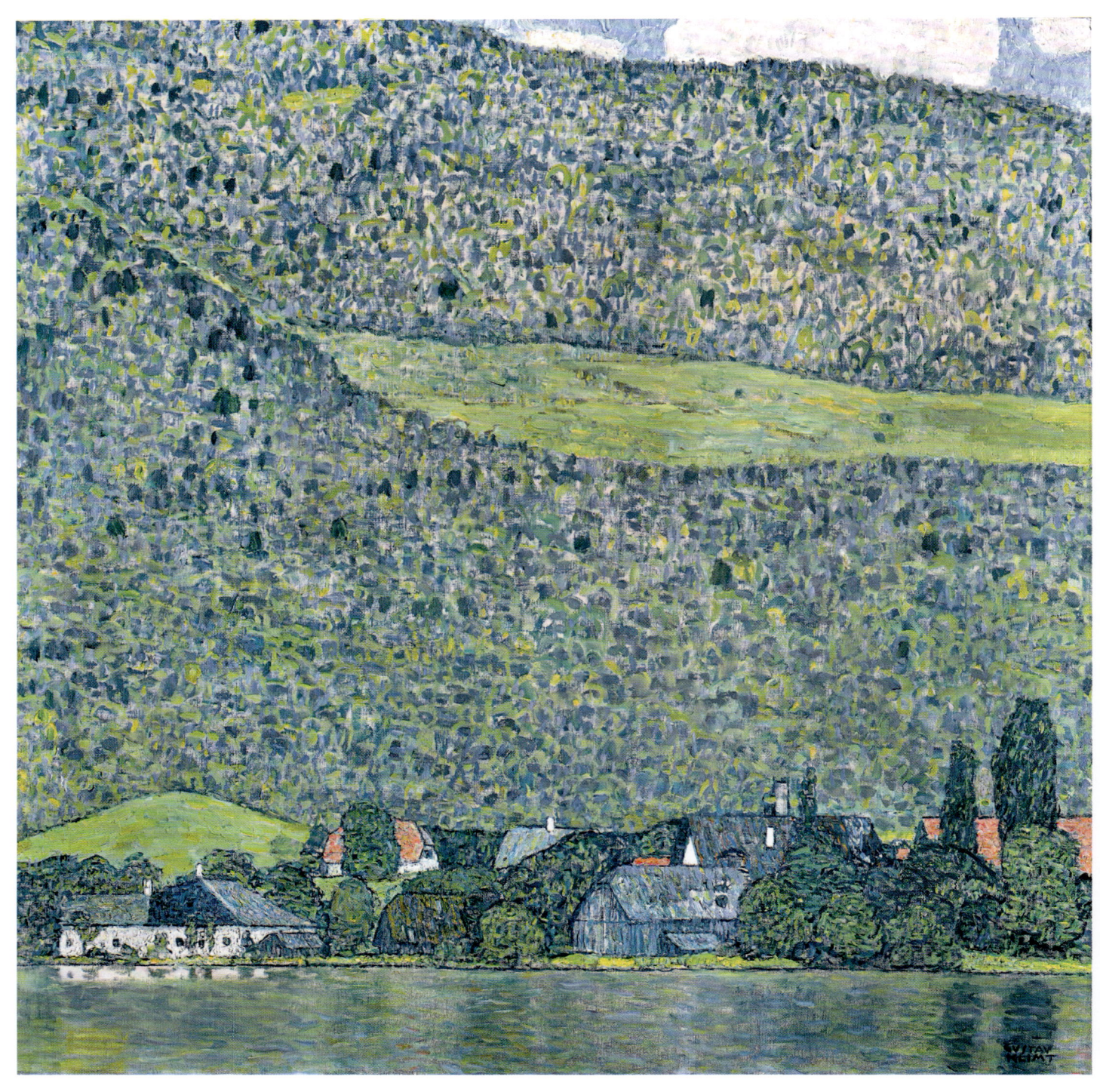

Litzlberg on Lake Attersee, *c.* 1915, oil on canvas, 110 × 110 cm, private collection

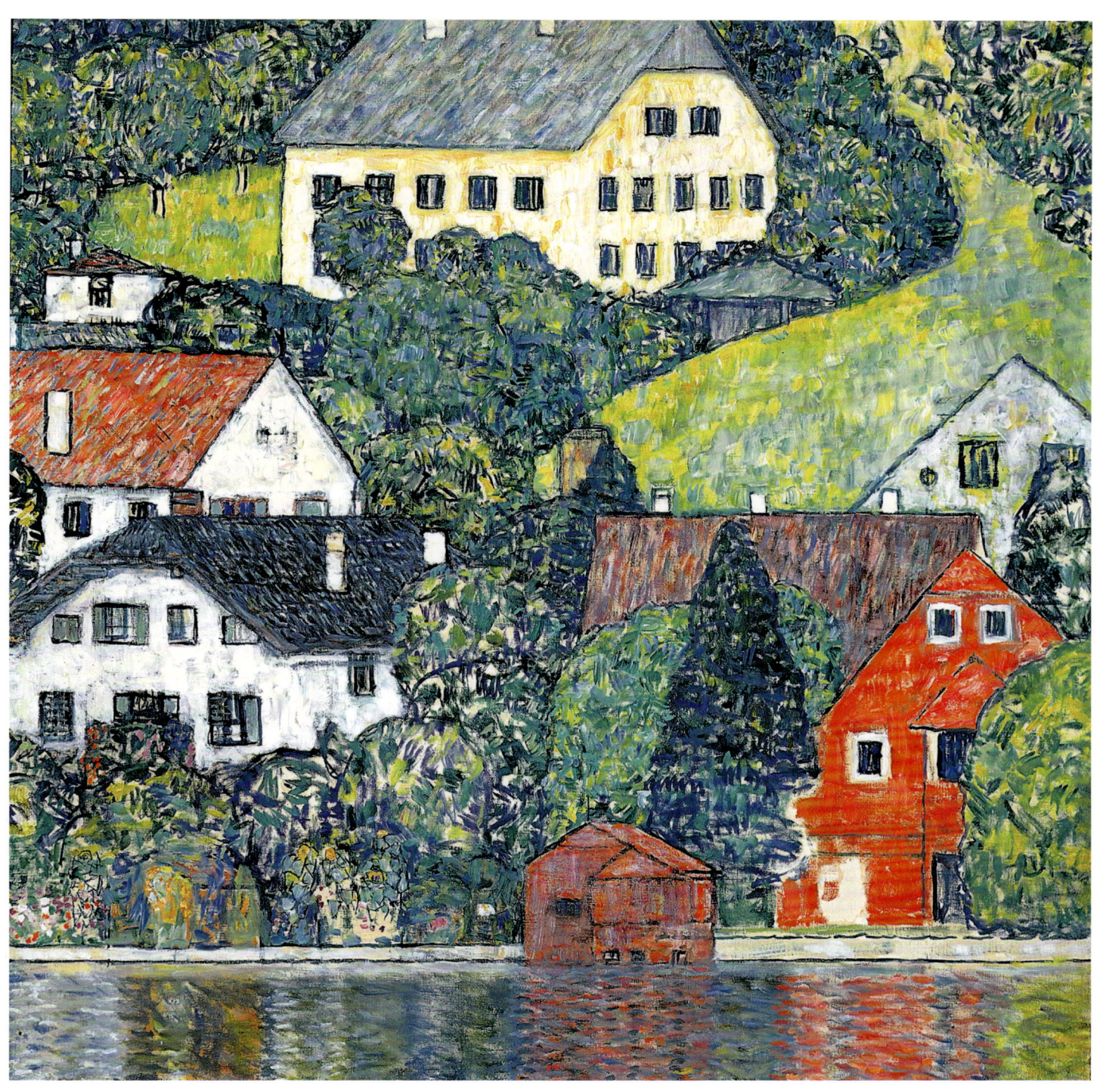

Houses in Unterach on Lake Attersee, 1915/1916, oil on canvas, 110 × 110 cm, private collection

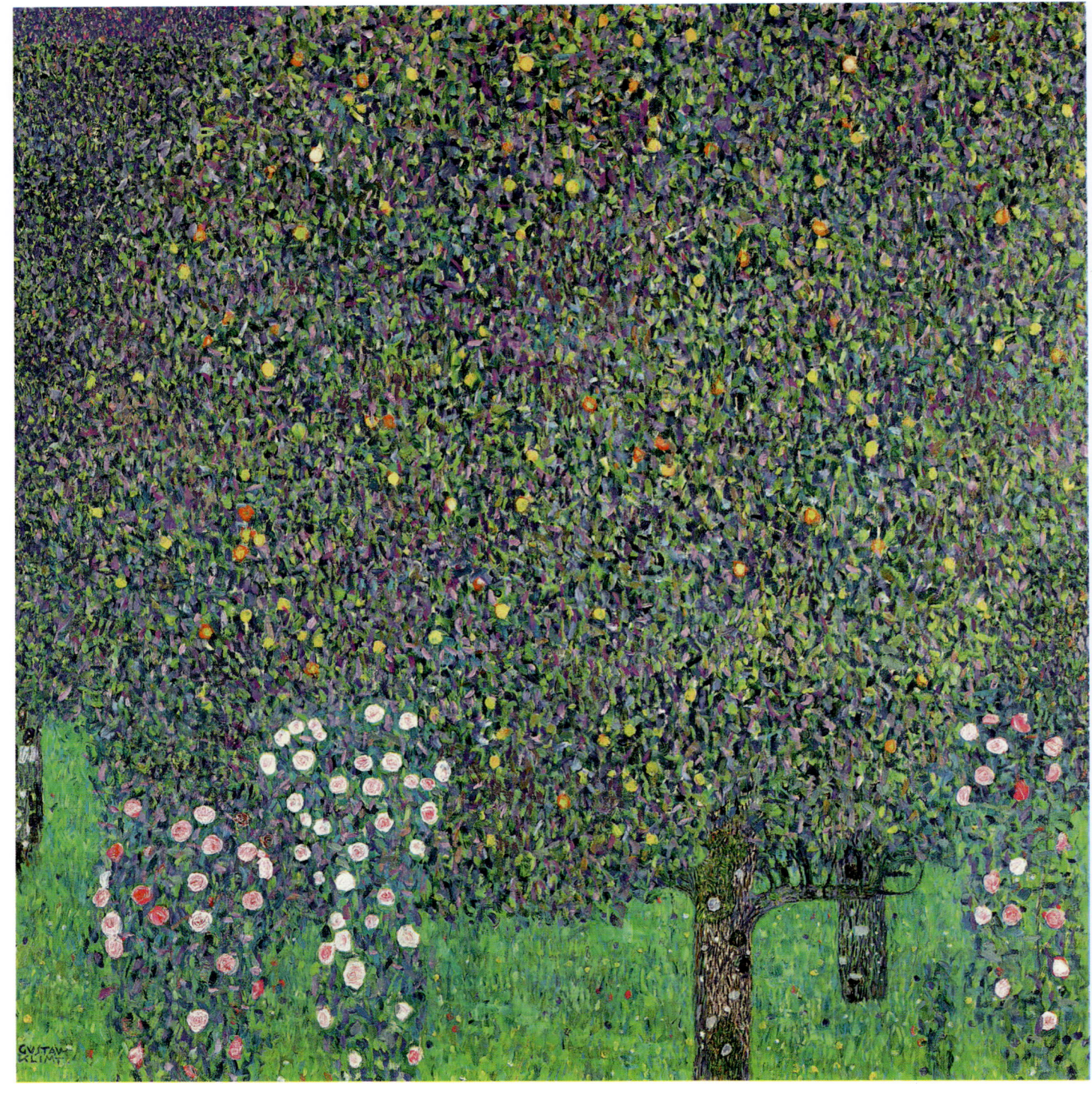

Rose Bushes Beneath Trees (Roses), *c.* 1904, oil on canvas, 110 × 110 cm, private collection (above)

Church in Cassone (Landscape with Cypresses), 1913, oil on canvas, 110 × 110 cm, private collection (right, detail)

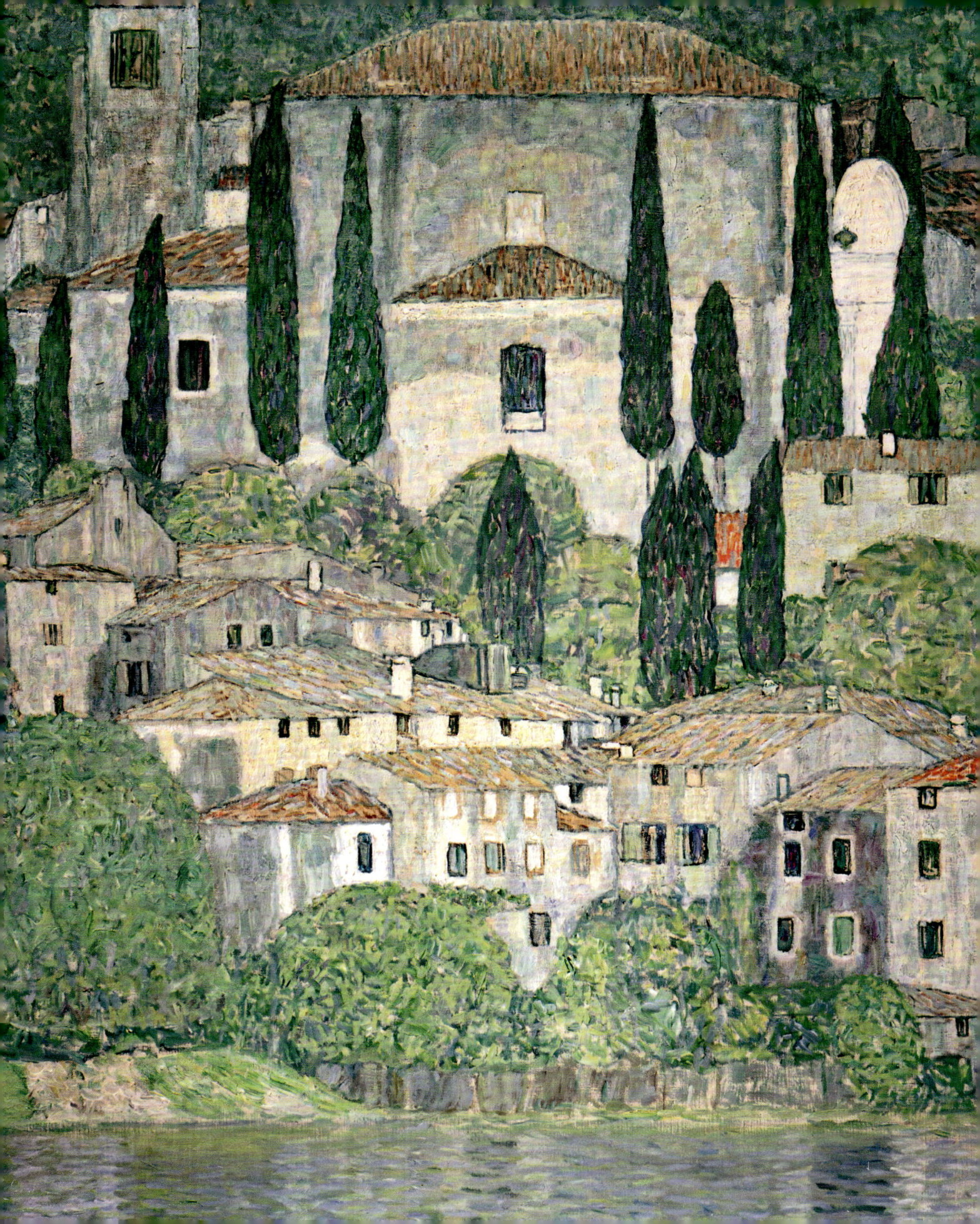

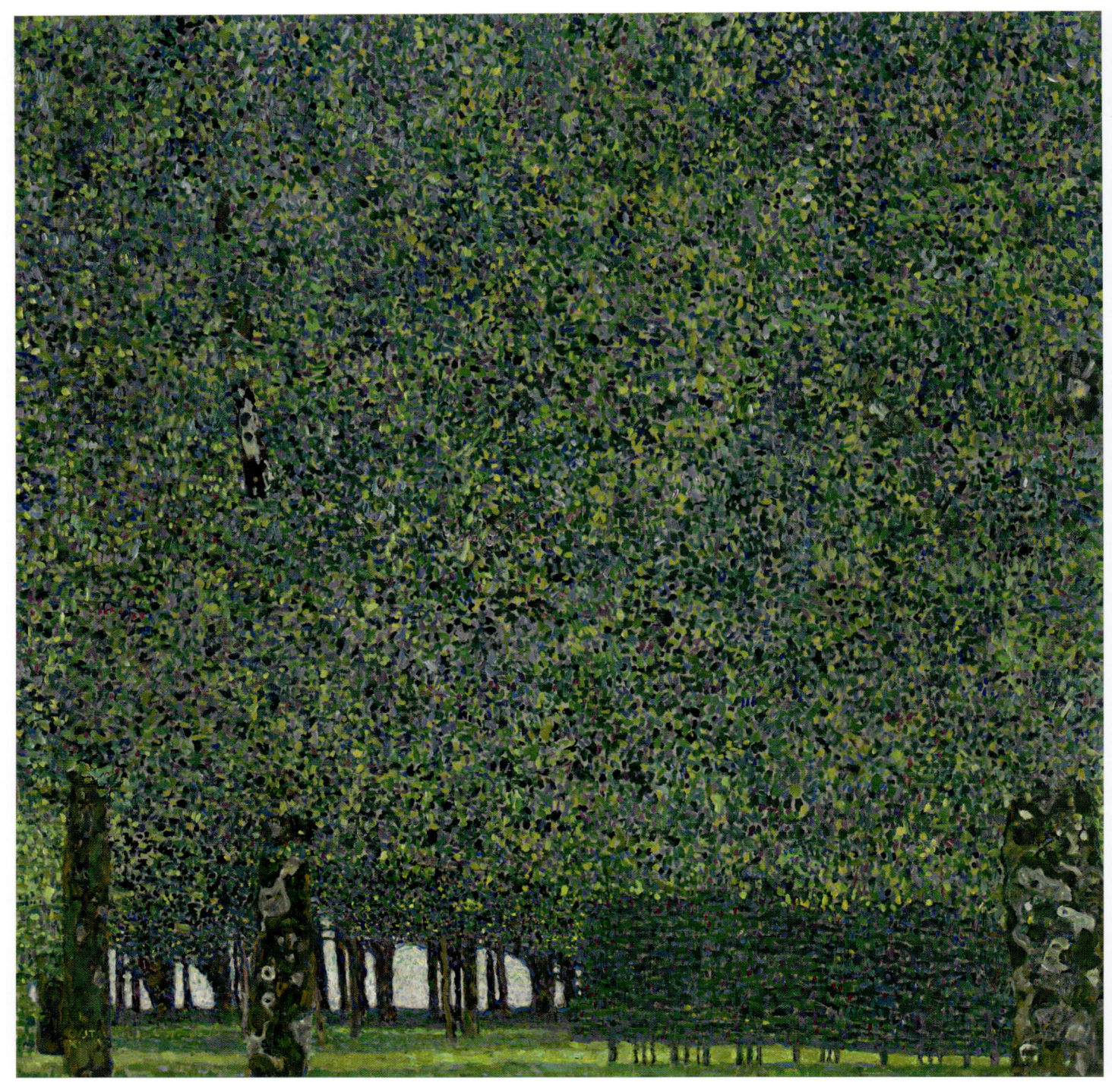

The Park, 1909, oil on canvas, 110.4 × 110.4 cm, Museum of Modern Art, New York (above)

Avenue in Front of Kammer Castle, 1912, oil on canvas, 110 × 110 cm,
Österreichische Galerie Belvedere, Vienna (opposite, detail)

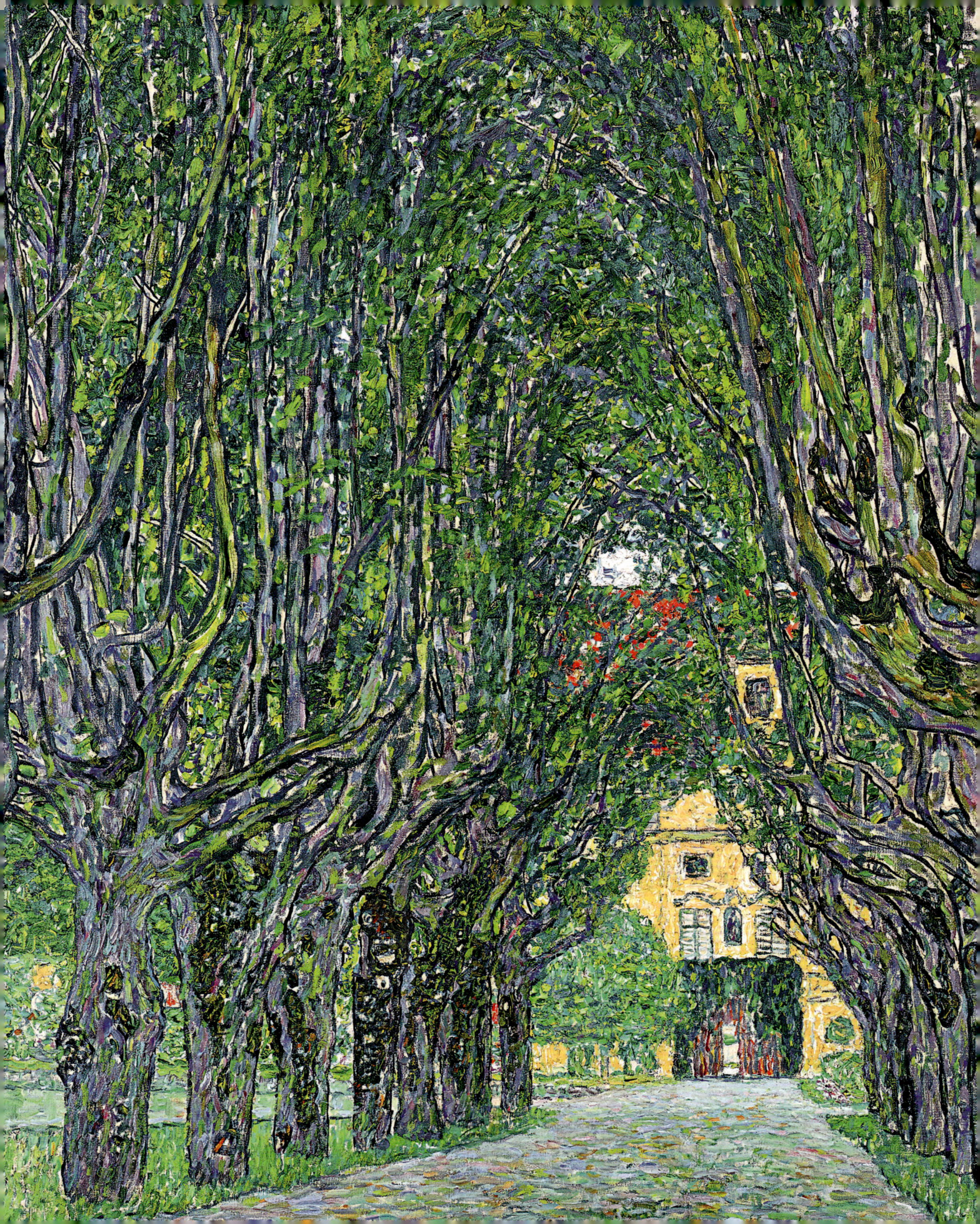

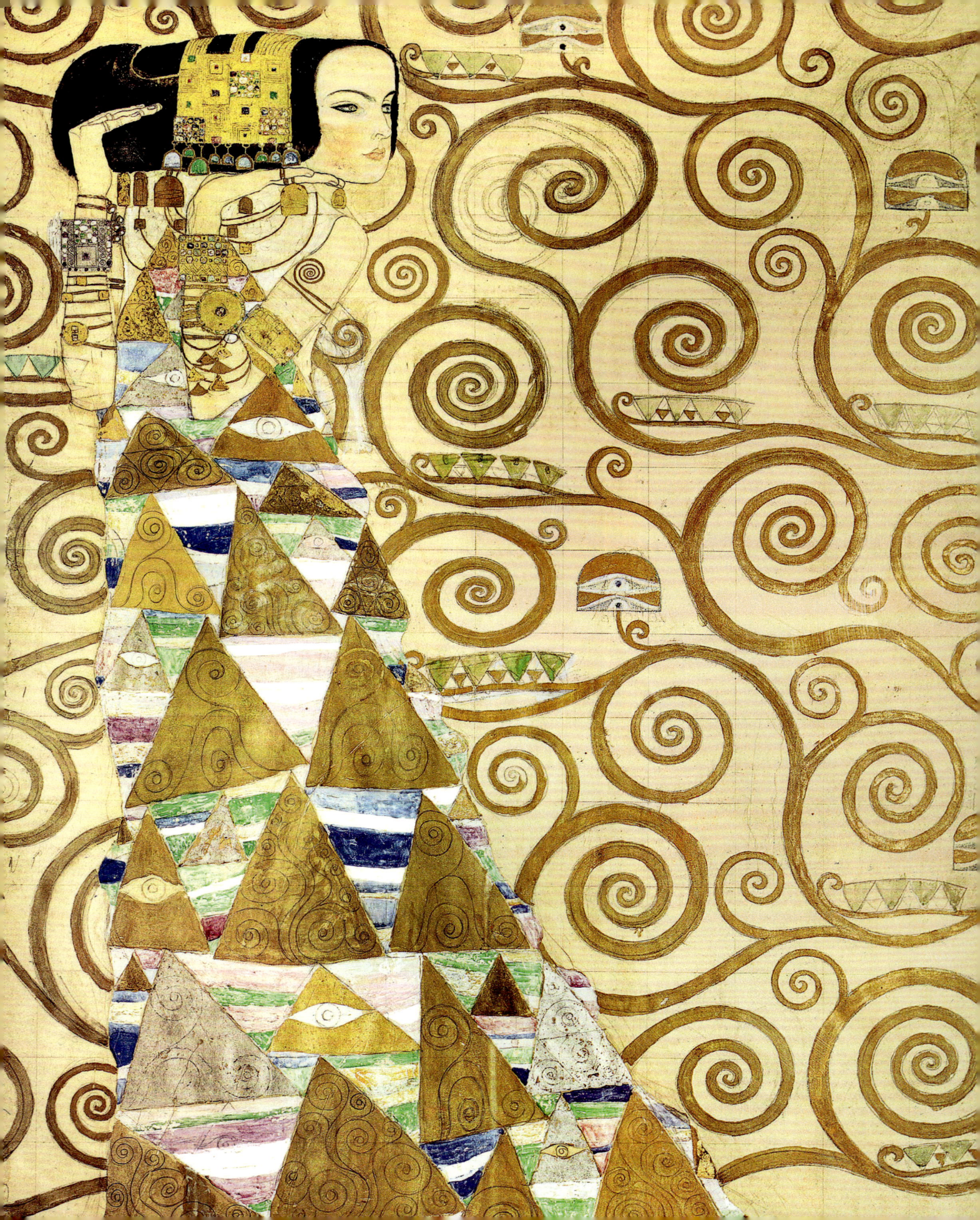

The Palais Stoclet

The Palais Stoclet occupies a special place in Klimt's oeuvre since Adolphe Stoclet (1871–1949), who commissioned it, was not a Viennese businessman or an industrialist but a Belgian engineer and financier – and furthermore his wife, Suzanne, was the niece of the society painter and portraitist Alfred Stevens. The couple lived in Vienna. In addition to his job at the Brussels-based railway company Compagnie internationale des chemins de fer, Adolphe Stoclet was a director of three Austrian companies, including the Wiener Lombard- und Escompte Bank, a large lending institution. Dazzled by the villas that Josef Hoffmann had recently constructed in the Hohe Warte quarter – particularly that of the painter Carl Moll, co-founder of the Wiener Secession – the Stoclet family contacted the architect about building and furnishing a residence.

In 1904, however, the Stoclet patriarch died, and Adolphe was obliged to return to Belgium to assume the direction of the prestigious Société générale de Belgique, then the preeminent Belgian bank and holding company. He nevertheless continued his plans, the actual cost of which is unknown. According to Peter Vergo, a prominent specialist on the Wiener Werkstätte, it is "a secret that Adolphe Stoclet took with him to his grave". But we do know that at one point, Stoclet let it be known that he would no longer make the requested advance payments and would only pay after inspecting the progress of the construction work.

This explains why a *palais* designed by Hoffmann from 1905 to 1909 now stands on Avenue de Tervueren in Brussels. Construction began in 1906 and was completed five years later. The building has a rectangular footprint and is 37.5 meters long by 13.5 meters wide. The street-facing façade is ten meters high, and the tower that rises above the terrace brings the total height to almost twenty meters. This two-storey tower is crowned by a metal dome adorned with stylized flowers. The second storey is in the shape of a cross; on each of the arms stands a monumental heroic figure, in copper, produced by the Austrian sculptor Franz Metzner (1870–1919). The building's façades are built of brick covered with panels of white Norwegian marble. The edges of the panelled areas are contoured with gold-and-black patinated metal moulding.

Hoffmann called on Klimt to decorate the dining room, located on the ground floor and opening directly onto the main hall, along with the music room, the smoking room and a small salon. The two creators had a deep connection. Not only had Hoffmann given Klimt free rein to use all his Secessionist decorative talents at the 1902 homage to Ludwig van Beethoven; he had also designed the exhibitions of Klimt's works at the 1900 Paris Exposition universelle, the St. Louis World's Fair in 1904, the Internationale Kunst-Ausstellung in Mannheim, Germany, in 1907, and the Kunstschau in Vienna in 1908. Moreover, admirers of Klimt's paintings often entrusted Hoffmann with both constructing their villas and doing the interior decoration of their apartments. Many photographs published in contemporary magazines give a partial yet precise sense of the extreme refinement of the spaces in designed by these aesthetes and of the care with which Hoffmann integrated Klimt's paintings. For example, in the music room in Sonja Knips's apartment at Gumpendorferstrasse 15, a niche above a window seat with direct natural light was designed especially to accommodate a Klimt landscape. In the house built on the Hohe Warte hill for Hugo Henneberg in 1900–1901, the portrait of the lady of the house hung above a fireplace of marble and gold-plated copper that was inserted in the wood-panelled room, which also featured photographs by the property owner.

For the dining room of the Palais Stoclet, Hoffmann did not rely on existing works by Klimt but commissioned new ones. The commission focussed on designing mosaics for the room's fourteen-meter-long side walls as well as the end wall, all of which were panelled in pale Porto Venere marble. The execution of the mosaics fell to the studio of Leopold Forstner (1878–1936), who often collaborated with the Wiener Werk-

Stoclet Frieze

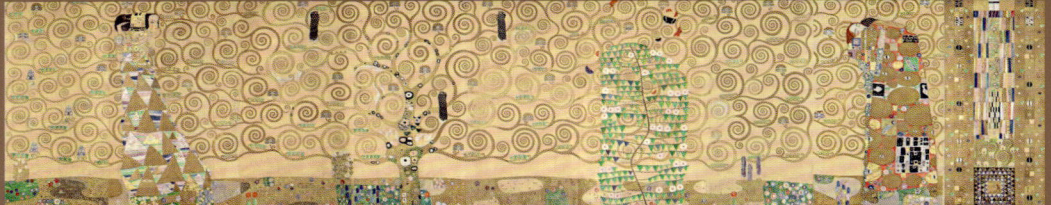

Klimt's role in the design of the dining room of the Palais Stoclet was to create cartoons for the mosaics adorning the marble-panelled walls. The exact date that he began work is not known, but it is generally accepted that his plans were first committed to paper as early as 1908. The mosaics of the central panel *(Knight)* and the left wall *(Expectation)* were installed in autumn 1911, and *Fulfilment* did not take its place on the right wall until early the following year. From his first drawings, Klimt had specific technical characteristics in mind for the planned works. That is, he did not design the frieze as a unified composition that would then be divided up according to the various kinds of tesserae chosen by the mosaicist. On the contrary, he created assemblies of decorative motifs, most of which were abstract. There is little doubt that he was considerably inspired by his 1903 study of the Byzantine mosaics with golden backgrounds at the Basilica of San Vitale in Ravenna. This fold-out features a photomontage created by the Museum für angewandte Kunst in Vienna, where the original cartoons by Klimt are kept.

Stoclet Frieze, cartoons for the dining-room mosaics of the Palais Stoclet, 1908–1911, tempera, watercolour, pencil, chalk, and gold and silver leaf on cardboard, 200 × 730 cm, Museum für angewandte Kunst, Vienna

Expectation, cartoon for the left-hand-wall mosaic, 200 × 102 cm (left leaf, detail)

Fulfillment, cartoon for the right-hand-wall mosaic, 200 × 102 cm (right leaf, detail)

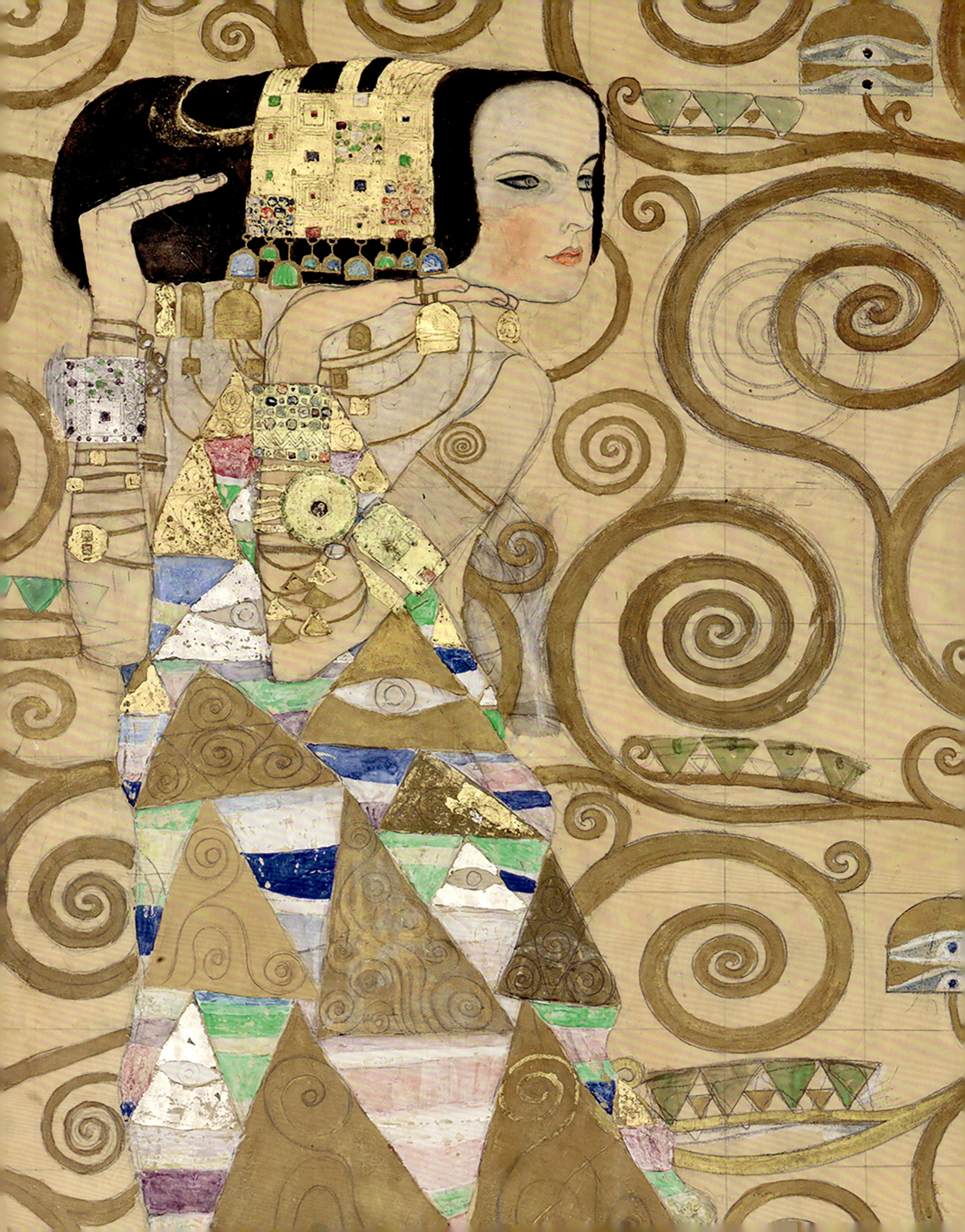

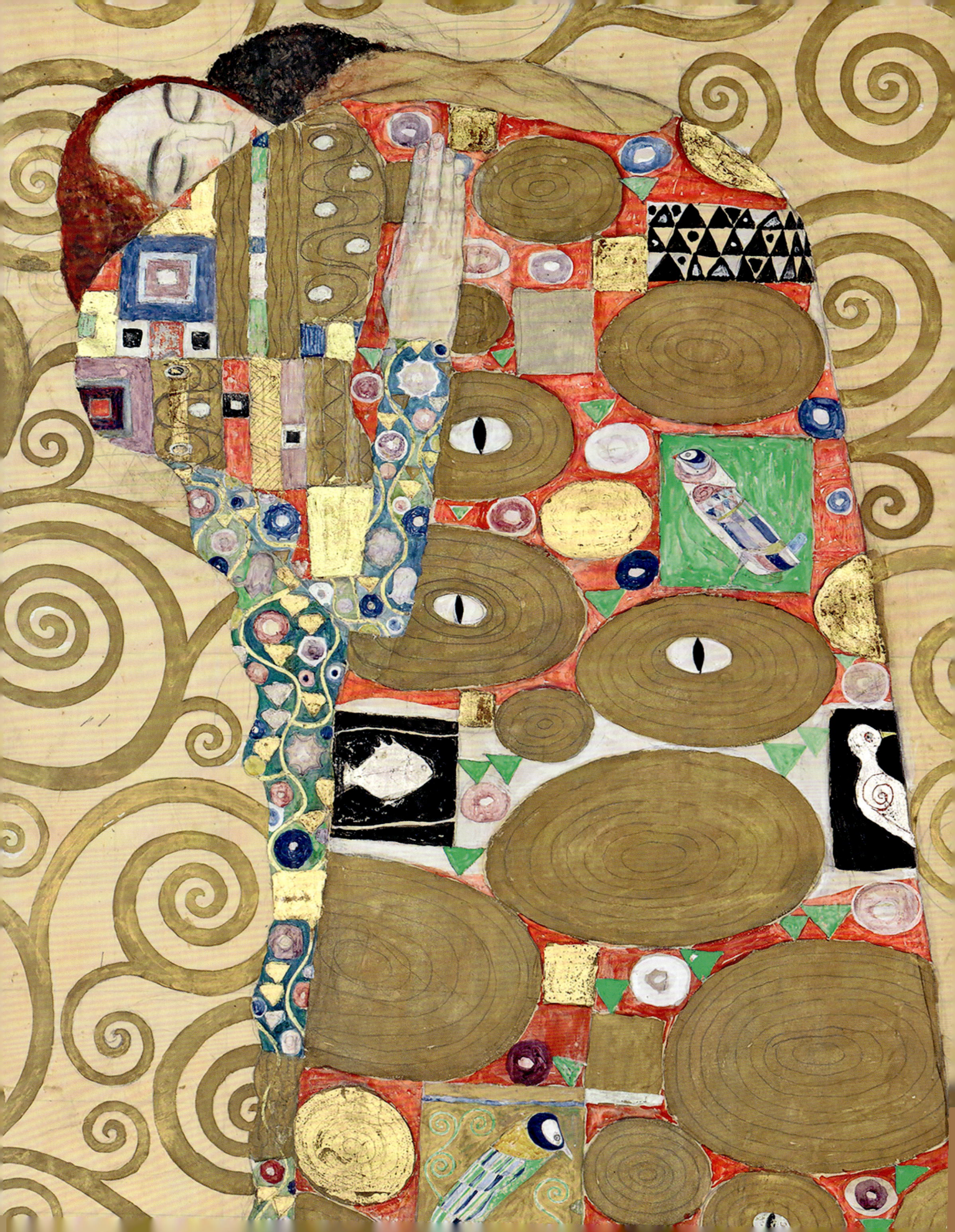

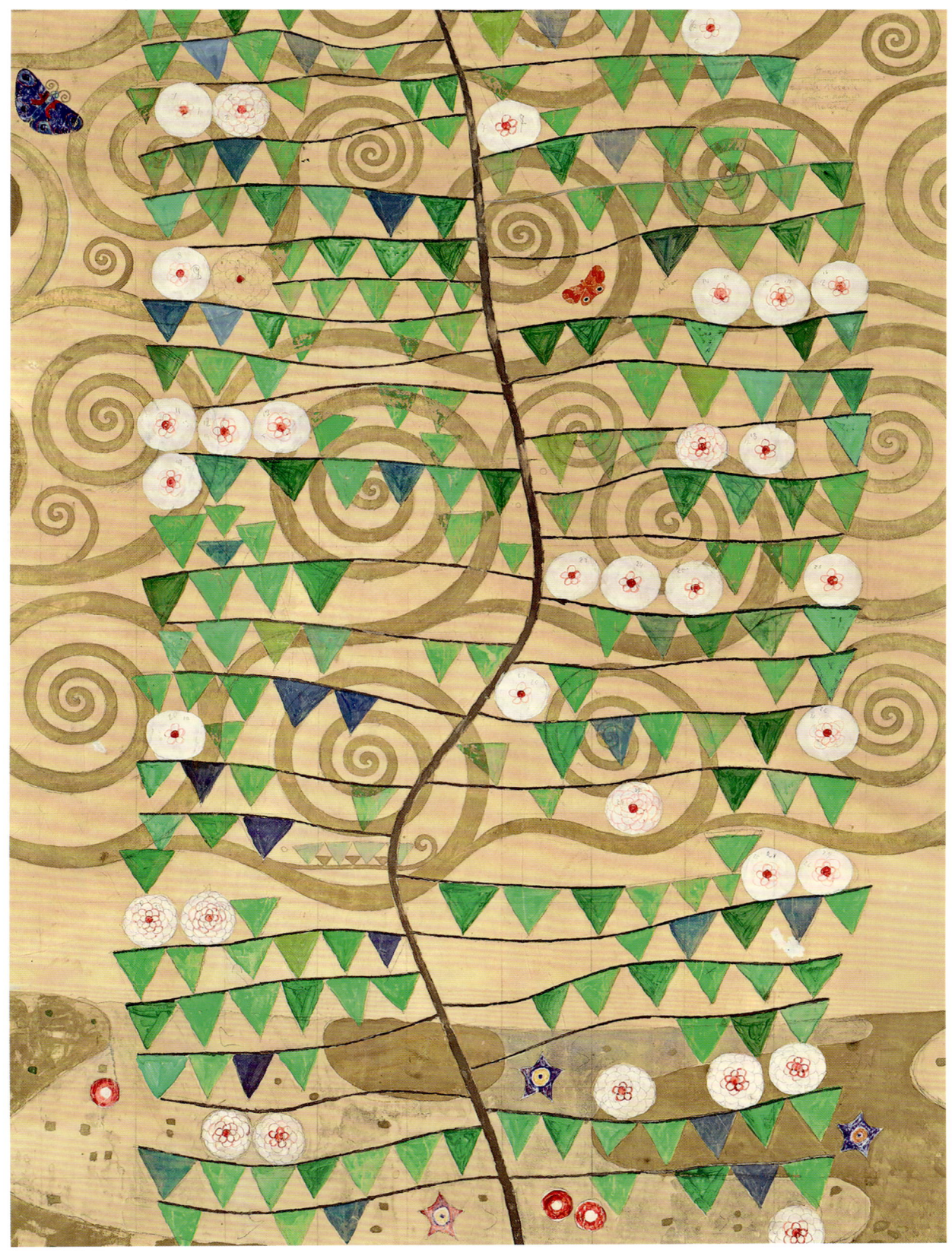

The Tree of Life, cartoons for the mosaic on the left wall of the Palais Stoclet dining room,
1908–1911, tempera, watercolour, pencil, chalk and silver and gold leaf on cardboard,
200 × 102 cm, Museum für angewandte Kunst, Vienna (detail)

stätte, which was responsible for the overall interior furnishings. Klimt's allegorical vision is infinitely less complex than that of the *Beethoven Frieze* (fold-out p. 50), due to the fact that he had done away with the dark, malevolent forces. There is nothing but light here: a central tree of life with impossibly long curls that lose themselves in beds of roses and link together the richly clothed human figures at the two ends of the composition: Expectation, symbolized by a young woman, and Fulfilment, the latest manifestation of the theme of embrace. Although the small central panel was long considered a purely decorative, even abstract composition (p. 122), Klimt always called it "my knight", perhaps implying that it was the guardian of this enchanted garden, protector of human happiness.

Expectation,
drawing for the mosaic on the left-hand wall of the Palais Stoclet dining room,
1908–1911, tempera, watercolour, pencil, chalk, and gold and silver leaf on cardboard, 200 × 102 cm,
Museum für angewandte Kunst, Vienna (p. 118, detail; and fold-out)

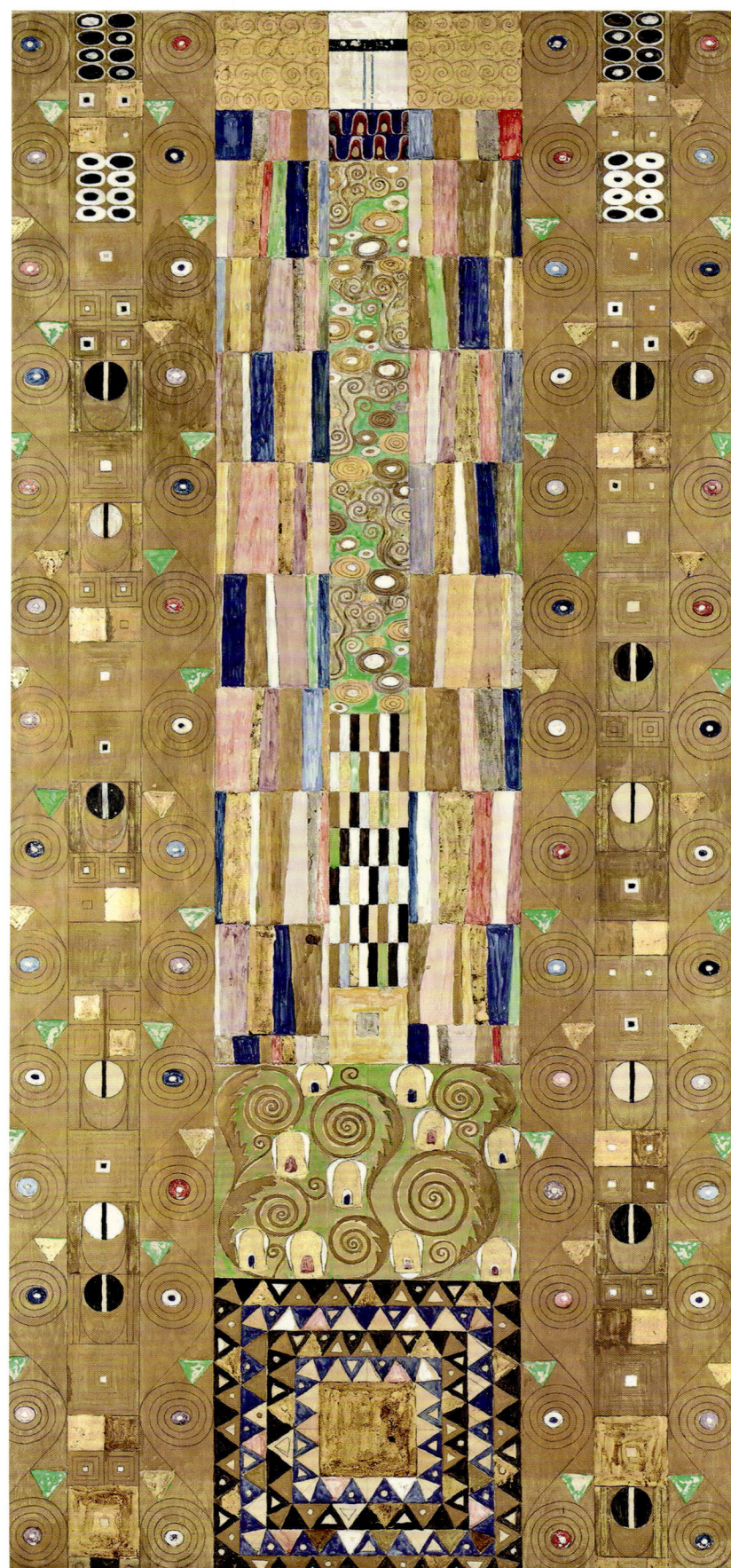

Knight,
drawing for the mosaic on the central wall of the Palais Stoclet dining room, 1908–1911, tempera, watercolour, pencil, chalk, and gold and silver leaf on cardboard,
197 × 89.9 cm,
Museum für angewandte
Kunst, Vienna
(right)

Fulfilment,
drawing for the mosaic on the right-hand wall of the Palais Stoclet dining room, 1908–1911, tempera, water-colour, pencil, chalk, and gold and silver leaf on cardboard,
200 × 102 cm,
Museum für angewandte
Kunst, Vienna
(opposite)

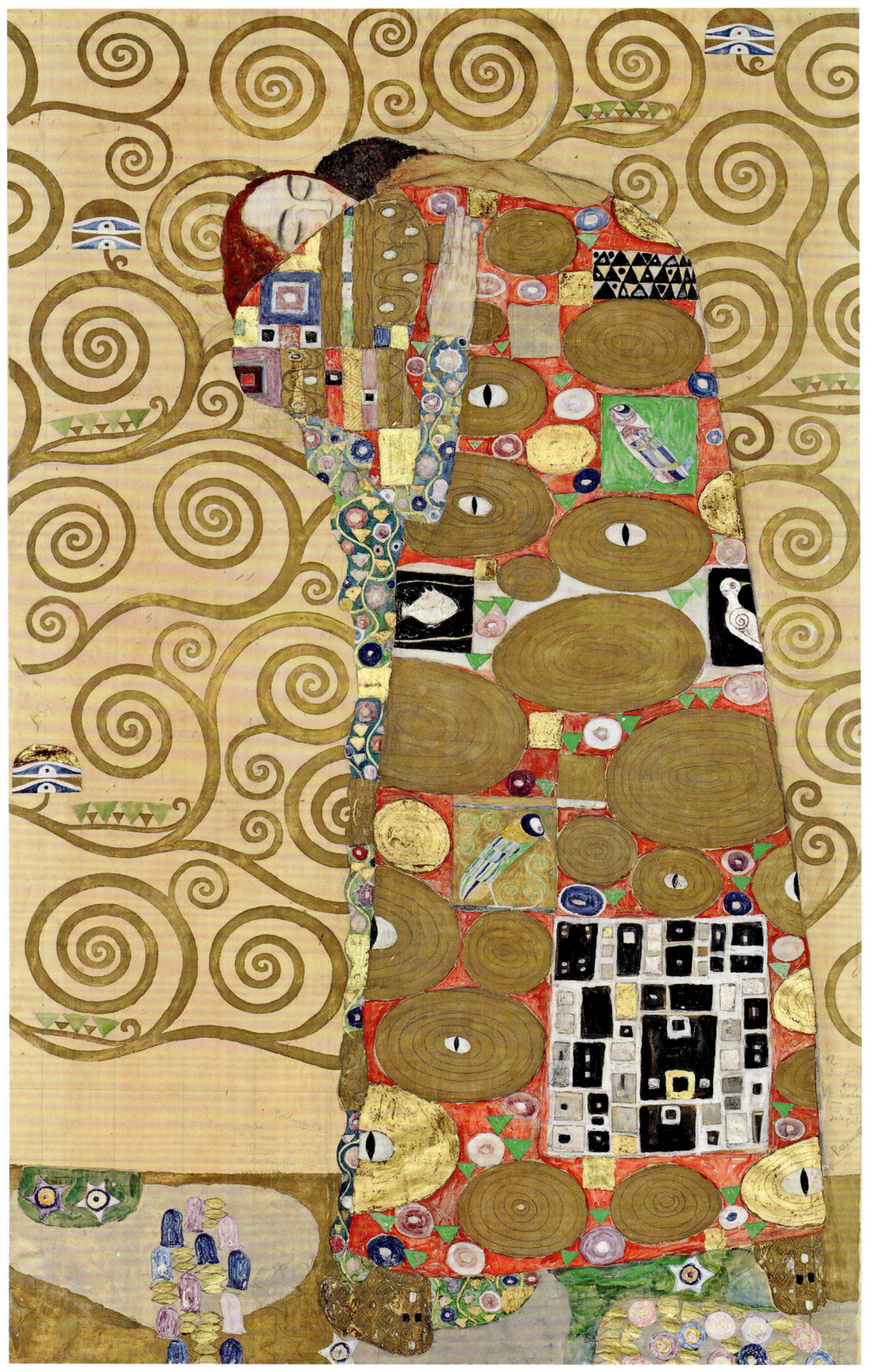

Image Credits

Heritage Image Partnership Ltd/Alamy Stock Photo: p. 23; Vidimages: p. 64; Gravure française: p. 65; Hirarchivum Press: p. 98

Bayerische Staatsgemäldesammlungen – Neue Pinakothek, Munich / CC BY-SA 4.0: pp. 36–37, 62

Belvedere, Vienna: pp. 38, 42, 44–49, 57, *Beethoven Frieze* fold-out p. 50, *Water Serpents I* fold-out p. 72; photo Johannes Stoll: pp. 40, 63, 74, 94–95, 96–97, 108, 109, 110, 117, cover

Bridgeman Images: pp. 4, 43, 56, 68, 70, 71, 72, 76, 80–81, 82–83, 86–87, 90–91, 100–101, 104–105, 106, 114, *The Kiss* fold-out p. 88, *The Virgin* fold-out p. 94; PVDE p. 6; photo © Fine Art Images: pp. 26–27, 28–29, 30, 58, 115, 116; Luisa Ricciarini: p. 112, *Adele Bloch-Bauer I* fold-out p. 72; photo © Christie's Images: pp. 52, 66, 113; Cameraphoto Arte Venezia: p. 41; photo © Leonard de Selva: p. 62; photo: Artothek: p. 69; photo © Sotheby's: p. 73; photo © NPL – DeA Picture Library: pp. 74, 88–89

Galerie Neue Meister, Dresden: p. 107

Kunsthaus Zug: p. 111

MAK – Museum of Applied Arts, Vienna / photo: © MAK/Georg Mayer: pp. 118, 122, 123, *Stoclet Frieze* fold-out p. 120

National Gallery of Art, Washington, DC / Gift of Otto and Franziska Kallir with the help of the Carol and Edwin Gaines Fullinwider Fund: pp. 92–93

National Gallery of Canada, Ottawa: pp. 84–85

The Metropolitan Museum of Art, New York / Gift of André and Clara Mertens, in memory of her mother, Jenny Pulitzer Steiner, 1964: p. 67

Wien Museum, Vienna: p. 39; CC BY 4.0, photo: Birgit and Peter Kainz: pp. 18–19, 20–21, 22, 14, 31, 32; photo: TimTom: pp. 59–61

First published in French
Klimt. L'art plus grand
© 2024 Éditions Hazan

Translation: Richard N. Block
Copy-editing: Tas Skorupa
Proofreading: Joann Skrypzak
Editorial direction Prestel: Katharina Haderer
Production Prestel: Martina Effaga
Typesetting: Sieveking Agentur, Munich
Separations: Hyphen Group, Orio al Serio, Italy
Printing and binding: C&C Printing

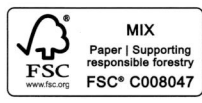

Penguin Random House Verlagsgruppe FSC® N001967

Printed in China

ISBN 978-3-7913-9399-5
www.prestel.com